Catholic Cults and Devotions

Catholic Cults and Devotions

A Psychological Inquiry

MICHAEL P. CARROLL

McGill-Queen's University Press
Kingston, Montreal, London

© McGill-Queen's University Press 1989
ISBN 0-7735-0693-4

Legal deposit first quarter 1989
Bibliothèque nationale du Québec

(∞)

Printed in Canada on acid-free paper

This book has been published with the help of a grant
from the Canadian Federation for the Humanities,
using funds provided by the Social Sciences and
Humanities Research Council of Canada. Publication
has also been assisted by a grant from J.B. Smallman
and Spencer Memorial Fund, University of Western
Ontario.

Canadian Cataloguing in Publication Data

Carroll, Michael P., 1944–
  Catholic cults and devotions
  Includes index.
  Bibliography: p.
  ISBN 0-7735-0693-4
  1. Catholic Church – Customs and practices – Psychological
aspects. 2. Catholic Church – Controversial literature. I. Title.
BX1970.C37 1989   282'.019   c88-090469-0

To the memory of
Herbert Thurston, S.J. (1856–1939) and
Sigmund Freud (also 1856–1939)

A chi vuol dar buon giudizio del suono, bisogna
il sentire l'una campana, e l'altra.

Baldinucci, *La Veglia*

Contents

Tables

Acknowledgments

I am keenly aware of the special debt I owe to my parents, William Carroll and Olga Ciarlanti, whose hard work and very real sacrifices when I was younger have in the end provided me with the opportunity and freedom to engage in scholarly investigations of the sort presented here. I extend them my thanks. I also want to thank my wife Susan for being my wife, and to thank my son Ian and my daughter Emily, mainly because I love them and know they both will enjoy seeing their names in print.

This book has been published with the help of a grant from the Canadian Federation for the Humanities, using funds provided by the Social Sciences and Humanities Research Council of Canada. The inclusion of photographs in this book was made possible by a grant from the Smallman Publications Fund administered by the Faculty of Social Science at the University of Western Ontario. The opportunity to investigate the contemporary blood miracles of Naples, discussed in Appendix C, was made possible largely through two grants. The first of these came with the Research Professorship awarded to me by the Faculty of Social Science at the University of Western Ontario in 1987/88; the second was from the Social Sciences and Humanities Research Council of Canada block grant administered by the Faculty of Social Science. I want to express my gratitude for all of this aid.

Engraving by Domenico Barriere of the *apparato* by Niccolò Menghini that was used in the Gesù at Rome in 1646. (Reproduced by permission of the Trustees of the British Museum.)

Cloverleaf, German, 15th Century   **Tower, German 16th Century**

Two examples of early monstrance design. Both Tower and Cloverleaf monstrances often have small statues of various saints included in various niches. These have been omitted in these examples in order to provide a clearer sense of the overall design. In the case of the Tower monstrance, the Eucharistic host was inserted into the lunette held aloft by the two angels. (Illustrator: Susan Turner)

Sunburst, French, 17th Century   **Sunburst, French, 19th Century**

Two examples of a Sunburst monstrance. Notice the concentricity apparent in both cases, even though the two designs differ in other details. For the psychological importance of this concentricity, see the discussion in chapter 6. (Illustrator: Susan Turner)

A composite religious medal widely sold in North America. The individual medals represented are, on the front (clockwise from left), St Joseph with the Infant Jesus, the Sacred Heart of Jesus, St Christopher, and the Miraculous Medal; on the back they are the Infant of Prague, Our Lady of Mount Carmel, St Anthony of Padua with the Infant Jesus, and the Miraculous Medal. (Photo: Alan Noon)

Religious medal, early twentieth century, collected in France, but probably of Italian origin. Face: Our Lady of Perpetual Help; back: St Alphonso Liguori praying the Rosary before a Crucifix, while an Angel looks on. (Photo: Alan Noon)

Mass-produced representation of the
Immaculate Heart of Mary, artist
unknown. (Photo: Alan Noon)

Example of the Dominican Rosary. In this case the beads are brown seeds of some sort, and the medal joining the tassel to the main string has an image of the Sacred Heart of Jesus on one side and an image of Our Lady of Mount Carmel on the other. Unscrewing the knob at the bottom of the crucifix allows the back of the crucifix to open, exposing a small space into which a relic may be inserted. (Photo: Alan Noon)

Some examples of the Brown Scapular of Our Lady of Mount Carmel. The large scapular at the top is handmade and probably dates from the early twentieth century. The two scapulars at the bottom were obtained in the 1980s, but similar designs have been available for decades. Notice the fairly straightforward and unconditional version of the Scapular Promise on these two: "Whoever dies wearing this Scapular will not suffer eternal fire." In all cases there is nothing sewn onto the back of the scapulars, so that the side worn next to the body is entirely and only composed of brown wool. (Photo: Alan Noon)

Cloth badge worn by members of the Apostleship of Prayer in League with the Sacred Heart. Founded originally in France in the late 1840s, the Apostleship was reorganized and expanded as a result of papal directives issued in the 1870s. The writing on the front refers to regulations issued on 14 June 1877, which grant a partial indulgence of one hundred days each time a member of this association (1) wears this badge on his person and (2) repeats the invocation "Thy kingdom come." This indulgence was applicable to the souls in Purgatory. (Photo: Alan Noon)

Plaster statue of the Sacred Heart of Jesus. Manufactured in Italy, statues of this type are still available in most stores selling Catholic religious goods in North America. (Photo: Alan Noon)

Catholic Cults and Devotions

Introduction

The failure of psychoanalysts to take any significant interest in the study of popular Catholicism is puzzling, since popular Catholicism seems ideally suited to psychoanalytic investigation. Imagine, for example, the heart ripped from the body of a man, wrapped tightly with a circlet of thorns, pierced with a knife, and then displayed on the outside of that man's chest. Not a stylized "Valentine" heart, mind you, but a real, physical heart, complete with aortic opening and asymmetrical shape. If such an image appeared recurrently, say, in a person's dreams or in hallucinations experienced by several individuals, psychoanalytic investigators would have little hesitation in deciding that they might be able to shed light on the processes that gave rise to these images. Precisely this image does lie at the core of the devotion to the Sacred Heart of Jesus, one of the most popular Catholic devotions. Yet I know of no psychoanalytic investigator who has studied this particular devotion.

Another example: imagine a person who was absolutely convinced that he or she had to wear a small piece of brown wool next to their skin in order to avoid a great calamity. Suppose further that the person insisted that the wool had to be brown and had to be worn continuously. Could there be a clearer case of obsessive behaviour? Yet though obsessive behaviour of just this sort was among the very first things studied by Freud, this particular obsession – which defines the Catholic devotion to the Brown Scapular of Our Lady of Mount Carmel – has been ignored by psychoanalytic investigators.

Or what about the Catholic insistence that the Angelus prayer only be said in response to the sounding of a loud church bell? Or the fact that the Rosary only became a popular devotion when the Rosary prayers were merged with the practice of fingering small hard beads? Or the very graphic emphasis upon the suffering of Christ evident in the Stations of the Cross? Why haven't such things been addressed by the psychoanalytic investigators, who find it so easy to address similar beliefs and patterns in connection with dreams, myths, neurotic behaviour, and so on?

One likely reason is that Freud's own work on religion has always been something of an embarrassment even to the most devoted of his disciples. This is because his most important statements on religion, "Totem and Taboo," (1912–13) and *Moses and Monotheism* (1939), are permeated with a psychological Lamarckism that virtually nobody is willing to defend.

In "Totem and Taboo," remember, Freud argued that the original band of brothers rose up and killed their father. Overcome by guilt after the deed was done, they first renounced the very thing that had led them to commit parricide, namely, sexual access to their mother and sisters; for Freud this was the origin of the incest taboo. Then they sought to atone for their crime by venerating a father surrogate, and this gave rise to totemism, the veneration of a animal totem thought to be the ancestor of the group. Freud then argued that the memory of this primal crime, as well as the resulting guilt and the desire to atone, were repressed and so driven into the unconscious of the original father killers.

Putting aside the not inconsequential issue of whether all this actually happened in history, there is nothing particularly controversial about the general theoretical principles that Freud invoked in making his argument to this point. But then he advanced the fatal hypothesis that virtually nobody has been willing to accept: that the repressed memory of the primal parricide, along with the resulting guilt and desire to atone, *was passed on to succeeding generations* and even now resides in the unconscious of all human beings. The history of religion, he continued, is a history of these unconscious memories "returning" to the conscious mind, with the result that over the millennia the image of the supernatural beings we venerate come more and more to resemble the image of the primal father. One reason it is so difficult to dismiss Freud's argument here as a momentary aberration is that in *Moses and Monotheism*, which he wrote intermittently during the last five or six years of his life, he very explicitly chose to reinforce and expand his earlier hypothesis.

Today *Moses and Monotheism* is most likely to be remembered for Freud's assertion that the historical Moses was not really Jewish at all, but rather an Egyptian who tried to promulgate the monotheistic religion of the Pharaoh Akhenaten among a group of non-Egyptian Semites living in Egypt at the time. But these assertions really play only a very small role in the argument Freud constructed. More important was his assertion that the Israelites had killed the historical Moses during the Exodus. An unrepentant Lamarckian to the end, Freud then argued that the memory of this Moses killing was repressed and passed on to succeeding Israelite generations. In the Israelite unconscious, the memory of the killing of Moses constantly reactivated and energized the memory of the primal father killing. The result was that the memory of that original parricide came closer to the conscious mind in the case of the Israelites than in the case of any other previous people. This ensured that Israelite monotheism – with its emphasis upon a single God clearly conceptualized as an powerful father – came to reflect the memory of the primal father more clearly than did any previous religion.

But for Freud the process did not stop with Judaism. This same "return of the repressed," that is, this same coming closer to the conscious mind of the unconscious memory of the primal parricide, gave rise to Christianity. The key event occurred when one particular Jewish leader, Saul of Tarsus (later to be called St Paul), added three elements to the beliefs surrounding a failed messianic leader called Jesus Christ. The first was that there had been an original sin against God the Father that demanded atonement; the second was that Jesus Christ was the Son of God; and the third was that the crucifixion of Christ had been foreordained as a means of redeeming humankind from that original sin. The new religion that Saul organized around these beliefs reflected even more than traditional Judaism the repressed primal memories. The idea of an original sin against God was for Freud only a barely disguised reflection of the memory of the original father killing, and the idea that the *Son* of God must atone for that original sin by his death was, Freud argued, a tacit admission that the *son* (or *sons*) had been guilty of the original crime against the primal father.

Though undeniably ingenious, Freud's argument in both books depends on the premise that unconscious memories can be passed on to succeeding generations, a premise that is simply unacceptable to psychoanalysts and just about everyone else. Why Freud clung to such an unpopular position is a question that has been addressed by several commentators. Sulloway (1983) in particular has offered some thoughts on why Freud relied so heavily upon psychological Lamarckism. I have myself speculated on the idiosyncratic processes that would have made the specific argument presented in *Moses and Monotheism* so appealing to Freud personally (Carroll 1987d). But such history of science issues aside, the fact remains that psychological Lamarckism does permeate both "Totem and Taboo" and *Moses and Monotheism*, and this has almost certainly brought the psychoanalytic study of religion into some disrepute.

RELIGION AS WISH-FULFILMENT

On the other hand, Freud did develop a second perspective on religion, and one that does not depend at all on Lamarckian premises. This second perspective, advanced mainly in "Obsessive Actions and Religious Practices" (1907) and "The Future of an Illusion" (1927) suggests that religious beliefs and rituals are shaped by unconscious infantile memories and are appealing because they gratify unconscious infantile wishes. This of course is more or less the same hypothesis that lies behind Freud's work on dreams (1900), on parapraxes or "Freudian slips" (1904), and on jokes (1905). Unfortunately, Freud's application of this hypothesis to the study of religion is uninteresting.

Freud was always at his best when he developed his theories in close association with the analysis of particular examples. The great appeal of his work on dreams, parapraxes, and jokes lies precisely in the fact that his theoretical arguments and interpretations are larded generously with analyses of particular dreams, particular parapraxes, and particular jokes. It is just this merging of the theoretical and the concrete that is missing from the discussions in which Freud presents his wish-fulfilment theory of religion. Nor have later psychoanalysts interested in religion done much to remedy the situation: all too often they have aped the master and likewise avoided the concrete.

There are, for instance, a great many works by psychoanalysts that purport to be about religion, but which never get around to analysing in detail particular religious beliefs or rituals associated with particular people in particular cultures. Though some may find these neo-philosophical discussions to be of value, I do not. Psychoanalytic analyses are not only more interesting when they involve the analysis of concrete materials, they are also more valuable. After all, our goal as social scientists is to explain what we find in the world around us, and that simply cannot be done without taking some concrete phenomenon as the object of explanation. The desire to bring the psychoanalytic method to bear upon concrete examples of religious belief and ritual was one of the factors that gave rise to this book. I have chosen to look at popular Catholicism in particular because, as I have said, the beliefs and patterns associated with popular Catholicism seem ideally suited to psychoanalytic investigation.

THE PSYCHOANALYTIC STUDY OF CHRISTIANITY

It would not be correct to say that Christianity in general has escaped psychoanalytic scrutiny. Ernest Jones, for instance, one of the co-founders of the psychoanalytic movement, did some excellent work on the Christian belief in the Holy Ghost, and I will be making use of parts of Jones's argument in chapter 2. Generally, however, what is striking about the psychoanalytic literature on Christianity is its "non-denominational" emphasis. By this I mean that it concentrates on the Christian beliefs that are shared by all Christian groups, which usually means an emphasis on the New Testament. The New Testament account of the Christ's crucifixion in particular, probably because of the castration imagery involved, seems to have caught the fancy of psychoanalytic investigators (see, for example, Bunker 1951, 29-33; Dundes 1981; Graber 1986; Carroll 1987b). Similarly, Tarachow (1955) relied heavily upon New Testament sources in developing his psychoanalytic account of St Paul. As interesting as these analyses might be, they generally ignore the great differences between the various forms of Christianity, and they certainly ignore the unique features of popular Catholicism.

One possible explanation for the failure of psychoanalysts to take a greater interest in popular Catholicism might be, quite simply, that they have not been aware of the unusual juxtapositions of elements that have defined so many popular Catholic cults and devotions. This raises an interesting question in the sociology of science, since it would suggest that perhaps Catholics are far less likely than others to be attracted to the logic of psychoanalytic thought, and this in itself would need to be explained. In any event, if I am correct here, the fact that the post-Vatican II period has seen a rapid decline in the popularity of most extra-liturgical cults and devotions in the Catholic Church should only make matters worse, since today these cults and devotions are unfamiliar even to many Catholics.

Most likely, then, if a good book on Catholic cults and devotions from a psychoanalytic perspective is ever going to be written, it will be written by someone raised in the Catholic Church before Vatican II and who has bucked the odds and developed an affection for psychoanalysis.

Catholic authorities have always made a distinction between "liturgical practices" and "popular devotions." For all practical purposes, a liturgical practice can be defined as a form of public worship that has been approved by the Church and which the Church sees as directly relevant to the Sacraments and the celebration of the Mass. A popular devotion by contrast is a pious practice that centres on the veneration of some sacred object or thing but which is not considered by the Church to a part of its official liturgy. Popular devotions can be celebrated in public or in private, and though they have often been encouraged by the Church, they can flourish and have often flourished without such encouragement. A cult is a group of people who all engage, individually or collectively, in some particular pious practice. My concern in this book is only with popular devotions and the cults associated with them.

In deciding which particular devotions to study, I have been guided by the judgments of Catholic commentators as to which devotions have been the most important, a issue on which there seems to be a great deal of agreement. Table 1 identifies the devotions listed as "Principal Devotions" in the *National Catholic Almanac* for selected years from 1939 to 1965.

Apart from the fact that all the devotions listed are extra-liturgical, most of them share two additional characteristics. First, they are all what Christian (1972, 46-7) has called "generalized devotions"; that is, they are all devotions whose practice now transcends national or cultural boundaries. Thus they are to be distinguished from Catholic devotions whose practice necessitates visiting some particular geographic location. Second, as we shall see in later sections of this book, most of these devotions first achieved some measure of popularity before being taken over and promulgated by the Church.

What all this suggests to me is that the popularity of these devotions cannot

TABLE 1

Extra-Liturgical Devotions Listed as "Principal Devotions" in the *National Catholic Almanac*, Selected Years

	1939	1945	1950	1955	1960	1965
Angelus	X	X	X	X	X	X
Benediction of the Blessed Sacrament	X	X	X	X	X	X
Brown Scapular	X	X	X	X	X	X
First Saturday	X	X	X	X	X	X
Five Wounds	X	X	X	X	X	X
Forty Hours Adoration	X	X	X	X	X	X
Holy Name of Jesus	–	–	–	–	X	–
Immaculate Heart of Mary	–	–	X	X	X	X
Infant of Prague	–	–	–	X	X	X
Miraculous Medal	X	X	X	X	X	X
Mother of Sorrows	X	X	X	X	X	X
Precious Blood	X	X	X	X	X	X
Rosary	X	X	X	X	X	X
Sacred Heart of Jesus	X	X	X	X	X	X
St. Joseph, Patron of the Dying	–	–	–	–	–	X
Seven Sorrows of Blessed Virgin	X	X	X	X	X	X
Stations of the Cross	X	X	X	X	X	X
Three Hours Agony	X	X	X	X	–	–

Note: *The National Catholic Almanac* was called *The Franciscan Almanac* from 1931 to 1939. In 1968 it changed its title again, this time to simply *The Catholic Almanac*, and no longer included a special section devoted to principal devotions. This last change is one of the many indications that the popularity and practice of all these devotions has declined dramatically since Vatican II.

be attributed solely to the idiosyncratic features of life in particular cultures or societies nor to the fact that they came to endorsed by the Church. On the contrary, it seems highly likely that the popularity of these "generalized" devotions is due in large measure to psychological processes that transcend particular socio-cultural boundaries. I am going to argue in this book that to a great extent these "transnational psychological processes" are those described by Freud in connection with his "wish-fulfilment" theory of religion. In short, the master hypothesis that will guide the analyses in this book is that the appeal of popular Catholic devotions derives largely from the fact that these devotions gratify one or more unconscious infantile wishes.

Most of this book will be concerned with explaining the appeal of the devotions in Table I that seem to me to have been most popular with lay Catholics over the past several centuries. The Rosary (perhaps the single most popular of all Catholic devotions) will be considered in chapter 1; the Angelus in chapter 2; the Stations of the Cross in chapter 3; the Forty Hours devotion in chapter 6; the Brown Scapular of Our Lady of Mt Carmel in chapter 7; and the devotion to the Sacred Heart of Jesus, and to a lesser extent devotion to the Immaculate Heart of Mary, in chapter 8.

Chapters 4 and 5 are somewhat anomalous, since neither deals with a generalized Catholic devotion. Chapter 4 deals with Neapolitan cults that are organized around liquefying blood relics, and chapter 5 with the stigmata. These blood-liquefaction cults have no real counterpart outside the Naples area, and although individual stigmatics have often become the centre of a cult, the experience of stigmatization itself is not usually considered a "pious practice." I have addressed these two subjects because both have long had a wide visibility among lay Catholics and because both can be explained by theoretical arguments that are strikingly consistent with the arguments developed in the rest of this book.

I should make it clear that although Freud's wish-fulfilment hypothesis will guide the analysis, I will not be relying on the standard psychoanalytic arguments that most readers probably associate with Freud's name. On the contrary, the first three chapters draw heavily upon Freud's analysis of anal eroticism, which is one of his less-known and less-used arguments. Indeed, one of my goals is to demonstrate that Freud's discussion of anal eroticism is probably more useful for understanding religious ritual than his better-known discussions of the oedipal period. Freud's work on the oedipal period, in fact, is really only used extensively in chapter 4. Chapters 5 to 8 virtually abandon the specifics of Freud's work altogether in favour of the theories developed by Melanie Klein. Indeed, as this investigation progressed, it became more and more clear to me that Kleinian theory, with its emphasis on the crucial role played by the infantile need to make reparation for attacks made in phantasy against the mother, provides a theoretical template that is extremely useful in helping to make sense of many Catholic devotions.

Chapter 9 deals with an issue that is raised at least implicitly by everything that precedes it: why do we find a proliferation of popular devotions, each characterized by the juxtaposition of fairly unusual and disparate elements, in the Catholic tradition but not in the Protestant tradition? The answer turns out to be as much sociological as psychoanalytic.

Finally, the book concludes with some thoughts on the lessons to be learned from all of this with regard to both the social scientific study of religion and the future place of popular devotions in the Catholic church.

CHAPTER ONE

The Anal-Erotic Origins of the Rosary

In one of the many critical essays that he wrote on popular Catholic devotions, Herbert Thurston, S.J., (1900d, 403) called the Rosary "the most widely spread and the most highly prized of all our modern popular devotions."[1] A later Catholic commentator, though just as willing as Thurston to be critical of some Rosary traditions, nevertheless felt compelled to begin his own study of the Rosary with an even more elegant panegyric: "The Rosary ... is the most satisfyingly complete form of Christian prayer outside the Mass and the Divine Office ... Every Catholic knows it, and probably most Catholics say it ... It is a staple prayer, the daily bread of devotion, on which the humble faithful nourish their spiritual lives ... It is a golden chain of praise and petition by which we go to God as God came to us, through His Blessed Mother" (Shaw 1954, vii). In her survey of the twenty-three most popular Catholic prayer books published in the United States in the period 1770–1880, Taves (1986, 24–5) found that virtually all of them mentioned the Rosary, and that no other devotion came close to being mentioned as often as the Rosary.[2] As recently as the late 1950s and early 1960s, it was common practice in many Catholic elementary schools throughout North America for the students to say the Rosary collectively at least once a day.[3] It was also common (and in some places still is) for Rosary beads to be entwined around the fingers of Catholic corpses lying in state, so that "praying the Rosary" was for many Catholics – at least superficially – their very last religious devotion. Finally, terms like "bead-snappers" and "bead-clackers" have long been used to denigrate Catholics (at least in the United States and Canada), thus indicating that non-Catholics also recognize, however unintentionally, the importance of the Rosary to lay Catholics. Like so many other popular Catholic devotions, the Rosary has declined in popularity since Vatican II. But even as late as the 1970s a survey conducted among a national sample of US Catholics found that 36 per cent of those surveyed had prayed the Rosary in the preceding thirty days (see Gallup and Polling 1980, Table H).

HISTORICAL BACKGROUND

Strictly speaking, the Rosary is a particular arrangement of prayers. The most common Rosary (there are more than one[4]), usually called the Dominican Rosary, consists in the recitation of 150 Hail Marys, arranged into groups of ten, or decades, with each decade being preceded by an Our Father and ending with a Glory be to the Father. Each of the fifteen decades of the Rosary is also associated with a "mystery," which is some event connected with the life of Jesus or Mary, and upon which the devotee is supposed to meditate while praying. The fifteen "mysteries" associated with the modern Rosary are (1) the Annunciation, (2) the Visitation of Mary to her cousin Elizabeth, (3) the birth of Christ, (4) the presentation of Christ at the Temple, (5) the finding of Christ in the Temple, (6) Christ's agony in the garden, (7) His scourging, (8) the crowning with thorns, (9) the carrying of the cross, (10) the crucifixion and death of Christ, (11) the Resurrection, (12) the Ascension, (13) the sending of the Holy Spirit, (14) the Assumption of Mary into heaven, and (15) Mary's coronation as Queen of Heaven. The first five mysteries are called the Joyful Mysteries, the second five the Sorrowful Mysteries, and the last five the Glorious Mysteries.

But the term Rosary is also applied, at least in common discourse, to the string of beads used as an aid in praying the Rosary. The Rosary as an object consists of a string of beads attached end to end form a continuous circle. These beads are arranged into five groups of ten (each group of ten beads corresponding to a decade of Hail Marys), with a single bead (on which is prayed an Our Father) separating each of the decades. Devotees move from bead to bead with their fingers and pray the appropriate prayer at each bead. The Glory be to the Father that closes each decade of Hail Marys is usually said "on" the space between the final bead of that decade and the following Our Father bead.[5] Obviously, a string of Rosary beads must be prayed three times in order to complete a full Rosary prayer.

I might note that modern Catholic commentators who discuss the Rosary often stress the Rosary as an arrangement of prayers and de-emphasize use of Rosary beads. For instance, in the "Rosary" entry in the *New Catholic Encyclopedia* (Hinnebusch 1967) the use of beads is mentioned only once and only in passing; it strikes me that someone could read this discussion of the Rosary several centuries from now without realizing that the Rosary prayer was so intimately associated with the use of prayer beads. This point is worth emphasizing, if only because I will later be arguing that the tactile experience of fingering small, hard beads is one of the very things that has made the Rosary such a popular devotion.

How did the Rosary originate? According to pious tradition the Virgin Mary herself gave the Rosary to St Dominic (1170–1221) during an apparition and told him that praying the Rosary would help him in his crusade against the Albigensian heretics. There is, however, absolutely no documentary reference to a tradition linking St Dominic to the Rosary until the late fifteenth century, nearly 250 years after this saint's death. In the twentieth century at least, even most Catholic commentators have seemed willing to concede that the story linking St Dominic to the Rosary is apocryphal.[6] Rather it seems clear that the Rosary as we know it developed slowly, and resulted from the merging of several different traditions.[7]

Even before AD 1000 Irish and Anglo-Saxon clerics had developed the practice of reciting the 150 psalms of the Old Testament in three groups of fifties. At some point, this arrangement of the Old Testament Psalter gave rise to the recitation of an Our Father Psalter, composed of three groups of fifty Our Fathers. By the thirteenth century it had become customary as well to pray a Psalter of Hail Marys,[8] that is, to pray a series of 150 Hail Marys, arranged into three groups of fifty.

Sometime after 1400, an event in the life of Jesus and Mary became associated with each of these 150 Hail Marys. Towards the end of the fifteenth century, the number of such events, called "mysteries," was reduced (from 150) and began to be standardized, until we arrive at the fifteen mysteries (each associated with a decade of Hail Marys) familiar to modern devotees.

Archaeological and artistic evidence (reviewed in Thurston 1901d) show that prayer beads were used, at least by some members of the clergy and the aristocracy, from the twelfth century onwards. Some commentators have suggested the use of such beads resulted from contact with Moslems, who had from a much earlier period used a string of prayer beds to aid in the recitation of the names of God, but there is no direct evidence to support this theory. What should be emphasized, however, is that there is *no* evidence that these early Christian prayer beads were used to aid in praying the *Marian* Psalter. On the contrary, the fact that in all parts of Europe these beads were called "paternosters" (Thurston 1901d, 398–9) suggests that they were used to pray Our Fathers.

We do not encounter unambiguous evidence of beads being used to pray a Marian Psalter until the fifteenth century, with the appearance of a number of books and poems on "Our Lady's Psalter" that explicitly mention the use of beads. This is significant because all commentators agree that it was only during the fifteenth century that the Rosary became a truly popular devotion, that is, a devotion practised by large numbers of Catholics. In other words, neither the use of prayer beads nor the praying of a Marian Psalter achieved a wide popularity in and of itself; rather, both become widely popular only when they were merged into a single practice.

Given that the Rosary, with its 150 Hail Marys, is so obviously a form of Marian devotion, it might reasonably be expected that the Rosary (and from this point on, I will use this term to refer simultaneously to the arrangement of prayers and to the use of an associated set of beads) would first have become popular in those places, like southern Italy and Spain, where the Mary cult has always been the strongest. Certainly that was my expectation. In fact, this was not the case.

Catholic commentaries usually attribute the relatively sudden emergence of the Rosary as a popular devotion to the proselytizing efforts of Alain de la Rouche (1428–75). (It was de la Rouche, incidentally, himself a Dominican, who first reported that the Rosary had been given to St Dominic). It is true that the first confraternity[9] established to promote devotion to the Rosary was the "Confraternity of the Psalter of Jesus and Mary" established by de la Rouche at Douai, in northern France, in 1470. Nevertheless, whatever the role of de la Rouche, two sets of evidence suggest that the Rosary first became a truly popular devotion in the German-speaking regions of Europe.

The second Rosary confraternity to be established, for instance, was established at Cologne in 1474, and quickly became the most important of all the Rosary confraternities in Europe.[10] Within four months of its foundation, the Cologne confraternity had five thousand members. By the end of its first year, that number had grown to fifty thousand. One contemporary report (cited in Thurston 1900f, 622) suggests that by 1479 the number of members registered with this one confraternity had increased to five hundred thousand. It is true that not all the members of the Cologne confraternity were German-speakers, since people from all over Europe could be registered in the confraternity. Nevertheless, the fact that the confraternity was centred at Cologne does suggest that German-speakers were the largest single linguistic group among the membership. This conclusion gains support from the fact that three of the next four Rosary confraternities to be established were also established in German-speaking areas. Thus a confraternity was established at Lisbon in 1478, at Schleswig in 1481, at Ulm in 1483, and at Frankfurt in 1486 (Willam 1953, 48).

The association of German Catholicism with the spread of the Rosary as a popular devotion is also seen in the fact that the first books that promoted this devotion were by German-speakers. The earliest manual of the Confraternity of the Holy Rosary, for instance, was a book written in German, drawn up by the Dominican Jacob Sprenger (better known now as one of the authors of the *Malleus Maleficarum*[11]) and printed at Cologne in 1476. More important perhaps, all commentators agree that the book which did the most to promote devotion to the Rosary was another German-language book, *Unser Lieben Frauwen Psalter* (*Our Dear Lady's Psalter*). Editions of this book were printed at Ulm by Conrad Dinckmuk in 1483, 1489, and 1492; at Augsberg by Anton Sorg in 1490 and 1492; and again at Augsberg by Luke Zeiselmaier in 1495 and 1502 (see Willam 1953, 56; Thurston 1900f, 624–9). Except for the absence of the "Glory be to the Fathers" and a few changes in the mysteries associated with each decade of Hail Mary's, the Rosary that was popularized in the *Unser Lieben Frauwen Psalter* was more or less the Rosary of modern times.

Having achieved its initial success in Germany in the late fifteenth century, the Rosary as a popular devotion did spread to other parts of the Catholic world, though with varying success. In the case of France, for example, Lançon's (1984) analysis of archival materials relating to Rosary confraternities in the old province of Rouergue suggests that such confraternities were rare there during the sixteenth century and only began to appear in great numbers during the early seventeenth century. On the other hand, although I know of no study of the early history of the Rosary in Italy, Marian shrines in Italy contain a great many ex votos dating from the middle to late sixteenth century and depicting people praying the Rosary.[12] Finally, Thurston (1927e, 55) has pointed out that books dealing with the Rosary appear often in catalogues that list the titles of books published in both England and Europe during the early part of the sixteenth century. All in all, then, with some clear exceptions, it seems that by at least the middle of the sixteenth century, the Rosary had established itself as popular devotion in a great many parts of the Catholic world. Nevertheless, its initial popularity came in the German-speaking parts of Europe, and this needs to be explained.

Rothkrug (1987, 243–7) accounts for the great popularity of the Rosary Confraternity in Germany by arguing that in establishing a uniform practice for the veneration of the Virgin, this Confraternity "could help to unite the peoples of the empire in a single form of worship." I suspect that Rothkrug is correct, in the sense that the spread of the Rosary probably did induce some political integration in German-speaking regions. But this sort of argument in no way explains the unique features of the devotion. In other words, for "political integration" purposes, any uniform devotion would have sufficed. Why did the Rosary in particular come to be so popular with German-speakers?

PSYCHOANALYTIC PRELIMINARIES

Early in his psychoanalytic career, Freud (1907) called attention to the similarities between a wide variety of religious devotions and the type of neurotic behaviour he called "obsessional." The most obvious common denominator, for Freud, was an emphasis upon repetition and doing things in one particular order. In that original essay Freud devoted most of his discussion simply to describing some of these similarities. He did suggest, however, that the similarities between religious devotions and neurotic obsessions might well result from the fact that a similar psychological process was operating in each case. In particular, he suggested that religious devotions, like neurotic obsessions, might result from an attempt to achieve a compromise between two opposing forces, namely, an unconscious desire to do something and a conscious prohibition against doing that very thing.

Some years later Freud's clinical observations caused him to refine his explanation of obsessional behaviour. In particular, he later came to conclude that neurotic obsessions were usually shaped very specifically by unconscious desires that had first developed during an anal-erotic stage of sexual development and that had been activated and intensified by events in later life (see, for instance, Freud 1913; 1926). By anal-erotic stage Freud meant a stage (usually experienced around the age of two or three years) during which children derive a diffuse sense of physical pleasure from such things as the act of defecation and the act of coming into contact with their feces. This meant (for Freud) that neurotic obsessions were shaped by processes quite different from those that shaped, say, hysteria, which he believed was shaped primarily by desires that developed during the oedipal stage.

Freud's conclusion about the anal-erotic origins of obsessional behaviour is obviously related to his work on the "anal personality" (Freud 1908b). Confronted with a number of patients who all seemed to exhibit the same cluster of character traits – an emphasis upon cleanliness, orderliness, parsimony, and obstinacy – Freud came to the conclusion that these traits had anal-erotic origins, in the sense that they were either reactions against particularly strong anal-erotic desires or disguised gratifications of those desires. Thus he saw an exaggerated emphasis upon order and cleanliness as reactions against a strong infantile desire to play with one's own feces, while obstinacy was a sublimation of the infantile desire to preserve control over one's excretory processes in the face of parental interference.

Freud's work on anality has had a mixed reception over the decades. On the one hand, his suggestion that there was an "anal personality," defined as a personality characterized by an emphasis upon parsimony, orderliness, and obstinacy, was well received by early investigators like Abraham (1921) and Jones (1918) and has since been validated by a relatively large number of clinical studies (reviewed in Kline 1981, 68–129). On the other hand, Freud's specific suggestion that these traits derive from anal-erotic experiences associated with early childhood has generated little apparent interest and few studies.[13] More important, at least given our purposes here, Freud himself seems never to have gone back and revised his early remarks on religious obsessions in light of his later remarks on the anal personality and the anal-erotic origins of obsessional behaviour.

Nevertheless, if his later theory is correct, it seems clearly to lead to the simple conclusion that a great many religious devotions, especially those characterized by an excessive emphasis upon repetition and orderliness, are likely to have an anal-erotic origin. This is the hypothesis that I want to consider here. What I am suggesting, in other words, is that praying the Rosary is a popular Catholic devotion because it represents the gratification of anal-erotic desires.

BEADS AND FECES

As a start, it seems obvious that the Rosary does emphasize two of the elements, namely, repetition and orderliness, which (if Freud is correct) derive from strong anal-erotic desires. The Rosary's emphasis on repetition is reflected in the fact that the recitation of a full Rosary necessities saying a single prayer, the "Hail Mary," 150 times. The emphasis on orderliness is seen in the fact that these 150 Hail Marys must be said in precise groups of ten and that each group of ten is associated with one of fifteen mysteries that must be considered in a precise order.

But remember that the Rosary did not become popular until the practice of saying 150 Hail Mary's (in sets of ten, interspersed with Our Fathers) was merged with the use of beads. Indeed the use of Rosary beads is now an integral part of the Rosary devotion, something that is very much evidenced by the ecclesiastical regulations that govern the use of the Rosary as a religious devotion.

Those regulations for instance, specify that any indulgences associated with a given Rosary are uniquely associated with the *beads* that compose that Rosary (see Beringer 1925a, 430–1). Thus, for example, replacing the string or chain along which the beads are strung does not invalidate an indulgence associated with particular Rosary. Similarly, on rosaries with tassels, the medal that joins the tassel to the main string can also be replaced without penalty. But if a significant number of the beads (and this seems to mean about five or more) from a Rosary are lost or destroyed, that Rosary does lose any indulgences with which it has been associated. This emphasis upon beads makes perfect sense if indeed the appeal of the Rosary is anal-erotic.

In an early and now classic article on the transformation of anal-erotic desires, Ferenczi (1914) pointed out that under the impact of the repression of all things anal (a repression that occurs regularly, at least in Western cultures), the infantile desire to play with feces undergoes a series of transformations. The desire to play with feces first transforms itself into a desire to play with odourless materials that have the same consistency as feces (mud, clay, and sand being the obvious examples), then into a desire to play with small, hard objects (like pebbles, marbles, and buttons) and finally, at least in some cases, into a desire to play with coins and, by extension, to possess money.

I am suggesting that the act of fingering small, hard beads during the course of a Rosary prayer, like the child's habit of playing with, say, small hard pebbles, represents the gratification of the infantile desire to play with one's feces. Remember too that a Rosary is usually prayed by pulling the Rosary beads, one bead at a time, between the thumb and forefinger of the right hand. Pulling small hard beads though the crevice formed by the thumb and forefinger bears, I suggest, a more than passing physical resemblance to the act of excreting feces through the anus.

MOTHERS AND EXTERNAL THREATS

Recall that the original practice was to pray a Psalter of 150 Our Fathers, not a Psalter of 150 Hail Marys. Remember too that prayer beads were originally used in Europe to count Our Fathers. Thus it seems obvious that there was a basis for developing a Rosary in which the central prayer was the Our Father, not the Hail Mary. Yet such a Rosary never became a widely popular devotion. The use of beads only became a popular devotion when such beads were used in connection with a form of prayer that honoured Mary.

The Rosary honours Mary not simply because it involves the recitation of 150 Hail Marys, but also because the logic of the fifteen mysteries associated with the Rosary gives equal status, at least implicity, to Mary and Jesus. After all, the mysteries dwell upon events from the lives of both Mary and Jesus, and when we get to the Five Joyful Mysteries at the end, events like the Resurrection and Ascension of Christ are mentioned with the Assumption of Mary and the Coronation of Mary as Queen of Heaven. The fact that these last two distinctively Marian events are mentioned at the very end of the Rosary, in the manner of a culmination, might even suggest that they were being given more prominence than the events associated with the life of Christ.

Why should a repetitive, orderly prayer, associated with the use of beads, only become popular when it becomes associated with the Virgin Mary? The key, I think, lies with Freud's early remark that a neurotic obsession is a compromise of some sort between an unconscious desire to do something and the conscious sense that the desired thing is prohibited. Under the interpretation offered in the last section, the unconscious desire that gives rise to Rosary devotion is the desire to play with ones own feces. But what is the conscious prohibition associated with this desire? Quite obviously it is the injunction not to play with one's feces. Now consider: who is it that the infant is most likely to associate with this prohibition? In almost all cultures, this prohibition is likely to be associated with an older female (who is often, but by no means always, the mother), since such females almost inevitably have primary responsibility for child rearing and thus for feces training.

I am suggesting then that an attempt to effect a compromise between an unconscious infantile desire to play with one's feces and the perception that this is forbidden by the mother (or a mother surrogate) gives rise to an obsessive practice, namely, praying the Rosary, which is approved by a mother surrogate (Mary) but which nevertheless involves (for the reasons given in the last section) the disguised gratification of that infantile desire to play with feces.

The suggestion that the Mary associated with the Rosary is the mother or mother surrogate who first attempted to interfere with the infantile gratification of anal-erotic desires also provides us with a basis for explaining another aspect of the Rosary devotion, namely, the tendency over the centuries to associate praying the Rosary with external threats to the Church.

In 1573, Pope Gregory XIII decreed that the Feast of Rosary should be celebrated in the city of Rome on 7 October to commemorate the defeat of the Turks at the battle of Lepanto on that date in 1571, a defeat that he (and many other Catholics) attributed to the rosaries prayed by members of the various Rosary confraternities. In 1716 Clement xi decreed that the Feast of the Rosary be extended to the entire Western Church to commemorate the efficacy of Rosary prayers in causing the defeat of the Turks at Peterwardein (in what is now Yugoslavia).

A more recent example of this same pattern is to be found in the association of the Rosary with the Church's fight against Communism. During the 1917 apparitions at Fatima, the Virgin Mary is supposed to have instructed Lucia Santos that Catholics would have to pray the Rosary to achieve the conversion of Russia. In actual fact, it appears that the original message of Fatima was that the faithful should pray for the conversion of the *world*, with the anti-Communist and anti-Russia element being added only in 1927 (Carroll 1986a 136–7). But the important point is that since the 1940s, when devotion to Our Lady of Fatima first began to be popular with Catholics throughout the world, those Catholic organizations that have been most concerned with spreading the message of Fatima have portrayed the Rosary as the most potent weapon that can be used to defeat Communism.[14]

In short, whether the threat to the Church is seen to come from Turkish Moslems or from godless Communists, there has been a tendency for the Catholic mind to see "praying the Rosary" as a potent weapon (if not the most potent weapon) against such external threats. Why should that be?

In psychoanalytic terms, the very young child faces all sorts of "external threats," some real, some imagined. One of the earliest of these threats is the attempt (usually by the mother) to control and regulate the child's toilet behaviour. What makes this particular threat so important to the child is the fact that excretion and urination are among the very few pleasurable processes over which the young child has almost full control. This makes these processes quite different from, say, nursing or eating, where the amount of pleasure experienced depends so much more upon the co-operation of the mother.

Therefore, it seems highly likely that when the *adult* mind is confronted with an external threat to something that is highly valued, like the Church, then this must inevitably reawaken infantile memories of that very early external threat represented by the mother's attempt to regulate anal sexuality. But this memory is in turn intimately associated with the now repressed anal-erotic desires that the mother was trying to control, and so these desires themselves would be activated.

If the appeal of praying the Rosary is indeed that this activity represents the disguised gratification of our repressed anal-erotic desires (and that is the basic hypothesis being presented here), then it makes perfect sense that people should turn to the Rosary when those anal-erotic desires are intensified, as occurs (under the interpretation just given) when Catholics believe there is an external threat to the Church.

GERMANIC ANAL EROTICISM

Although I have attributed the appeal of the Rosary to the hypothesis that praying the Rosary represents the disguised gratification of anal-erotic desires, I do not mean to suggest that these desires are for some reason more intense in Catholics than Protestants. If Freud's reconstruction of our sexual development is even approximately correct, almost everyone experiences anal-erotic desires and in almost all cases (at least in the Western cultural tradition) these desires come to be repressed. This suggests (under my hypothesis) that praying the Rosary should to some degree have a universal appeal. Nevertheless, I assume that in the usual case these repressed anal-erotic desires are not sufficiently strong by themselves to maintain an obsessive religious practice like praying the Rosary. If Catholics rather than Protestants pray the Rosary, it is not only because this gratifies anal-erotic desires, but also because the Church has given institutional support to the practice for centuries. If such support were withdrawn for a significant length of time, I assume that praying the Rosary would die out as a popular religious devotion. In fact, something very much like this has happened.

Although a significant number of Catholics still pray the Rosary, it seems clear that the proportion of Catholics who do so has declined significantly over the past two decades. By 1983, for instance, one Catholic commentator, writing in a Catholic periodical, could even describe the Rosary as an "old-fashioned Catholic practice" (Finley 1983). At least in part this is due to the Church's general de-emphasis of most extra-liturgical devotions since Vatican II.

But while official encouragement from the Church, together with the Rosary's weak universal appeal, might *maintain* the Rosary as a popular devotion, such an argument cannot account for the initial establishment of the Rosary as a popular Catholic devotion. In other words, the historical record shows that the Rosary first achieved widespread popularity among Catholics in the late fifteenth century and was only then taken over and encouraged by the Church hierarchy. What accounts for that initial upsurge in popularity before the Church began to support the practice wholeheartedly?

If we remember that the Rosary first established itself as a popular devotion in German-speaking regions of Europe, then Alan Dundes's (1984) study of German culture provides us with an argument that meshes perfectly with the argument developed here. Very simply, Dundes's extensive analysis of the cultural traditions in various German-speaking regions of Europe over the centuries leads him to conclude that these traditions are overwhelmingly pervaded with anal-erotic themes. Anal-erotic themes of course appear to some degree in all cultural traditions; Dundes' point is only that a relative emphasis upon such themes is so much greater in the cultural traditions of German-speaking areas.

It is impossible to summarize here all the data that Dundes presents in support of his argument, since those data consist of hundreds of examples – including a variety of slang terms, jokes, poems, and practices associated with German popular culture, beliefs associated with folk medicine, folktales, and so on. The simple presentation of this material accounts for most of Dundes's book. For the sake of illustration, however, I might only mention that direct references to "shit" or "ass-licking" (in one form or another) seem far more prevalent in obscenities and profanities of Germanic origin than in obscenities and profanities of, say, American or Canadian origin (which tend to be characterized by a greater emphasis on genital themes of the "fuck you" variety); that traditional German toilets were built in such a way as to take into account a Germanic predilection for directly inspecting one's feces (supposedly for reasons of health) immediately upon excretion; that there are relatively large number of German folktales in which feces are particularly important, and in particular, a relatively large number of German folktales that rely heavily upon a "feces into gold" equation; and so on. Dundes does establish, I might add, that this emphasis upon anality and anal-eroticism has been a feature of the culture in the German-speaking regions of Europe for centuries.

Having established the strong emphasis upon anal-erotic themes in Germanic culture, Dundes uses this to explain a wide range of associated customs and beliefs – ranging from food preferences (for example the Germanic fondness for sausages and chocolate) to musical preferences (in particular, the preference for music made with wind instruments) to, more seriously, traditional Germanic attitudes towards Jews. Some readers might dismiss Dundes's argument out of hand, on the grounds that it smacks too much of now discredited "national character" studies. For my part, I seen nothing inherently implausible in the suggestion that different cultures might emphasize the same themes to different degrees.

In any event, if we accept Dundes's conclusion as a given, namely, that the cultural traditions associated with the German-speaking regions of Europe have for centuries been characterized by a relatively strong emphasis upon anal-erotic themes, then this would seem to suggest that people raised in German-speaking areas have relatively strong anal-erotic desires. This is in fact what Dundes argues, and he does consider some aspects of child-rearing in these areas that might have produced this condition. But in the end he concludes – wisely I think – that the data needed to link particular child-rearing practices to this apparent intensification of anal-erotic desires are not available.[15] In other words, it seems clear that *something* about child-rearing in German-speaking areas over the centuries has intensified anal-erotic desires, but just what that something is is not yet known.

If we grant that anal-erotic desires are and have been especially strong in German-speaking areas, then the fact that the Rosary first established itself as a popular devotion in these same parts of Europe is entirely consistent with the argument offered here. Although I have argued that the appeal of praying the Rosary lies in the fact that it represents the disguised gratification of anal-erotic desires, I have also argued that these desires are not usually strong enough to maintain the Rosary except when it is encouraged by the Church. Thus, the only situation in which we might except to find the Rosary establishing itself as a popular devotion without official encouragement from the Church would be a situation in which anal-erotic desires were significantly stronger than usual, and this is precisely the situation that exists (and has existed for centuries, if Dundes is correct) in the German-speaking parts of Europe.[16]

PEBBLES, COINS, BEADS, AND MEDALS

A sacramental is an object or action that is not one of the seven sacraments that Catholics believe to have been instituted by Christ but which in the eyes of the Church can be used by the faithful for their spiritual benefit. The Rosary is a sacramental. Apart from the Rosary, other objects that have long been among the most popular sacramentals are crucifixes, cloth scapulars of various sorts, and religious medals. I have dealt elsewhere with the emergence of a graphic emphasis upon the crucifixion (Carroll 1986a, 86–9), and cloth scapulars will be considered in chapter 7 of this book. It seems appropriate to discuss religious medals here, however, because there are good theoretical reasons for believing that the appeal of these medals has the same anal-erotic origins as the appeal of the Rosary.

Catholic religious medals must be made of a hard, durable substance, which usually means that they are made of some hard metal. It is not permissable, for example, to make medals of wood, ivory, or soft metals like lead or pewter. Medals are almost always circular or oval and bear one or more images on their surfaces. In recent centuries the vast majority of Catholic medals have born the image of Christ, the Virgin Mary (under one of her various titles), or one of the saints. Church regulations issued in the nineteenth century, in fact, forbade the placing of an image of an uncanonized person (such as, for instance, a reigning pope) on a medal unless an image of Christ, Mary or a saint was also present (Beringer 1925a, 430). The most popular medal in modern times is almost certainly the Medal of the Immaculate Conception, more commonly known as the Miraculous Medal, but most stores carrying Catholic religious goods usually have two dozen or so other medals in stock.

"Composite" medals are also widely available from such stores. These are single medals, of various shapes, that are stamped with the designs of several different medals. The medals whose images most often appear on the composite medals I have seen, presumably because they are judged to be the most popular of all Catholic medals, include the Miraculous Medal and medals associated with the Infant of Prague, St Joseph with the infant Jesus, the Sacred Heart of Jesus, St Christopher,[17] and Our Lady of Mount Carmel.

The fact that Catholic religious medals are roundish bits of hard metal means that they are very similar to coins. In fact this similarity is so strong that Catholic commentators inevitably make a reference to coins when defining medals:

A religious medal is a piece of some solid substance generally but not necessarily metallic, in the form of a coin, adorned with some religious inscription or image, usually fitted to be worn suspended from the neck. (Mulhern 1967, 546)

A medal may be defined to be a piece of metal, usually in the form of a coin, not used as money, but struck or cast for a commemorative purpose, and adorned with some appropriate effigy, device or inscription. (Thurston 1913c, III)

This similarity to coins allows us to establish a theoretical link between the Rosary and the use of medals.

Recall the transformations that according to Ferenczi (1914), disguise the infantile desire to play with one's feces: the desire to play with feces becomes a desire to play with odourless materials that have the same consistency as feces (sand, mud, and so on), which in turn becomes a desire to play with small hard objects. In this analysis I have argued that fingering Rosary beads gratifies the now transformed desire to play with small hard objects. But in Ferenczi's original discussion small hard objects meant first pebbles and then coins. The insight that coins were symbolic feces was especially important in Ferenczi's discussion because it is a strong fascination with coins that gives rise to the concern with money and with parsimony that is so characteristic of the anal personality. Dundes (1984) also relies on the coins = feces equation to explain the prevalence of the feces-into-gold motif in Germanic folklore.

But if playing with coins, like fingering Rosary beads, gratifies the infantile desire to play with feces, then the strong similarity between coins and medals leads us to expect that the wearing of religious medals should gratify the same infantile desire. At the very least this leads us to predict that the Rosary and the wearing of religious medals should have emerged as popular Catholic devotions during the same historical period and in the same places. Is that what happened?

There is some evidence that religious medals were used in the early Christian Church, since archaeologists have recovered several medals of likely Christian origin from various Roman sites.[18] One particularly famous medal, for instance, usually dated to the fourth century, depicts on one side a scene in which a person (usually assumed to be St Lawrence) is being roasted on a gridiron by a Roman magistrate, and on the other a structure that seems to represent a tomb. Surrounding the first scene are undeniably Christian symbols: the Alpha, the Omega, and the Chi-Rho. Evidence of the use of medals by early Christians also comes from several documentary sources, usually written by Christian leaders intent upon discouraging the wearing of medals on the grounds that such medals were too reminiscent of the magic amulets worn by pagans. But although some early Christians seem to have worn medals, there is no clear evidence as to how common the practice was.

Commentators do agree that by the Middle Ages the wearing of medals was relatively *uncommon*, except in two circumstances. First, as early as the twelth century pilgrims to various shrines were often sold a badge to prove that they had visited the shrine in question, and the manufacture and sale of these badges became an important source of income for these shrines. Such pilgrim badges, however, unlike modern medals, were usually made of soft metals like lead or pewter, and were not indulgenced. The second circumstance involved *jetons*, thin pieces of metal stamped with some device or inscription that identified the bearer. These *jetons* seemed to have functioned in much the same way that business cards function today. They are relevant to the discussion here only because nearly half the *jetons* that have survived from the Middle Ages are also stamped with a pious inscription of some sort. But they too, like pilgrim badges, were not indulgenced.

Pilgrim badges and *jetons* notwithstanding, commentators agree that the wearing of coin-like medals for devotional purposes, that is, as aids to the veneration of figures like Christ, Mary or the saints, and as objects that would provide spiritual benefits to their wearers, did not become widely popular in the Catholic world until the last half of the sixteenth century (Thurston 1913d, 114; Mulhern 1967, 547). Certainly it was only at this time that the practice of blessing religious medals and associating them with indulgences became widespread.

What this means, then, is that the widespread use of religious medals for devotional purposes emerged less than a century after the emergence of the Rosary as a popular devotion. Unfortunately, to decide whether this fact lends support to the present argument is complicated by the fact that the century in question was particularly important. The sixteenth century, after all, was witness to the Reformation and the Counter-Reformation; and certainly, in later chapters I will be arguing that the Counter-Reformation had psychological effects upon lay Catholics, effects that had nothing to do with anal-eroticism. What we need to decide, in other words, is whether the widespread use of medals by Catholics that began in the late sixteenth century was a reaction of some sort to the Reformation or the Counter-Reformation, or whether the appeal of this practice derives from the same anal-erotic origins as the Rosary, a pre-Reformation devotion.

In this connection, remember that one of the strongest pieces of evidence in favour of the hypothesis that the Rosary has anal-erotic origins is that the Rosary first emerged in that part of Catholic Europe, namely, the German-speaking Catholic states, where there was an especially strong and overt anal-erotic emphasis. If the wearing of religious medals has the same anal-erotic appeal, we would expect that this devotion too should have first become popular in the German-speaking areas of Europe. Did it?

The first indulgenced medal seems to have been a medal struck by the Spanish government in response to the use of a blessed medal struck by rebels in Flanders in 1566. Subsequently, Pope Sixtus V (who reigned from 1585 to 1590) attached indulgences to some old coins that had been found beneath the Scala Santa in Rome and which he mounted in fine settings and sent to various prominent people in Europe. Thus legitimated, the use of indulgenced medals rapidly became a popular devotion. Thurston's (1913d, 114) review of various historical documents relevant to the use of religious medals in Europe leads him to conclude:

[After the late 16th century] ... the custom of blessing and indulgencing medals is said to have rapidly extended under the sanction of the popes ... [and] the use of these devotional object spread to every part of the world. *Austria and Bohemia* [emphasis added] seem to have taken the lead in introducing the fashion into Central Europe, and some exceptionally fine specimens were produced under the inspiration of the Italian artists whom the Emperor Maximilian invited to this court.

Austria of course is a German-speaking nation, and Bohemia had a large German-speaking minority (about one-third of the total population).

However coincidental it may have been, then, history seems to have mimicked the developmental sequence that Ferenczi posited for individuals: just as Ferenczi argued that strong anal-erotic desires in individuals first give rise to a fascination with pebbles, buttons, and marbles, and then to a fascination with coins, the strong anal-eroticism associated with the German-speaking regions of Europe seems to have provided a social milieu which fostered first the emergence of a popular devotion that used pebble-like beads (that is, the Rosary), and then the emergence of a devotion centred on coin-like medals.

THE NAME OF THE ROSARY

We are now in a position to consider one final characteristic of the Rosary, and one so far unmentioned: the recurrent association of the Rosary with a "garland of flowers," more specifically with a "garland of roses." At one level this association hardly seems problematic. The word Rosary itself is derived from medieval terms that mean "garland of roses," and a great many medieval legends (discussed in Thurston 1908a; 1908b) describe how someone (such as a knight or a cleric) honours Mary by presenting her with a garland of flowers (usually roses) and how this practice (usually at Mary's instruction) evolves into the practice of saying a Marian Psalter (that is, the Rosary). On the other hand, it seems equally plausible that these legends developed precisely to provide a conscious rationalization for an already existing association between the Rosary and flowers.

In any event, such medieval legends aside, the use of flowers or flowery garlands as a symbol for the Rosary is still very widespread. The continuing tendency to think of a string of Rosary beads as a garland of flowers would suggest, on the face of it, that there is some inherent similarity between these beads and flowers. But what?

As a start, let us draw up a list of the characteristics that are most associated with flowers. Most people would certainly include a pleasant fragrance. Flowers, in other words, have a distinctive smell – and that is the clue to the psychological link between flowers and the Rosary. After all, under the interpretation developed here, Rosary beads are substitute feces, and feces, like flowers, exude a distinctive smell. True, the smell is fragrant one case, and malodorous in the other, but the fact remains that *both* flowers and feces are strongly associated with a distinctive smell.

Incidentally, an emphasis on the Rosary as a flowery garland that exudes a distinctive smell often finds its way into official pronouncements. Thus, Pope Leo XIII, writing on the Rosary in 1901, suggested, "For as often as we greet Mary with the angelic salutation "full of grace" ... just so often in repeating that tribute of praise do we offer the Blessed Virgin, as it were, roses exuding the sweetness of the most pleasant perfume" (Oligny 1980, 152). Some may find it difficult to see in the act of offering up to the Virgin Mary the sweet-smelling roses of the Rosary the young child's desire to offer to his mother a gift of his or her own feces, but that, I suggest, is exactly what is happening.

CONCLUSION

Psychoanalytic arguments can only rarely be subjected to the sort of precise quantitative testing so favoured by philosophers of science. Cheshire (1975), however, has argued that psychoanalytic arguments can be evaluated, at least with respect to one another, by using a "comprehensibility" criterion. By this he means evaluating such arguments by determining the degree to which they do what psychoanalytic arguments have always done best: order a range of disparate elements into a coherent pattern. What then, in summary, are the disparate observations about the Rosary that are brought "into a coherent pattern" by the hypothesis that has been offered in this chapter, namely, that the appeal of the Rosary lies in the fact that praying the Rosary allows for the disguised gratification of anal-erotic desires?

First, the hypothesis presented here, when combined with Freud's arguments on the anal-erotic origins of obsessional behaviour, allows us to explain (1) why praying the Rosary is characterized by excessive repetition and an emphasis on orderliness, (2) why praying the Rosary involves the use of beads, which are carefully fingered by the devotee, and (3) why Catholics have traditionally associated the Rosary with external threats to the Church. Second, when merged with the work done by Dundes, the argument presented here can explain why the Rosary first became popular in German-speaking regions of Europe. Finally, the same argument that explains the appeal of the Rosary also explains the appeal (to Catholics) of wearing religious medals.

CHAPTER TWO

The Angelus

In the *Hibernian Magazine* for August 1778, an anonymous Englishman described a play he had attended during a recent visit to Spain:

> Everything in this country must have the air of devotion, or rather superstition; even during the representation of the piece [the play] just mentioned, I heard a bell ring, and immediately all the spectators fell upon their knees. The comedians set the example, and the two actors who were upon the stage in the middle of the scene stopped, moved their lips, and muttered some words in a whisper with the rest of the people. This ceremony over, they all got up, and the play went on. On inquiring, I was told that this was an office of devotion called the *Angelus*. (quoted in Thurston 1902b, 531)

The writer's use of words like "superstition" and "muttered" leaves no doubt as to his low opinion of this very public devotion. Indeed, he goes on to denigrate the devotion even further by suggesting that it was only a money-making scheme on the part of a local convent to gain a portion of the proceeds from the play. In fact, the Angelus was not a purely local devotion, nor even a peculiarly Spanish one. By the eighteenth century it had been widely observed in almost all Catholic countries for centuries, and it remained popular well into this century. Even in the United States, for instance, at least before Vatican II, it was customary for Catholic schools to ring the Angelus bell at noon and for all schoolyard activity to cease. Apart from those readers of this book who may have actually experienced the Angelus, many will be familiar with this devotion on account of the famous and widely reproduced painting by Jean-François Millet (1814–75), entitled *The Angelus*, which shows two French peasants in their field, observing the midday Angelus with bowed heads.

THE DEVOTION

Formally, the Angelus is a devotion in honour of the Incarnation, the moment at which God become man. In Catholic mythology this occurred when the angel Gabriel announced to Mary that she would bear the Son of God; the scene is described in Luke (1: 26–38). For centuries, the Angelus was observed three times each day in the Catholic parts of Europe: in the morning, at midday, and in the evening. On each occasion, a church bell was rung and the devout said three "Hail Marys." In the sixteenth century, each Hail Mary came to be preceded by a short verse from Luke's account of the Annunciation. Later still the final Hail Mary was followed by a short prayer to Mary and then a somewhat longer prayer to Christ.[1] Though called the "Ave Maria" in many parts of the Catholic world (notably Italy) and "le Pardon" in France, it came generally to be called the "Angelus" because the first of the three short verses added in the sixteenth century began with the Latin phrase "*Angelus* Domini nuntiavit Mariae" ["The Angel of the Lord announced to Mary"].

HISTORICAL DEVELOPMENT

The origins of the Angelus are somewhat obscure. But since the Angelus involves the recitation of multiple Hail Marys, it is obvious that the devotion (at least in anything like its present form) cannot have existed before the use of that prayer became widespread. This means that it cannot have developed earlier than the twelfth century, since the earliest extant documents suggesting that the Hail Mary be added to the list of prayers (which then included the Our Father and the Apostles' Creed) that all Catholics should know date from the late twelfth and early thirteenth centuries.[2]

The first part of the Angelus to develop seems to have been the *evening Angelus*.[3] Although some commentators have suggested that the evening Angelus crystallized around the ringing of the bell that sounded the curfew in many European towns, Catholic commentators have usually argued that it crystallized around the bell rung at the end of the Hour of Compline in various European monasteries (see Thurston 1901f; 1902a; Henry 1924, columns 2069–73). Certainly a number of documentary references from the late thirteenth century suggest that various religious orders were trying to popularize an evening devotion that involved the recitation of multiple Hail Marys at the sound of a bell and that was associated with the Incarnation. In 1318, and again in 1327, Pope John XXII granted an indulgence of ten days to those who participated in a devotion of this sort, and he implied that such a devotion was already well established in several places.

Somewhat less popular, but still widespread by the fourteenth century, was the morning Angelus. Both Thurston (1902b, 519–20) and Henry (1924, columns 2073–4) argue that this part of the devotion developed around the ringing of the bell that ended the Hour of Prime at the beginning of the monastic day, just as the evening devotion had developed around the bell-ringing associated with Compline at the end of the day.

The midday Angelus was added to the devotion only after the practice of the evening and morning Angelus had become widespread, and it had a quite different origin.[4] One of the earliest documents relating to something that resembles the midday Angelus was issued originally by a synod held at Prague in the late fourteenth century: "The Lord Archbishop ordains by this letter that on every Friday ... one of the greater bells should be rung in every church in honour of the Passion of the Most High. He recommends and exhorts that then all men, both clergy and laity, putting aside any work on which they may be engaged, and even interrupting their dinner, should say upon their knees five Our Fathers in honour of the Sacred Wounds" (quoted in Thurston 1902a, 521). Quite apart from the fact that this devotion is concerned with the Passion, not the Incarnation, it is different from the modern Angelus in that it involves the recitation of Our Fathers (not Hail Marys) and is said weekly (not daily). Nevertheless, it does appear that this devotion, which is described in terms similar to the above in other documents from the same period, did give rise to the midday Angelus.

Through a careful analysis of various ecclesiastical documents published during the fifteenth and early sixteenth centuries, Thurston (1902a, 521–5) traces the steps in the transformation of this original midday Angelus: first, the recitation of three Hail Marys was joined to the recitation of the original Our Fathers; then the midday devotion was associated with the morning and evening Angelus (thus tending to make it a daily devotion, and associating it with the Incarnation); finally, the Our Fathers and any reference to the Passion were eliminated altogether. It is Henry's (1924, column 2077) view that by the sixteenth century the transformation was complete: all three recitations of the Angelus – in the morning, evening and midday – consisted of the recitation of three Hail Marys; all three were practised daily; and all three were in honour of the Incarnation.

It should be noted that church authorities attempted to establish a popular devotion that associated bell-ringing with the passion and that this attempt failed. This suggests that there is something particularly appealing about the juxtaposition of the concepts bell-ringing and Incarnation, something that is not evoked by the juxtaposition of bell-ringing and Passion. This, as we shall see, provides us with an important clue as to the psychological appeal of the Angelus. But before pursuing that clue, there is a methodological issue that must be confronted.

NECESSARILY ANAL-EROTIC

Though I am personally convinced of the great explanatory value of psychoanalytic arguments, a great many intelligent and thoughtful scholars are not. One of the most common criticisms directed against psychoanalytic arguments is that they are little more that "just so" stories, glibly spun off by psychoanalytic devotees who can easily impose pre-existing psychoanalytic hypotheses on whatever data happen to be at hand. The criticism may not always be stated as baldly as this, but it does exist and has always impeded the wider acceptance of the psychoanalytic perspective. Psychoanalytic investigators who refuse to confront this criticism directly are doing no service to the tradition of which they are a part. They are also forgetting that Freud himself was careful to reach a broad audience, especially in his work on dreams (1900), parapraxes (1901), and jokes (1905).

One way to reduce the seeming arbitrariness of this sort of criticism is to use the above-mentioned criterion proposed by Cheshire, namely, to evaluate psychoanalytic arguments in relation to one another by looking at the degree to which each interpretation orders a wide range of seemingly disparate elements into an coherent pattern. A second methodological guideline that is useful to the psychoanalytic investigator is to pay scrupulous attention to theoretical consistency. Nothing so reinforces an anti-psychoanalytic bias as the fact that similar phenomena are given radically different interpretations by different psychoanalytic investigators (or, worse, by the same investigator in different studies).

All of which brings us back to the Angelus. In the last chapter I pointed out that on the basis of clinical evidence a number of psychoanalytic investigators, starting with Freud himself, have concluded that an emphasis upon orderliness and repetition has anal-erotic origins. This conclusion was adduced in support of the hypothesis that the Rosary, a devotion characterized by an excessive emphasis on repetition and orderliness, was popular because it gratified unconscious anal-erotic desires. But having made that argument in connection with the Rosary, I am compelled by theoretical consistency to make a similar argument in connection with the Angelus.

The Angelus, after all, is also a devotion characterized by excessive orderliness and repetition. That is, it must be said at three precise times during the day and, even then, only at the sound of a bell. Similarly, as in the case of the Rosary, the core of the devotion is the multiple recitation of a single prayer, the Hail Mary.

But simply asserting that the orderliness and repetition of the Angelus derive from anal-erotic origins does not satisfy the demands of theoretical consistency. On the contrary, in the case of the Rosary we were able to use the anal-erotic-origins hypothesis to explain other features of the devotion (for example the emphasis on fingering small hard beads) and we were able to specify which particular anal-erotic wish was being gratified (the wish to play with feces). We should be able to do something similar in the case of the Angelus, and it would certainly be useful if the resulting argument were consistent with already existing psychoanalytic arguments concerning anal-eroticism.

THE MADONNA'S CONCEPTION
THROUGH THE EAR

Although I know of no previous psychoanalytic investigator who has considered the Angelus, Ernest Jones (1914) came close. Jones sought to explain what he claimed was once a widely prevalent Catholic legend: the belief that the Incarnation took place when the breath of God the Father, in the form of the Holy Ghost, entered the ear of the Virgin Mary. Jones begins by pointing out that the idea that breath or wind are agents of impregnation is by no means limited to Catholic tradition. On the contrary, it is a motif found in a great many mythological traditions, and he presents a grab-bag of examples from various sources to make this point. Today, even more examples could be found by examining the listings under Motif T524 ("Conception by wind") in Thompson's (1955) *Motif Index of Folk Literature*.

For Jones the key question was *why* breath or wind should be seen as a fertilizing agent. Because breath is so clearly an indicator of life to the conscious mind of the adult, it might seem obvious that breath would come to be seen as having life-giving properties. But Jones rejects this line of reasoning. He takes it as a pre-existing psychoanalytic truth that myth and legend are shaped mainly by unconscious *infantile* images and argues that the infantile images that are routinely uncovered by practising psychoanalysts like himself do *not* show evidence of any strong association between breath and impregnation. But, says Jones, psychoanalysis have routinely uncovered an infantile concern with a different sort of wind and this other sort of wind *is* associated with impregnation. That different sort of wind is flatus, the air expelled from the anus.

Freud (1908c) had already pointed out that during the anal-erotic stage, children are very much concerned with where babies come from. He had also argued that children believe, at least for a time, that babies are born through the anus. Jones adds to this by arguing that during this same period children come to speculate not simply on the way in which babies are born, but also on the way in which babies are made. His own work with patients had convinced him that at some point during the anal-erotic stage children come to believe that conception occurs when the father's flatus flows into the mother's anus. This theory, like the theory of anal birth, is eventually abandoned, but the memory of it remains in the unconscious. For Jones, the unconscious memory of this theory lies behind the legend of the Madonna's conception through the ear.

In Jones's reconstruction, the "impregnation by anal wind" theory routinely undergoes a number of transformations that make the elements of the theory more acceptable to the conscious mind. First, flatus is dissociated from its disagreeable odour, and then (by means of the "displacement upwards" mechanism so familiar to psychoanalysts) becomes associated with the father's mouth rather than his anus. The result: a belief that a fertilizing breath issues from the mouth of the father. In the case of Catholic tradition, this fertilizing breath underwent a further transformation and "condensed" into the image of the Holy Ghost as a dove. Similarly, the mother's-anus element in the original theory becomes the more acceptable mother's ear. The final result is a legend in which the Virgin Mary is impregnated when the Holy Ghost, riding along the breath of God the Father, enters her ear.

In discussing the various transformations designed to make the infantile memory of flatus more acceptable to the conscious mind, Jones also argues that when flatus loses its disagreeable odour, some of its other characteristics come to be emphasized. One of these is sound. What happens, in other words, is that the concept "loud sound" comes to be associated with impregnation and birth. Though Jones gives a few examples of various classical and primitive myths in which this motif occurs, he does not really make much of this particular association. Over sixty years later, however, Dundes (1976) used this part of Jones's argument to shed light on the use of the bullroarer in various initiation ceremonies held by several Australian aboriginal groups. Briefly, Dundes focused upon several things associated with the bullroarer, including (1) the use of the bullroarer to make loud noises, (2) the association of this object with initiation ceremonies that are conceptualized as ceremonies of rebirth, and (3) the recurrent use of mud and often feces in these same initiation ceremonies. He argued that these associations make sense if we see them as symbolic expressions of the impregnation-by-anal-wind theory discussed by Jones.

A moment's reflection will show that both Jones and Dundes overlooked a powerful piece of evidence in support of the arguments they were advancing. That evidence is the popularity of the Angelus.

A dominating feature of the Angelus devotion is, after all, its association with a loud sound, namely, the ringing of a church bell. Although it is customary in the Catholic tradition to ring church bells to summon the faithful to Mass or to mark the moment of consecration during the celebration of the Mass, the Angelus is in fact the only extra-liturgical popular devotion in which the sounding of a church bell occupies a central position. Remember too that the Angelus is explicitly described as a devotion in honour of the Incarnation, the moment at which Christ become man. We have in the Angelus, then, even more than in the obscure legend that Jones himself considers, or in the initiation ceremonies considered by Dundes, a very strong association between loud sounds and conception.

Adopting the general theoretical argument developed by both Jones and Dundes, I am suggesting that the Angelus devotion has been shaped by memories of the infantile belief, formed during the anal-erotic period, that the father's flatus (with its associated sound) can impregnate the mother.

WISH-FULFILMENT

Even granting that the Angelus devotion has been shaped by infantile memories of the impregnation-by-anal-wind theory, that does not explain the appeal of the devotion. Presumably, at least given the master hypothesis that underlies this book, this devotion is appealing because it gratifies an unconscious wish or desire. In the case of the Rosary, I argued that the wishes being gratified were (1) the desire to play with feces, and (2) the desire to behave in accord with the maternal injunction not to play with feces. This interpretation was supportable given that praying the Rosary involves the fingering of small hard beads, and that beads (in light of Ferenczi's work) can be seen as symbolic feces. But I see nothing in the practice of the Angelus that even remotely resembles the handling of symbolic feces.

Jones (1914, 353-5) himself argued that the imagery associated with the legend of the Madonna's conception through the ear gratified two wishes having to do with castration anxiety. On the one hand, the son wants to identify with the castrating father (which would mean having intercourse with the mother), while on the other hand the son's fear of castration leads him to fear that genital intercourse with the mother would lead to penis detachment ("castration" in Freud's sense), which the son wants to avoid at all costs. By identifying with God the Father (in the legend) the son can vicariously impregnate the mother (equals the Virgin Mary); yet the fact that the impregnation is by means of anal wind (under Jones's interpretaiton) avoids the anxiety about penis detachment that would be activated by a fantasy more clearly involving genital imagery.

While I see nothing inherently unreasonable about this argument, I don't think that it is correct. At the very least, we should demand of psychoanalysts who invoke ideas like castration and castration anxiety as explanatory concepts that they point to some evidence of castration imagery in the material being analysed. Yet this sort of imagery is noticeably absent from the legend that Jones is considering. Where in this legend, for example, is there any mention of bleeding or wounding, the severing of limbs, the cutting up of phallic-shaped objects, or any of the other motifs long recognized in the psychoanalytic literature as representing castration? In fact, this sort of imagery is just not present.

The key to understanding the Angelus, I think, lies rather in remembering that, unlike the Rosary, is intimately associated with only one event: the Incarnation.[5] If participation in the Angelus gratifies an infantile wish, it seems likely that it would be a wish somehow associated with the imagery conjured up by Catholic ideas and beliefs about the Incarnation. To discover just what those ideas and images are, it will be convenient to start by considering a blatant error in Jones's original essay.

After reviewing a few documentary references to the legend of the Madonna's conception through the ear, Jones argues that traces of the legend can be found in medieval art. He first lists four paintings of the Annunciation, each by a different artist, in which the dove is portrayed as entering the Madonna's ear (or at least, moving towards her head). In discussing where the doves in these paintings originate, Jones (1914, 270) says; "In the first named [of these four paintings], the dove emanates from the right hand of the father, in the second from his bosom; more typically however as in the picture of Simone Martini's here reproduced, one which will presumably be more fully discussed, *the Dove emanates from the mouth of the Father*" (emphasis added). The only painting reproduced in Jones's article is the *Annunciation* by Simone Martini (1284–1344), one of the most famous of all medieval paintings. The reproduction is a fuzzy black and white picture, and Jones (1914, 356) complains that the "marvelous colour [of the original] cannot be here reproduced," a remark which obviously implies that he is familiar with this painting. All the more strange then that although Jones says explicitly that the dove in the Martini *Annunciation* "emanates from the mouth of the father," it does no such thing. On the contrary, the dove in this particular picture is set directly in the top of the centre panel and is enclosed within a circular field defined by a series of "winged heads" (cherubs). "God the Father" is not in the picture. Furthermore, not only is the dove not emanating from the mouth of the father, but it is nowhere close to the Virgin's head, let alone her ear. In short, this particular painting, upon which Jones lays so much stress, shows absolutely no trace of the legend he is discussing.

I should hasten to point out that traces of this legend do exist in other representations of the Annunciation. In a stone relief at the Würzburg Cathedral (executed *c.* 1430–40), which Jones also mentions, the infant Jesus slides along a tube leading from the mouth of God the Father to the ear of the Virgin Mary. There are also a fair number of depictions of the Annunciation, not mentioned by Jones, in which a dove travels to Mary (though not always to her ear) along a gust of wind originating in the mouth of the father. This includes a thirteenth-century mosaic by Jacopo Torriti at S. Maria Maggiore in Rome; the Grabow altar executed by Master Bertram in 1379; an altar-piece executed by Melchior Broederkam in 1397; the central panel of a triptych executed *c.* 1440–43 by the Master of the Aix Annunciation; and a tapestry from the Lower Rhine executed *c.* 1500. All of these works are reproduced in connection with Schiller's (1966, 33–55) study of the iconography of the Annunciation (see plates 96, 104, 105, III, and II4), and they all lend support to Jones's argument. The point is only that Martini's *Annunciation* does not.

On the other hand, though Jones saw something in the Martini *Annunciation* that he wanted to see but that was not there, he overlooked something that was. It happens that something is entering the Virgin's ear in that painting, and that something does originate from a mouth. The something is a string of words, the Angel's salutation to Mary, which Martini depicts as a straight line running from Gabriel's mouth to Mary's ear. Spoken words, of course, are a form of sound, and given the analyses developed by both Jones and Dundes, sound entering an woman's ear is as easily seen as a symbolic expression of impregnation by anal wind as breath entering a women's ear. But this would suggest that the Martini *Annunciation* contains some graphic evidence that Gabriel, not God the Father, is impregnating Mary. I think this is exactly the idea being conveyed by the picture, and it is an idea that ties in quite nicely with established psychoanalytic theory.

Neither Freud nor any other psychoanalyst ever claimed that young children always have a clear, or even a conscious, awareness of the link between sexual intercourse and the process by which babies are born. Still, he did argue (see, for example, Freud 1931) that both boys and girls desire close physical contact with their mother in the pre-oedipal period. Furthermore, he also argued that children do perceive some sort of link between close physical contact and the making of babies. This in turn suggests that the desire for physical contact with the mother would bring with it a desire to make a baby with the mother. To be sure, the dynamics of the oedipal period intensify this wish in males and undermine it in females. But during the anal-erotic stage (and I have already argued that the general features of the Angelus devotion suggest that it is being shaped by desires formed during this stage), this desire should emerge in both the son and the daughter, and indeed there is clinical evidence that it does.[6]

If we now grant that the three main characters in the Annunciation drama, at least the three characters who routinely appear in Annunciation scenes in human form, are God the Father, the Virgin Mary, and the Angel Gabriel, then it is not difficult to see these as symbols respectively, of the father, the mother, and the son, or more generally, the child. This would mean that the imagery evoked by Martini's *Annunciation*, with its suggestion that Gabriel is impregnating the Virgin, is gratifying the child's pre-oedipal wish to impregnate the mother. I now want to argue that exactly this same wish underlies not only Martini's particular painting but, more generally, the Angelus as well.

As a start, we must understand why Martini painted the actual words of the Angel in the Annunciation scene. At one level, he did this because it was a well-established inconographic convention. Depictions of the words of the Angel issuing from Gabriel's mouth occur frequently in medieval art. But this convention itself derives from a long-standing Catholic tradition, namely, that Mary conceived Christ immediately after hearing and replying to the words of the Angel. The belief, in other words, is that Christ was conceived in Mary's womb just after Mary heard the Angel's words and answered with the phrase, "Behold, I am the handmaid of the Lord" (Luke 1: 38).

In light of this tradition, consider a question that is not really as self-evident as it first appears: who really caused the Virgin Mary to conceive a child? The doctrinally orthodox reply seems clear: it was God the Father, since he sent the Hold Ghost to Mary to effect conception. Yet because Catholic tradition holds that Mary only conceived upon hearing and responding to the words of the angel, there is some basis for arguing that the Angel Gabriel was at least the proximate cause of Mary's conception.

This ambiguity, I grant, is only implicit, but it is reinforced by official accounts by the Church of the Incarnation, which routinely pair statements making God the Father responsible for the Incarnation with a second statement that links the Incarnation to Mary's hearing the words of the Angel. The old *Baltimore Catechism* (see Schumaker 1954, 70–4), for instance, whose simple questions and answers about Catholic doctrine had to be learned by rote by innumerable Catholic schoolchildren in the United States, first gave the more orthodox view of the Incarnation:

Q. 86. How was the Son of God made man?
A. The Son of God was conceived and made man by the power of the Holy Ghost in the womb of the Blessed Virgin Mary.

But this was quickly followed by a reaffirmation of the continuing Catholic belief that the Incarnation occurred when Mary heard the Angel's words:

Q. 87. When was the Son of God conceived and made man?
A. The son of God was conceived and made man on Annunciation day, the day on which the Angel Gabriel announced to the Blessed Virgin Mary that she was to be the Mother of God.

This same dual emphasis, first upon the Incarnation as resulting from the Holy Ghost sent by God the Father and then upon the efficacy of the Angel's words, is likewise found in a catechism used in French-speaking dioceses of eastern Canada in the late nineteenth century:

81. Comment s'est accompli le mystère de l'Incarnation?
– Le mystère de l'Incarnation s'est accompli dans les entrailles de la bienheureuse Vierge Marie par l'opération du Saint-Esprit, c'est-à-dire, par un miracle de la toute-puissance divine.

85. Quel jour le Fils Dieu s'est-il fait homme?
– Le Fils de Dieu s'est fait homme dans le sein de la bienheureuse Vierge Marie, à Nazareth, le jour de l'Annonciation, lorsque l'archange Gabriel annonça à la Sainte Vierge qu'elle serait mère de Dieu. (*Le Catéchisme* 1888, 16–17)

This implicit ambiguity that Catholic tradition has built into the mythology surrounding the Incarnation, about who was the proximate cause of Mary's impregnation, explains the popularity of the Angelus. This ambiguity, in other words, means that participation in the Angelus and identification with the Angel Gabriel, can gratify the pre-oedipal desire to impregnate the mother, without doing violence to the perceived infantile "reality," namely, that it is really the father (God the Father) who impregnates the mother (Mary).

GENUFLECTION

In 1724, when Benedict XIII augmented the indulgences associated with the Angelus, he attached only two conditions: the Angelus must be said at the sound of a bell and it must be said on bended knee.[7] Though the bended knee seems to have given way to simply bowing the head in the modern era (Millet's picture is some evidence of that), the fact remains that for centuries the Angelus *was* said on bended knee. Though "praying on bended knee" is hardly uncommon in the Church, it has never, as far as I know, been made a requirement of any other popular devotion. Why was this done only in the case of the Angelus? Here again, we must refer to iconography of the Annunciation.

If we look over the various depictions of the Annunciation that accompany Schiller's (1966, 33–55) analysis, it is clear that at least during the Middle Ages the only main character in the Annunciation scene to be consistently portrayed on bended knee was the Angel Gabriel. Mary, by contrast, was usually portrayed sitting down. This "Gabriel on bended knee" element has no basis in Luke's account of the Annunciation, and it does not appear in depictions (also reproduced in Schiller's book) executed before AD 1000, which usually show the Angel standing next to Mary. But the fact that Gabriel was usually portrayed on bended knee during the Middle Ages means that this was the iconographic convention during precisely the period when the Angelus first emerged as a popular devotion.

Given this iconographic convention, the fact that practitioners of the Angelus routinely knelt when reciting the Hail Mary can be seen as reinforcing the identification with Gabriel which (under my hypothesis) makes the devotion appealing.

A THEORETICAL PROBLEM

So far I have argued that the theory of impregnation by anal wind underlies the imagery evoked by the Angelus, and that this infantile theory allows the "Mary conceived after hearing the Angel's words" element to fulfil the child's desire to impregnate the mother. But why should this desire be expressed in just this way? Children devise all sorts of answers to the question of how babies are made, of which the anal-wind theory is only one. Why wasn't one of those other infantile theories about conception invoked in shaping a popular Catholic devotion that centred on the Incarnation?

The answer lies in the one conclusion about the Angelus upon which all commentators agree: this devotion developed around the ringing of a church bell. The ringing of the bell, in other words, was primary. Now what infantile memories would most likely be evoked by the ringing of a Church bell? If Jones's reconstruction of the anal-erotic period is even approximately correct, then the loud sound of a church bells would almost certainly reactivate the particular loud sound that figures so prominently during the infantile period, namely, the sound associated with flatus.

But if infantile memories of flatus are reactivated, then this must inevitably activate memories of the impregnation-by-anal-wind theory which children develop (if Jones is correct) during the anal-erotic stage. Thus it would be particularly appropriate to associate the ringing of a church bell with an impregnation fantasy, and that is precisely what happened, for we know the ringing of the bell became associated with the Incarnation.

This is not to presuppose that the structure of the Angelus reflects a conscious design. On the contrary, I assume that it developed by something akin to natural selection. We already know, for instance, that an unsuccessful attempt was made to associate the midday Angelus with the Passion. We can now understand why: since the connotations evoked by the Passion are more with death than with impregnation or birth, there was no particular appropriateness about the psychological association between the Passion and the ringing of a church bell. But given the theory of impregnation by anal wind, the association between an impregnation fantasy like the Incarnation and the ringing of a bell *is* especially appropriate, and so this particular association became the basis for all three of the daily devotions centring on the ringing of a bell.

THE GERMAN CONNECTION

In the last chapter, the hypothesis that the appeal of the Rosary had anal-erotic origins, together with Dundes's work on the intense anality that seems to be a *leitmotif* of German culture, led to the prediction that the Rosary should have first established itself in the German-speaking parts of Europe. The fact that this prediction was correct was taken as support for the overall argument. But here again, as at the beginning of this chapter, a concern for theoretical consistency would seem to force us to make a similar prediction about the Angelus. Since I have traced the appeal of the Angelus to processes that occur in the anal-erotic stage, consistency would seen to require that I predict that the Angelus, like the Rosary, would first emerge in places where the experiences associated with the anal-erotic stage were particularly intense. The prediction, in other words, is that the Angelus, like the Rosary, would have first emerged as a popular devotion in German-speaking places. Unfortunately, the geographical origins of the Angelus are difficult to investigate.

We know that by the late fourteenth century the Angelus was widely practised throughout Europe. In other words, the Angelus first emerged in a historical period (the thirteenth and early fourteenth centuries) that is much farther removed from us than the period (the late fifteenth century) in which the Rosary emerged as a popular devotion. Consequently, the historical record is much scantier, which presumably is why most modern discussions of the Angelus simply ignore the question of geographical origins (see, for example, Latourette 1953, 536; De Marco 1967). But this question was addressed, at least indirectly, by Thurston, and his conclusion is remarkably consistent with the prediction made here.

In discussing the likely thirteenth-century origins of the Angelus, Thurston (1902a, 69–72) argued that the virtual absence of documents relating to this issue could be somewhat offset by the archaeological evidence, in particular, the evidence of church bells. The fact that such bells were often cast with dated inscriptions makes them a valuable source of information. Though the number of bells surviving from thirteenth century Europe is not large, several of those that have survived carry an inscription that invokes the Virgin Mary. While Thurston is well aware that such inscriptions do not necessarily mean that these bells were Angelus bells, he does argue that this is a reasonable inference.

More relevant to our concerns here is that fact that of the five particular thirteenth-century bells whose inscriptions Thurston discusses, three are from Germany, one is from France, and one from Majorca. The oldest of these five bells, which is dated 1234, is in fact a German bell found at Helfta, near Eisleben. This particular bell carries the inscription "AVE MARIA GRATIA PLENA, DOMINUS TECUM." Since these are the opening words of the Hail Mary, it seems especially likely that this particular bell was an Angelus bell. In short, limited though the evidence is, it does suggest that the Angelus was practised in Germany a full century before it became a European-wide devotion.

In a later article, Thurston (1904a) returned to the issue of church bells as a source of information about the early practice of the Angelus. He first notes that there is a relatively large number of German bells that can be dated to the thirteenth century and that carry an inscription containing the word "peace." A fairly common example is "O REX GLORIAE CHRISTE VENI CUM PACE ("O King of Glory Christ Come with Peace")." While conceding that there is no way to know with certainty what these German bells were used for, Thurston argues that there are two reasons for believing that they were Angelus bells.

First, we know that later in the Middle Ages the phrase "pro pace schlagen" ("to ring the peace") was in universal use throughout German-speaking regions as referring to the Angelus, just as that devotion was called "le pardon" in France and the "Ave Maria" in Italy. Furthermore, the bells rung as part of the Angelus during this later period (in Germany) were actually called "peace" bells. On analogy with this later practice, then, the inscription on these thirteenth-century bells that includes the word "peace" (as in "veni cum pace") suggests (to Thurston) that they too were probably Angelus bells.

Second, and more important, a few German bells from the late thirteenth century link the "veni cum pace" formula quite explicitly with the Virgin Mary, as in the following three inscriptions that appear on three different bells: "AVE MARIA AMEN + O RX GLORIE VENI CUM PACE"; "MARIA VOCOR. O REX GLORIAE VENI CUM PACE"; and "AVE MARIA GRATIE PLENA; VENI CUM PACE." Here again this leads Thurston to argue that "veni cum pace" bells were Angelus bells.

Finally, Thurston notes that the "veni cum pace" formula is somewhat less common on French bells and virtually unknown on English bells. He concludes that some form of the Angelus (at least in the sense of a popular devotion that involved the ringing of a bell and the saying of Hail Marys) was popular in Germany during the thirteenth century.

There is no denying the weak spots in Thurston's argument. There is, after all, no certainty that "veni cum pace" bells were Angelus bells or even that most of them were associated with the saying of the Hail Mary. Even granting that these bells might have been Angelus bells, there is no way of knowing if the Angelus in question was a truly popular devotion.

Still, however tenuous Thurston's argument, the fact remains that Thurston – in one of the few attempts to determine the geographical origins of the Angelus and with no particular theoretical axe to grind – came to precisely the conclusion that best supports the argument made in this chapter: that the Angelus first established itself as a popular devotion in Germany.

CHAPTER THREE

The Stations of the Cross

A great many things have changed in the Catholic Church since Vatican II, and several of those changes are apparent if Catholic churches built after Vatican II are compared with those built before. Many new churches, for instance, contain none of those plaster statues of various saints before which so many pious Catholics used to pray. Similarly, whereas it used to be common for a Catholic church to contain several different statues of the Virgin Mary, many churches now contain only one such statue, and often even this one statue has been banished from the main body of the church to the small enclosed room where mothers are supposed to sit with their crying babies. Formerly the central and dominating feature of any Catholic church was a crucifix, that is, a cross to which is attached an image of the crucified Christ, but even that has changed. In at least a few Catholic churches the cross that hangs suspended over the alter is now just a plain cross (without the body of Christ), something that would have almost certainly told pre-Vatican II Catholics that they were in a Protestant church. But in the midst of all this change, I have yet to visit a Catholic church, new or old, that did not have attached to its interior walls the fourteen plaques marking the Stations of the Cross, the popular devotion that is the subject of this chapter.

Since the Stations of the Cross is a devotion organized around Christ's various sufferings on his way to Calvary, it is one of the few popular devotions in the Catholic Church that is overwhelmingly Christocentric. This fact probably explains why this devotion is still (quite literally) built into the structure of Catholic churches. Though Catholic commentators rarely say it outright, the fact is that Vatican II severely undermined the Mary cult and, by extension, all those devotions like the Rosary, the Angelus, and the Brown Scapular that have Mary as their focus.

The Council's relatively sudden de-emphasizing of the Mary cult stands in marked contrast to the preceding century and a half, which was clearly a period of Marian advance. It was during this period for instance that the

Church choose to proclaim officially two important Marian doctrines (regarding the Immaculate Conception and the Assumption), each of which established Mary's specialness in the Christian pantheon, and it was also during this period that the well-known apparitions of the Virgin Mary at Paris (1830), LaSalette (1846), Lourdes (1858), and Fatima (1917) each gave rise to very popular cults.[1]

Why the Church hierarchy suddenly chose to bring this long period of Marian advance to a close is an important question and one that has not received much attention from sociologists of religion. But whatever the causes of this de-emphasis, the result has clearly been that since Vatican II the Church has given far less encouragement to popular devotions organized around the Virgin Mary than it used to. In connection with those popular devotions organized around Christ, however, like the Stations of the Cross, the Church has had more room to manoeuvre, since encouraging such devotions can actually strengthen the Christocentric emphasis so strongly endorsed by Vatican II.

THE STATIONS OF THE CROSS: WHAT ARE THEY?

According to Catholic tradition, the fourteen Stations of the Cross commemorate fourteen separate incidents associated with Christ's Passion, starting with Pontius Pilate's pronouncement of his judgment and ending with the interment of Christ's body in the tomb. Each of these fourteen incidents is portrayed in a picture or bas-relief attached to the interior walls of the church. Traditionally, seven of these plaques were affixed along one side wall, the other seven along the other side wall. Dehne (1975, 456), however, reports that in many new churches all the plaques are affixed to the rear wall (though all the new churches that I have seen use the traditional arrangement). The titles associated with these fourteen incidents are listed in Table 2.

The devout move from station to station (that is, from plaque to plaque) and meditate upon the particular scene portrayed. If there is a large number of people in the church, it is customary for most people to remain in the pews and for the officiating priest and his assistants to move from station to station. Apart from the necessity of stopping at each station and meditating upon each scene, there is nothing else that is formally required of participants. But it is usual to say at least one Our Father, one Hail Mary, and one Glory be to the Father at each station; other prayers are also sometimes added (see for instance the prayers in the Roman Missal; Cabrol 1947, 1436–41).

PILGRIMAGES TO JERUSALEM

Most earlier research on this devotion has been concerned with uncovering its historic origins, and on this issue there is now a great deal of scholarly con-

TABLE 2
Titles of the Fourteen Modern Stations of the Cross

First Station	Jesus is condemned to death.
Second Station	Jesus receives his cross.
Third Station	Jesus falls the first time under his cross.
Fourth Station	Jesus meets his afflicted mother.
Fifth Station	Simon of Cyrene helps Jesus to carry his cross.
Sixth Station	Veronica wipes the face of Jesus.
Seventh Station	Jesus falls the second time.
Eighth Station	Jesus speaks to the women of Jerusalem.
Ninth Station	Jesus falls the third time.
Tenth Station	Jesus is stripped of his garments.
Eleventh Station	Jesus is nailed to the cross.
Twelfth Station	Jesus dies on the cross.
Thirteenth Station	Jesus is taken down from the cross.
Fourteenth Station	Jesus is laid in the sepulchre.

Source: Cabrol 1947: 1435–41.

sensus. It is immediately apparent, for instance, that the Stations of the Cross is not directly derived from the traditions preserved in the New Testament. Five of the Stational incidents (the three falls of Jesus, his meeting with his mother, and his meeting with Veronica) are not mentioned in the New Testament at all, and a sixth (his being stripped of his garments when reaching Golgotha) is at best referred to only indirectly.[2]

Devotional guidebooks (for example, Cabrol 1947; 1435; Pegis 1961, 209) often suggest that the Stations of the Cross represents a vicarious pilgrimage, that is, that it simulates the behaviour of Christian pilgrims who visited various sites in the Holy Land. While statements of this sort might provide useful insight into the conscious motivation that leads individual Catholics to participate in this devotion, they cannot be taken at face value. However the devotion originated, it did *not* derive from the practices of pilgrims to the Holy Land.[3]

Pilgrims from the West had visited the Holy Land since the earliest centuries of the Christian era, and there were even a few attempts to recreate at European locations what Ousterhout (1981) has called "memento Jerusalems," which were usually churches whose design was based on the design of the Church of the Holy Sepulchre in Jerusalem. The most famous of these recreations was the group of churches dedicated to Santo Stefano in Bologna, but others existed on Cambridge in England, Brindisi in southern Italy, Østerlar in Denmark, and Torres del Rio in Spain (Ousterhout 1981, 311).

Furthermore, it does appear that these "memento" churches were associated with at least a few popular devotions. Using the architectural and archaeological data from the Santo Stefano site in Bologna, for instance, Ousterhout (1981, 316–7) argues that three popular devotions in particular were especially important. The first was a type of Palm Sunday celebration; the second was an *Adoratio Crucis*, a ceremony in which a relic of the True Cross was venerated; the third was an Easter Week ceremony in which a host or a cross or both were symbolically entombed in commemoration of Christ's entombment. Though a study of these devotions might be interesting in itself, the point to be made here is that none of them resembles the modern Stations of the Cross.

These memento churches aside, nothing like the Stations of the Cross seems to have been celebrated in Jerusalem itself during the medieval period. A careful inspection of the accounts left by pilgrims to the Holy Land up until the end of the Middle Ages reveals that although these pilgrims visited hundreds of sites in the Holy Land, the sites associated with Christ's journey from Pilate's house to Golgotha were not in any way grouped together or seen as a set separate from the other sites.

Only in pilgrims' accounts written between 1300 and 1500 do we first begin to find references to a distinct "Way of the Cross," that is, references suggesting that the sites associated with incidents that took place between Pilate's house and Golgotha were thought of as a "set." Even then it was only one of many such sets. In addition to the Way of the Cross, for instance, there were the sites located in and around Bethlehem, the sites located within the precincts of the Church of the Holy Sepulchre, the sites associated with a rambling journey around Jerusalem that the Virgin Mary is supposed to have made regularly after Christ's death, and so on. No particular set, and certainly not the Way of the Cross, was singled out as being more important than the others. Each set was rather just a separate "tour" that pilgrims to the Holy Land were expected to take.

We also know that the sites associated with the Way of the Cross were visited in reverse order; that is, Golgotha was visited first and Pilate's house last. Thurston (1906, 22–3) suggests that the Franciscans, who by papal decree had been made custodians of Christian holy sites for the Roman Church, settled on this order because it ensured that Christian pilgrims would visit the sites in the centre of Jerusalem at times of the day when these places were least frequented by the Moslem inhabitants of the city. Peters (1985, 107–8) suggests simply that the topography of the city made it more convenient to visit the sites in this order. Only in the early 1500s did pilgrims begin visiting these sites in the chronological order now evident in the Stations of the Cross. Even so, in conformity with Islamic beliefs regarding idolatry, Turkish authorities forbade the placing of representational images at any of these sites and forbade the Christian pilgrims who travelled the Way of the Cross from stopping, or even slowing down, at any particular site.

What this means is that two of the most prominent elements in the Stations of the Cross as a popular devotion, namely, graphic portrayals of each of the fourteen incidents, and stopping and meditating at each station, were not part of the experiences of actual pilgrims who visited the Way of the Cross in Jerusalem.

Finally, I should make it clear that although a distinct Way of the Cross had indeed appeared in Jerusalem by the end of the fifteenth century, there is by no means any clear agreement in pilgrims' accounts about the sites to be included in this group. Several incidents preserved in the modern Stations of the Cross (notably, the three falls) are not found in most pilgrim accounts, whereas many of those accounts do mention sites (like the house of Dives[4], and the houses of Herod and Simon the Pharisee) that have no place in the modern devotion. The events that do appear in most pilgrim accounts, are not always put in the same order. Some accounts, for instance, suggest that the meeting with Simon of Cyrene occurred before the meeting with Veronica, whereas others suggest just the reverse; some have Christ meeting Simon of Cyrene before meeting the women of Jerusalem, some suggest just the reverse; and so on.

In summary then, the actual practice of pilgrims in Jerusalem cannot explain: (1) why the Way of the Cross (rather than some other set of sites) was singled out and made the basis for a popular devotion, (2) why one particular set of events associated with the Way of the Cross came to be incorporated in the Stations of the Cross, while others were left out, (3) why the modern devotion relies so heavily upon graphic portrayals of the events commemorated, or (4) why the modern devotion emphasizes stopping and meditating at each station.

THE EMERGENCE OF
THE DEVOTION

All commentators agree that the Stations of the Cross first emerged as a popular devotion in the latter half of the fifteenth century (see for instance Thurston, 1906, 62–75; Schwemmer 1958, 34). Early examples of the Stations of the Cross can be found in several German cities, but the most well-known is the set of Stations erected by Adam Krafft in Nuremberg in about 1490. Krafft's plaques were initially set on a series of pillars erected outdoors rather than inside a church (as in the modern practice). The project was sponsored by a private citizen, not by ecclesiastical authorities, and remained in private hands for several centuries.

There were only seven stations in Krafft's scheme, which was a variant of a more general scheme called the "Seven Falls." The Seven Falls devotion was so named because it commemorated a series of events in the Passion in each of which Christ was prostrate (and thus "fallen") as a result of, say, falling under the weight of the cross, being taken down from the cross, being laid

TABLE 3

Titles of the Stations in Adam Krafft's "Seven Falls" System (Nuremberg, c. 1490) and in Peter Sterckx's "Seven Falls" System (Louvain, 1505)

Krafft's System	
First Station	Jesus meets his mother.
Second Station	Jesus is helped by Simon of Cyrene.
Third Station	Jesus meets the women of Jerusalem.
Fourth Station	Jesus meets Veronica.
Fifth Station	Jesus sinks under the cross and is belaboured by the Jews.
Sixth Station	Jesus is prostrate under the cross (after having been crucified).
Seventh Station	Jesus is laid in the arms of his Blessed Mother.
Sterckx's System[a]	
First Subject	Jesus is condemned to death.
Second Subject	Jesus falls the first time under the weight of the cross.
Third Subject	Jesus is helped by Simon of Cyrene.
Fourth Subject	Jesus meets Veronica.
Fifth Subject	Jesus falls the second time under the weight of the cross.
Sixth Subject	Jesus meets the women of Jerusalem.
Seventh Subject	Jesus falls the third time under the weight of the cross.
Eighth Subject	Jesus is stripped of his garments.

[a] Although Sterckx's scheme involved eight separate subjects, it is unclear whether the number of separate stations, or stopping places, was eight or some lesser number; see Thurston (1906, 65).

in the tomb, and so on. Since each of Krafft's plaques gives the distance from Pilate's House, and since there was a chapel and a crucifixion scene that were apparently visited after the seventh fall, it seems clear his system actually had nine stations. Table 3 lists the names associated with each of the Seven Falls in Krafft's system, as well as those associated with each of the falls in another Seven Falls system erected by Peter Sterckx at Louvain, Belgium, in 1505.

It is obvious that these two variants of the Seven Falls system are not in agreement with each other, let alone with the modern form of the devotion (see Table 2), with regard to either the content or ordering of the events.

After much historical sleuthing, Thurston (1906, 76–95) concluded that the modern arrangement of Stations was most likely the invention of Jan Pascha, an early sixteenth-century Flemish writer from Louvain. In Thurston's reconstruction, Pascha merged the incidents mentioned in one of the Seven Falls systems with some of the traditional incidents mentioned regularly by pilgrims to Jerusalem. Pascha assumed that four of the seven falls in the Seven

Falls system corresponded to four of these traditional incidents (the meeting of Christ with his mother, with Simon of Cyrene, with Veronica, and with the women of Jerusalem), and in these four cases the explicit mention of a fall was suppressed. The three remaining falls were kept, and do in fact appear in the modern Stations of the Cross.

But Pascha's system was by no means the only system of arranging the Stations of the Cross that existed in the sixteenth and seventeenth centuries, and we can reasonably ask why his particular system came to predominate. To Thurston (1906, 136–7) the answer seemed clear:

The curiously complicated development of the Stations of the Cross seems to the present writer to illustrate, in a conspicuous way, the working of a law akin to that of the survival of the fittest, a law which meets us more often than might be expected, in this and many other similar matters of popular piety. If one particular set of Stations has prevailed in preference to another, this I conceive, is ultimately to be attributed to the fact that the one appeals more strongly that the other to the pious imagination or to the devotional needs and feelings of the faithful at large.

This is an uncharacteristic lapse into psychology for Thurston, who was usually far more concerned with the historical origins of various Catholic devotions than with their psychological appeal. But the passage expresses perfectly one of the guiding threads of this book: the key to understanding the popularity of certain Catholic cults and devotions is to be found primarily in the psychological appeal of those cults and devotions to ordinary Catholics.

Thurston himself did not attempt to uncover the general psychological appeal of the Stations of the Cross, except to say that Christ's meeting with his mother and his meeting with Veronica are probably appealing because they express the sort of maternal care and affection that we all desire. The general hypothesis that guides the analyses in this book, however, suggests that if this devotion has proven to be popular, then this is likely due to the fact that it gratifies an unconscious desire of some sort.

A MAN BEING BEATEN

Even a casual inspection of the pictures appearing on the plaques at each Station or of the commentary so often supplied to the faithful as an aid to their meditation upon these pictures, will reveal that the Stations of the Cross emphasizes the suffering of Christ in great physical detail. Consider for instance, the following commentaries taken from the Roman Missal (Cabrol 1947, 1435–41):

Third Station ... Consider the first fall of Jesus under his cross. His flesh was torn by the scourges, his head crowned with thorns, and he had lost much blood.

Sixth Station ... Consider how the holy women named Veronica, seeing Jesus so ill-used, and his face bathed in sweat and blood, offered him her veil ...

Seventh Station ... Consider the second fall of Jesus under the Cross; a fall which renews the pain of all the wounds of his head and limbs.

Ninth Station ... His weakness was extreme, and the cruelty of his executioners very great, trying, as they did to hasten his steps.

Tenth Station ... Consider the violence with which Jesus was stripped by his executioners. As his inner garments adhered to his torn flesh, they dragged him off so roughly that the skin came with them.

And so on. Every one of the commentaries on each of the fourteen Stations describes the suffering of Christ in great (and often gory) detail, but the five commentaries just quoted are particularly important because they describe incidents not mentioned in the New Testament. In these cases, then, the details concerning the suffering of Christ can most easily be seen as fantasies that arise from the unconscious.

If we analyse the scenes commemorated in this devotion in the same manner as Freud (and other psychoanalysts) have analysed dreams, the emphasis on suffering suggests that we are dealing with a devotion whose appeal is either sadistic or masochistic. To decide which, we must look carefully at the attitude adopted by devotees.

Certainly if devotees were encouraged to identify with Christ and thereby share his suffering, at least vicariously, we would most reasonably conclude that the devotion gratifies a masochistic impulse. But they are *not* encouraged to identify with Christ and share his suffering. Rather they are encouraged simply to meditate upon each instance of suffering (hence the formula in the Roman Missal: "Consider now the ...").[5] This suggests that there is something about the simple perception of a man being beaten and abused that is appealing, which in turn suggests that participation in this devotion gratifies a sadistic desire.

Conceptualized as a sadistic fantasy, the Stations of the Cross seems remarkably similar to a fantasy that, according to Freud, appeared regularly in a large number of his patients. This was a fantasy in which "a child was being beaten" (Freud 1919). In this fantasy the patient dreams or imagines that a child is being beaten by a father or father surrogate. The child in the fantasy is not the patient, and in fact the child being beaten is usually male whether the patient is male or female. In other words, in this common beating fantasy a young male is beaten by a father or father surrogate, just as in the Stations of the Cross Jesus Christ is beaten, scourged, and so on by order of

Pontius Pilate. The two fantasies are similar enough to suggest that they might result from the same underlying process.

In Freud's reconstruction, the conscious beating fantasy just described is only the final stage in a series of transformations that derive ultimately from a son or daughter's oedipal desire for the father. In the first stage, the oedipal desire for the father – by which Freud only means the child's desire to be touched, held, caressed, and so on by the father – gives rise to the belief that this love is returned. Since beating implies the negation of love, the child imagines that the father is beating other children, who represent actual or potential siblings (e.g., "My father loves me and me only, and so is beating other children").

Inevitably, for a variety of reasons, the child's oedipal desire for the father comes to be repressed. But though repression pushes the desire into the unconscious, the desire still exists, and the existence of this now forbidden desire for the father results in guilt, which leads the child to want to punish himself or herself. This desire for self-punishment produces the next transformation, in which the child sees himself or herself as the child being beaten. This second phantasy remains unconscious and appears only under intense analysis.[6]

In the case of the son, the child being beaten in this unconscious phantasy is the son himself and thus male. In the case of the daughter the situation is more complex. The child being beaten is indeed the daughter herself, but under the influence of the overall oedipal process and the resulting penis envy, the daughter thinks of herself (Freud argued) in masculine terms, which means that the child being beaten is also male.

The final transformation of this phantasy occurs as a result of a regression to the infantile memories that were formed in the period just before the oedipal period. In the last two chapters, this earlier stage has been described as one in which anal-erotic desires were particularly important. That description was correct but incomplete and must now be expanded in order to understand Freud's analysis of the beating fantasy.

Freud argued that during the same period in which the young child is most concerned with the gratification of anal-erotic desires, the child (whether girl or boy) is also greatly concerned with achieving a mastery over its immediate environment. This drive for mastery easily results in sadistic phantasies, since such phantasies, involving as they do total control over someone or something else, are seen as the ultimate expression of a mastery over the environment.

Because this stage in the child's development is characterized simultaneously both by fairly strong anal-erotic desires and by these strong sadistic desires, Freud most commonly labelled it either the "anal-erotic" or the "anal-sadistic" stage, depending upon which type of desire he wanted to emphasize. Although the anal eroticism and the sadism of this stage develop more or less independently, the two tendencies do become fused, by which Freud means only that they become strongly associated. This ensures that acts of sadism can activate the feelings of diffuse physical pleasure (or at least the memory of these feelings) and so can be pleasurable in themselves.

It is this fusion of anal eroticism with sadism that is used to transform and disguise the now repressed oedipal desire for the father into something more acceptable to the conscious mind. This occurs by changing the unconscious "I am being beaten by my father" phantasy into a conscious "a child is being beaten by a father figure" fantasy. Because the child being beaten is not in any obvious way a representation of the real child, this fantasy is not recognizable by the conscious mind as an expression of the child's oedipal desires. Yet by virtue of the association between sadism and sexual pleasure the clearly sadistic nature of this fantasy does induce feelings of sexual pleasure, and so provides some gratification of the repressed desire for the father.

Not all people will experience the conscious fantasy, that is, the dream or daydream about a child being beaten, even though Freud did find that this fantasy was exceedingly common. The critical factor seems to be the ease with which a regression to the anal-erotic (or anal-sadistic) stage is effected. In other words, since the appeal of the final fantasy depends so heavily upon the association between anal-eroticism and sadism, those individuals who can regress to the anal stage most easily are most likely to experience that fantasy. On the other hand, Freud does say clearly that the underlying unconscious processes on which the fantasy rests do develop, at least to some degree, in almost everyone. This would suggest that if the fantasy were presented – fully formed – to most individuals, they would find it appealing.

This argument, with virtually no modification, leads easily to a hypothesis that would explain the psychological appeal of the Stations of the Cross, and it is this: the appeal of this devotion is that it is a sadistic fantasy that by virtue of a regression to the anal-sadistic stage, produces a diffuse sense of sexual pleasure and so gratifies vicariously the repressed desire for the father that develops in all children.

EXPLANATIONS

The hypothesis that the Stations of the Cross is a popular devotion because it is a sadistic fantasy would explain, first of all, the observation with which we started, namely, the emphasis that this devotion places upon a detailed and visual consideration of the suffering of Christ. It would explain, in other words, the injunction to meditate carefully upon various events associated with the suffering of Christ and the use of so many graphic portrayals of this suffering as an aid to this meditation. It would also explain why the devotions deals only with the Passion of Christ, something that has attracted criticism from some modern Catholic theologians (see the discussion in Brown 1967,

833), who argue that an emphasis upon the Passion that is not simultaneously associated with an emphasis upon the Resurrection is theologically incomplete. After all, if the sadistic content of the devotion is what makes it appealing, then the inclusion of something about the Resurrection (an event that emphasizes renewal and rebirth, not suffering) would only undermine that appeal, the cavils of liberal Catholic theologians notwithstanding.

Now consider another feature of the devotion that has always been problematic: the emphasis on falling. In a historical sense, there are three falling scenes in the modern devotion because Jan Pascha (under Thurston's reconstruction) took them over from the original system of Seven Falls. But as mentioned earlier, Pascha's system of Stations was only one of many, and the historical argument hardly explains why a version of the Stations with so many falls became so popular.

Freud found that falling dreams were among the most common of all the dreams that he encountered, and his investigations led him to conclude that such dreams usually reflected the gratification of a sexual desire. In particular, he argued that falling dreams usually reflected the infantile memory of the diffuse sense of physical pleasure that young children experience from games in which they were raised and lowered, as for instance when a parent lifts a child into the air, bounces the child upon the parent's knee, and so on (see for example Freud 1900, 392–5). I suggest that the emphasis on recurrent falling in the Stations of the Cross – an emphasis, remember, that has no clear basis in either the New Testament or the accounts of actual pilgrimages to Jerusalem – derives from the same infantile sources.

Remember that the sadistic fantasy evident in the devotion is pleasurable because it gratifies the oedipal desire for the father. But in so doing , it must inevitably rewaken the infantile memory of those early sexual experiences with the father that gratified this desire in a direct way, and many of these early experiences, as Freud noted, are associated with falling. This means that the inclusion of a falling emphasis in the devotion can also (like the emphasis on sadism) provide for the vicarious gratification of the now repressed desire for the father.

The hypothesis offered here also allows us to account for something else that is problematic about the Stations of the Cross: why they begin with the condemnation of Christ by Pilate. The rationale for starting with this event is by no means obvious. It is not, for instance, the event that has traditionally been seen as the beginning of the Passion of Christ. That is usually taken to be the Agony in the Garden at Gethsemane. Then too, any number of other events are traditionally considered to be part of the Passion and yet precede the decision by Pilate. These include Christ's sense of abandonment both when he discovers the apostles asleep at Gethsemane, and, later, when the apostles flee upon his arrest; the denial by Peter; the mockery and abuse he suffered when brought before the High Priest and Herod; and so on.

Nor is Pilate's decision pivotal in any theological sense to the sequence of events that led to Christ's crucifixion. Whatever the historic Christ might have thought about the matter, it has been a firm Christian belief at least since St. Paul's theology established itself in the Church that the crucifixion was fore-ordained by God the Father as a way of redeeming humankind.

Given all this, the question remains: why start with Pilate's final judgment?

Under the hypothesis offered here, remember, the child's oedipal desire for the father is gratified in this devotion. For Freud this is the reason why the father is the person doing the beating in the first and second stages in the development of the "child is being beaten" fantasy, and therefore the reason why the person doing the beating in the final fantasy is either the father or a father surrogate (like a teacher). If the same psychological process that gives rise to beating fantasies is also the process that makes the Stations of the Cross an appealing devotion, we would indeed expect that an authoritative father figure would be made ultimately responsible for the beatings and other suffer-ing experienced by Christ. That is precisely what the first station does, since it implies that Pontius Pilate is the single person most responsible for all of Christ's subsequent suffering. This implication would be weakened if the devotion started with the traditional beginning of the Passion (the Agony in the Garden) or any other of the Passion events that precede the meeting with Pilate.

SPREAD OF THE DEVOTION

Although the Stations of the Cross emerged as a popular devotion in certain European locations during the late fifteenth century, it was not until the late seventeenth century that it spread to almost all parts of Catholic Europe. There seems little mystery about what caused this late seventeenth-century increase in popularity; it was almost certainly due to the fact that only dur-ing the seventeenth century did various popes began to associate the Stations of the Cross with indulgences. The nature of an indulgence and the reason why its association with a religious devotion would greatly increase the popularity of that devotion cannot be understood without knowing something about Catholic beliefs regarding sin and punishment.

In the traditional Catholic world view, the commission of a serious sin oc-casions a fall from the "state of grace" that was established at Baptism. Should a Catholic die while in this condition, he or she will go to Hell. A state of grace can be re-established by receiving absolution for one's sins in the sacrament of Confession (now called the Sacrament of Reconciliation). But though ab-solution ensures that the person involved will not go to Hell (should they die), it does not remove the punishment (called the "temporal" punishment) that God will mete out for the sins that have been committed. This temporal punishment will be experienced either during a person's life here on earth or, after death, in Purgatory.[7] The effect of an indulgence is to reduce this temporal punishment.

Indulgences are of two types: a "plenary indulgence" cancels all the temporal punishment associated with all sins to that point in the sinner's life, and a "partial indulgence," as the name implies, only reduces that punishment to some degree. Partial indulgences are usually expressed in standard calendrical units ("thirty days indulgence," "ten years indulgence," and so on). This does *not* mean that the amount of temporal punishment is reduced by that number of days or years. It means rather that God will reduce your temporal punishment by an amount equivalent to what he would have reduced it by had you practised penitential mortifications (of the sort that prevailed in the early Church) for that number of days or years. Indulgences are usually associated with the recitation of particular prayers, visits to particular sites (like certain sites in the Holy Land, or certain churches), or participation in certain devotions.

I seriously doubt whether most lay Catholics have ever fully understood all the nuances of the Church's official doctrines regarding indulgences (which have only been cursorily summarized here[8]). But almost all Catholics would certainly know that an indulgence reduced the pain and suffering that a person might otherwise expect to experience in this life or the next for committing sin – and so it was something to be desired. Associating a devotion with an indulgence therefore provides a tremendous incentive for ordinary Catholics to participate in that devotion, and this is precisely what began to happen in the seventeenth century with regard to the Stations of the Cross.

In 1686 Innocent XI granted the Franciscans the right to erect Stations of the Cross in their churches and declared that the Franciscan themselves and the members of the lay organizations affiliated with their order could gain indulgences by visiting these stations. This privilege was confirmed by Innocent XII in 1694 and extended to all Catholics by Benedict XIII in 1726. Finally, in 1731 Clement XII decreed that these indulgences could be gained by visiting any Stations of the Cross that had been properly erected; that is, the indulgences were not limited to Stations erected in Franciscan churches.

In 1750, Benedict XIV erected the Stations of the Cross in the ruins of the Coliseum at Rome, and the devotion was conducted there every Friday from that time until 1870, when Rome came under the control of the Italian government. Given this strong papal endorsement, and the indulgences now associated with the devotion, the popularity of the devotion spread rapidly through Italy and the rest of Catholic Europe.

It thus appears that in the late seventeenth and early eighteenth centuries the Church did what it has often done: it incorporated and began to endorse strongly a devotion that had already achieved a certain measure of popularity.

But this raises the same sort of question that was raised in the last two chapters: what accounts for the initial popularity of the devotion, in the period before it was so strongly endorsed by the Church?

Remember that under Freud's original argument a sadistic fantasy gratifies the infantile desire for the father by means of a regression to the anal-sadistic stage, since it is only by virtue of a such a regression that the strong association between sadism and sexual pleasure is activated. Freud in fact often discussed the conditions that would facilitate a regression to the anal-sadistic stage. Generally, he argued that such a regression was facilitated if either of the anal eroticism or the sadism experienced during this stage had been especially intense, something that itself could result from one of two causes. First, in certain individuals sadistic or anal-erotic desires might be especially strong for "constitutional" reasons, by which Freud meant that it was part of their biological heritage. Second, and more importantly for us, he argued that either type of desire might also be intensified by the peculiarities of the child's interaction with his or her parents.[9]

What all this means then is that if the child-rearing practices prevalent in a region did systematically intensify either the anal-erotic or the sadistic desires experienced by young children during the anal-sadistic stage, then Catholics in such places (as compared to Catholics raised elsewhere) would find it easier to regress to this stage later in life. Since such a regression enhances the psychological appeal of the Stations of the Cross, these same places should be the ones where this devotion is most likely to became popular even without official encouragement from the Church.

When this conclusion is put alongside the discussion in the preceding two chapters, it seems to lead inexorably to a fairly precise prediction. After all, following Dundes, I have already argued that something about the child-rearing practices in the German-speaking regions of Europe intensifies anal-erotic desires in those regions. But if this is correct, German-speaking Catholics would find it easier to regress to the anal-sadistic stage, and should therefore find the Stations of the Cross especially appealing. The final prediction then is that the Stations of the Cross, like the Rosary and the Angelus, first emerged as a popular devotion in the German-speaking regions of Europe.

It turns out that this prediction is only partly correct. I have already mentioned that one of the first and most well-known Stations of the Cross was the one erected by Adam Krafft at Nuremberg (in Bavaria) in 1490. Other early Stations erected in German-speaking regions are those erected at Görlitz (Prussia) in about 1470 and at Bamberg (Bavaria) in 1507. The evidence seems to suggest that the Stations of the Cross began to emerge as a popular devotion in Germany during the latter part of the fifteenth century (see the discussion in Thurston 1906, 62–5; Schwemmer 1958, 34–6).

On the other hand, another well-known Stations of the Cross was erected at Louvain, in a Flemish-speaking region of what is now Belgium, in 1505, and seems to have been imitated throughout the Low Countries. Though it is tempting to conclude that the devotion developed first in Germany during the closing decades of the fifteenth century and then spread to the Low Countries in the early decades of the sixteenth century, Thurston's (1906) discussion rather creates the impression that it emerged more or less independently in both areas. The most justifiable conclusion would seem to be Thurston's (1906, 76), which is that in the early sixteenth century the Stations of the Cross was popular mainly in the German states and the Low Countries.

Since I have no reason to suspect that anal eroticism is particularly strong in the Low Countries (certainly Dundes does not make that argument), I cannot explain the early popularity of the Stations of the Cross in this region. On the other hand, the fact that the German-speaking states of Europe were at least *among* the first places to embrace this devotion before it was strongly endorsed by the Church does provide partial support for the argument developed here.

SUMMARY AND CONCLUSION

In summary, my argument is that the Stations of the Cross is a sadistic fantasy that, by virtue of the fusion between sexual pleasure and sadism that occurs at the anal stage, allows for the vicarious gratification of the an unconscious sexual desire for the father. The value of this hypothesis is that it can account for a range of observations associated with this devotion: the fact that the devotion places so much emphasis upon a detailed consideration of the sufferings of Christ; why other subjects (like the Resurrection) that Catholic theologians usually link with the Passion are not emphasized; why the Stations begin with Pilate's Final Judgment, an event that is not the traditional starting point of the Passion; why there is so much falling imagery in the devotion; and why the German-speaking regions of Europe were among the first places in which the Stations of the Cross emerged as a popular devotion.

It should also be emphasized that the psychoanalytic argument on which this explanation rests is not *ad hoc*; that is, it was not specially constructed to account for the appeal of the Stations of the Cross. It is instead virtually the same argument used by Freud to explain the beating fantasies that he encountered in so many of his patients. If this particular Freudian argument is unfamiliar to many readers, even to those who have a passing familiarity with the psychoanalytic literature, it is probably because Freud's work on anal eroticism has not attracted as much interest as, say, his work on phallic and genital sexuality.

Quite apart from the fact that psychoanalytic arguments can be used to order a range of observations into a coherent pattern, such arguments often have another strength: they can lead to the recognition of previously unrecognized patterns. Consider for instance the three devotions discussed in these first three chapters: the Rosary, the Angelus, and the Stations of the Cross. On the surface, these devotions would appear to have little in common. Certainly I know of no Catholic commentator who has suggested that there is any special link between them.

Nevertheless, the psychoanalytic arguments in the first three chapters have led to the conclusion that these devotions should be similar in at least one way: in the period before they were officially endorsed by the Church, they should all have been especially popular in regions where infantile anal-erotic experiences were especially intense. Since Dundes has identified the German-speaking parts of Europe as regions of just this sort, we were led to expect that these devotions should have Germanic origins. It turns out that there is some such evidence, however imperfect, in all three cases. Although Catholic commentators, in discussing these devotions individually, have touched lightly upon the Germanic origins of each, they had not thought to suggest this was particularly important. Certainly no one has previously suggested that the Germanic origins of these three devotions might provide a clue to their psychological appeal.

CHAPTER FOUR

The Blood Miracles of Naples

Of all the books written by Sigmund Freud, the one that seems to have proven the most popular with the general public (after, possibly, *The Interpretation of Dreams*) is his *The Psychopathology of Everyday Life* (1901). This book is concerned with "parapraxes," a broad term that includes "Freudian slips" (slips of the tongue and the pen); the sudden forgetting of otherwise familiar terms and memories; the bungling of usually simple tasks; and so on. There is very little theory in the book (Freud's only theoretical point is that parapraxes result when an unconscious thought or desire overcomes and influences a conscious action). Most likely it is this very absence of theoretical discussion, coupled with the colourful examples that Freud presents, which has ensured the book's popularity.

The analysis cited most often in the book is the one that takes up most of the second chapter, "The Forgetting of Foreign Words" (Freud 1901, 8–14). Freud begins with a personal anecdote: While travelling through Italy by train, he once shared a compartment with a young man who, like Freud himself, was Jewish. They began discussing the status of Jews in Europe. After complaining that the current generation of European Jews would not be allowed to fulfil their potential, the young man wanted to end the conversation with a dramatic flourish. He tried to do this by quoting a line from the *Aeneid*, a line in which Dido commits the next generation to vengeance. But he couldn't get the Latin quotation just right; he knew a word was missing but couldn't remember what word it was. In frustration, he asked Freud to supply it. Freud did: the missing word was "*aliquis*."[1] The young man, who obviously knew something about Freud's work, then challenged Freud to explain his inability to remember correctly such a well-known quotation. Freud good-humouredly took up the challenge.

As in all psychoanalytic investigations (including those in this book) Freud started with associations, and so he asked the young man to free-associate with the word *aliquis*. The primary associations turned out to be an association between "aliquis" and "liquefy" (based obviously on the phonetic similarity between the two words) and between "aliquis" and "relics." These two words (liquefy, relics) then reminded the man of the Blood Miracle of St Januarius at Naples, when the dried blood of that saint suddenly turns from a solid to a liquid. This in turn reminded the young man of story involving Garibaldi. It seems that Garibaldi was present on an occasion when the blood relic did *not* liquefy. The assembled crowd grew restless, thinking that a calamity was imminent. Garibaldi then "suggested" to the officiating clergymen that the blood had better start liquefying "or else," and the liquefaction promptly occurred.[2] This story in turn reminded the young man of something else, but something he was reluctant to discuss.

Freud intervened at this point and guessed the secret: the man was involved in a sexual relationship with a woman, that woman had missed her period, and he was now afraid she was pregnant. His unconscious anxiety over the social calamity that might follow upon this "failure of menstrual blood to flow" had reminded him about the incident involving "the failure of St Januarius's blood to flow," which (by way of the associations with "relics" and "liquefy") had blocked his memory of the Latin word "*aliquis*."

As far as I know, this is the only instance where Freud mentions the Blood Miracle of St Januarius, and I can find no studies of this miracle by later psychoanalysts. This seems surprising given the visibility of Freud's *aliquis* analysis, given that this miracle is so widely known in Europe, and given the ease with which the miracle can be connected to psychological concerns (like a concern with menstrual blood) usually considered to be important in the psychoanalytic tradition.

I concede that the St Januarius cult is different from the other cults and devotions considered in this book, for virtually all similar blood miracle cults are located in or around Naples. Such cults therefore do not have the "transnational" appeal of the other cults and devotions considered in this book. The only justification that I offer for considering this exception is that the psychoanalytic argument that explains the appeal of blood miracle cults is strikingly consistent with the explanations offered elsewhere in this book.

THE MIRACLE ITSELF

Grant (1929, 47–8) gives a good description of the reliquary containing the blood of St Januarius:[3]

Within this reliquary there are two ampollas (vials), the larger of which contains a varying quantity of a substance which is believed to the Blood of the Saint; the smaller of the two is almost empty ... These two ampollas are enclosed in a reliquary composed as follows: Two flat circular sheets of glass form the back and front of this receptacle; they are securely held by a circular metal band, the two ampollas being firmly set between these two sheets of glass in such a manner as to be immovable. The top of the reliquary is closed by means of a stratum of gum mastic. The base of the reliquary forms a handle.

I might only add that each of the two inside vials is set into a putty-like substance in the bottom of the reliquary, that the top of each vial is sealed with a coil of solder; and that there is some ornamentation (a crown supported by cherubs) set onto the top of the reliquary. This relatively small reliquary spends most of the year inserted in a much larger monstrance (a picture of which can be found in Petito 1983, figures 12 and 13).

The reliquary of the saint's blood is kept in a vault located in the Tesoro (treasury) of the Duomo at Naples. Though called a "side-chapel" in many accounts, the tesoro is by North American standards the size of a small church and is richly decorated with mosaics, statues, frescoes, and so on. Also in the tesoro vault is a life-sized half-figure statue of St Januarius. This too is a reliquary and it contains what is supposed to be the head of this saint. It is an essential belief of the St Januarius cult that the blood relic will only liquefy if it is close proximity to the saint's head, and so the two reliquaries are routinely exposed together.

Traditionally, the two reliquaries are exposed on eighteen different occasions during the year: on the Saturday before the first Sunday in May[4] and on each of the succeeding eight days; during the celebration of the Saint's Octave in September (that is, on the saint's feast day, 19 September, and the following seven days); and on 16 December.[5] On the first Saturday in May the reliquary containing the head is brought in procession to the Church of Santa Chiara in Naples, and a few hours later a second procession brings the blood relic to the same church. On all other occasions, the two relics are exposed together at the main altar of the Tesoro.

On the vast majority of these occasions the blood[6] does liquefy. Since the blood is sealed inside a vial, which is sealed inside the reliquary, what "liquefaction" usually means is that when initially shaken or turned upside down, the substance in the vial either does not move at all or rattles around like a solid; when shaken or turned later, it seems to flow like a liquid. Sometimes a change in the colour of the blood is also reported during these liquefactions, and on occasion it is also supposed to "boil" and "froth."

The officials at the Tesoro have kept a record of each year's liquefactions since 1632 for the December ceremonies and since 1648 for the ceremonies in May and September. Kehoe (1871) inspected these records and published the relevant information to 1860. His data are summarized in Table 4. "Liquefied" means that the relic was either fully or partly liquid when taken out of the vault that day, while "uncertain" refers to those cases in which the vial was

TABLE 4

Liquefactions of Blood Relic of St Januarius, Seventeenth to Nineteenth Century

| | Number of Years in Which Relic | | | | |
	Was Liquid When Removed from Vault	Liquefied during Ceremony	Never Liquefied	Uncertain	Total
May Ceremonies, 1648–1860					
Sat.	23	189	1	–	213
Sun.	13	200	–	–	213
Mon.	––	213	–	–	213
Tue.	––	209	–	4	213
Wed.	4	176	–	33	213
Thur.	3	155	–	56	214[a]
Fri.	3	141	–	68	212[a]
Sat.	1	137	–	75	213
Sun.	2	136	–	73	211[a]
September Ceremonies, 1648–1860					
19 Sept.	12	200	–	––	212[b]
20 Sept.	21	191	–	––	212
21 Sept.	21	190	–	1	212
22 Sept.	20	191	–	1	212
23 Sept.	22	188	–	2	212
24 Sept.	18	193	–	1	212
25 Sept.	17	194	–	1	212
26 Sept.	14	196	–	2	212
Ceremony on 16 Dec. for Years 1632–1860	1	181	43	3	228

Source: Kehoe (1871, 24–5)

[a] The total should be 213, but Kehoe does not explain the discrepancy.

[b] Kehoe makes it clear that for the September ceremonies the period covered, 1648–1860, is not inclusive, but he does not indicate whether the data are missing for 1648 or for 1860.

"full," that is, in which the substance inside the vial covered the vial's entire inside surface, making it impossible to decide if that substance was liquid or solid.

While these data make it clear that liquefaction almost always does occur, at least during the May and September celebrations, other data presented by Kehoe indicate that the time it takes for the relic to liquefy varies quite widely: often liquefaction occurs in a few minutes, often only after an hour or two, and in a substantial number of cases, only after two to five hours or more.

Information on more recent liquefactions can be obtained from Ambrasi (1970), who discusses the liquefactions that occurred during the December ceremony and on the first day of the ceremonies in May and September, for the years 1920–70. Since Ambrasi reproduces the actual diary entries made on these occasions, it is possible to categorize his data by the same classification scheme used in Table 4. This is done in Table 5. As is evident, the dominant pattern in these more recent data is more or less the same as in the data gathered by Kehoe: for the May and September ceremonies, at least, liquefaction almost always occurs. If there is any pattern evident in comparing Tables 4 and 5, it is that "failure to liquefy" during the December ceremony has become even more common in the twentieth century.

Mention here should be made of the *Zie di San Gennaro*, the Aunts of St Januarius. This is a group of women ranging in age from fifty to eighty years who attend each exposure of the relics. Membership in the group is hereditary, passing from mother to daughter, and it is believed that they are lineal descendants of St Januarius himself. Should the blood not liquefy promptly, it is customary for these "aunts" to try to hasten the liquefaction by cries and shouts that are often quite shrill and sometimes even obscene, something that has been a source of embarrassment to Catholic commentators.[7]

The historical St Januarius was a Christian bishop and martyr beheaded for his faith in town of Pozzuoli (which is just up the coast from Naples) in AD 305. But even the most ardent defenders of the cult (see for instance Petito 1983, 164) concede that the first known reference to the blood miracle is in a document dated 1389. Since there is no mention of the miracle in documents relating to the liturgy at the Naples Duomo around 1350 (Grant 1929, 47), it seems almost certain that the cult emerged sometime in the late fourteenth century. In the fifteenth and sixteenth centuries there are several references to the miracle, including one by Enea Silvio de'Piccolomini (1405–64), who became Pope Pius II, and by the Renaissance humanist Pico della Mirandola 1463–94). Since the early seventeenth century, as I mentioned, detailed records of the miracle have been kept by the Tesoro officials. There are also any

TABLE 5

Liquefactions of Blood Relic of St Januarius, 1920–70

	Number of Years in Which Relic				
	Was Liquid When Removed from Vault	*Liquefied during Ceremony*	*Never Liquefied*	*Uncertain*	*Total*
First day of May ceremonies	19	29	3	0	51
First day of September ceremonies	1	50	0	0	51
16 December	0	27	24	0	51

Source: Ambrasi (1970)

number of eyewitness accounts of this miracle written in the nineteenth and twentieth centuries by both Catholics and non-Catholics.

IMAGERY

There is an enormous scholarly literature dealing with the Blood Miracle of St Januarius. Thurston himself published nine different essays on this and related subjects, and the articles on the blood-miracle cults of Naples probably number in the thousands. Almost all of this literature, however, is concerned with trying to decide if the miracle is of natural or supernatural origin, and if of natural origin, what the precise natural process is.

Thurston's own view, expressed time and again, was that the miracles were indeed a natural phenomenon. He freely admitted that he did not know the nature of that process, but the very regularity of the miracle (something that devotees of the cult take as evidence of its supernatural origin) was for Thurston the very thing that made a supernatural origin unlikely. Simply put, Thurston did not believe in a God who would be such a showman as to perform so regularly what seemed (to Thurston) to be a pointless miracle.

In this case, as in all others in this book, I am going to avoid the issue of whether the miracle is natural or supernatural in origin. (But see appendix B.) I assume the liquefaction is produced by some natural process. Furthermore, I will not be concerned in this chapter with trying to discover the nature of that natural process. If the legions of experts who have subjected the relic to any number of scientific tests have not been able to do that, I certainly cannot.[8] Given that the blood is seen to liquefy, my concern is purely with the psychological appeal of the St Januarius cult. Why in other words, is a blood relic that liquefies regularly so appealing that a cult organized around such a relic is one of the most popular Catholic cults in the Naples area?

As usual the place to start is with the psychological associations evoked by this blood relic. In Freud's *aliquis* example, the liquefaction of the blood relic was associated with menstruation. While this may indeed have been an association in the mind of the young man to whom Freud was speaking, I can find nothing in the traditions and rituals surrounding the St Januarius cult that might reasonably be seen to evoke or reinforce menstruation imagery. On the other hand, there is one association that those same traditions and rituals do go to great lengths to establish and which must be considered here. This is the strong association between the blood relic and the head of St Januarius.

Remember that according to the traditions of the cult, the blood relic will only liquefy when it is in close proximity to the head, which is why the two relics are displayed together. It is of no concern here whether the relic would or would not liquefy in the absence of the head. What matters is the strong cultic insistence that the two relics be associated. Since St Januarius' head was severed during his execution, there seems a basis for suggesting that there is a strong association between the blood relic and decapitation. This association is reinforced by the fact that the blood in the blood relic is supposed to be the very blood that flowed during this decapitation.

An emphasis on decapitation puts us on familiar psychoanalytic ground. Freud routinely argued that as a result of "displacement upwards" the head was one of the dream symbols most commonly used to represent the penis (see for instance Freud 1915-16, 339–40). A severed head would thus be a severed penis, that is, castration.[9] In fact, in his own analysis of a dream in which a severed head appeared, Freud (1900, 366) saw it as a castration symbol.

But if the blood miracle of St Januarius is the ritualized re-enactment of the some sort of castration fantasy (which is what the above analysis would suggest), this would seem to lead to a bizarre conclusion. After all, I have argued repeatedly in this book that Catholic cults and devotions are popular because they gratify some unconscious desire. Applying the same logic here, and given the characterization of the St Januarius miracle as a castration fantasy, we would be forced to conclude that the St Januarius cult is popular because it gratifies an infantile desire to be castrated. Actually, however strange this conclusion may at first seem, I think it is indeed correct. But before demonstrating that, it will be useful to establish more firmly the psychological association that exists in the Neapolitan mind between the liquefaction of blood and castration by considering other blood liquefaction cults in the Naples area.

OTHER BLOOD MIRACLES

Miracles involving a saint's relics and some sort of blood flow are actually quite common in Catholic tradition. In order to ensure the comparability of the cases being analysed, I will discuss here only blood miracles similar to the St Januarius miracle, that is, miracles in which a blood relic is reported to have turned from a solid to a liquid state, and back again, regularly and predictably over a period of several decades, and that has been the object of ritual activity involving church authorities.[10].

This means that I will not be considering the dozens of cases (discussed in Thurston, 1927a; 1927b; 1952, 283–93) in which blood flowed when an attempt was made to remove some part of the body of a saint (usually shortly after death) and never flowed again. Nor will I be considering cases in which a relic exuded blood sporadically, at unpredictable and irregular intervals. This means excluding some cases that other commentators have discussed in connection with the St Januarius miracle, like that involving St Nicholas of Tolentino (whose severed arms, preserved in a reliquary, are supposed to have bled occasionally in the sixteenth and seventeenth centuries) and St Clare of Montefalco, whose blood relic is also supposed to have liquefied half a dozen times or so in the sixteenth and seventeenth centuries. Finally, I will not be dealing with the hundreds of blood relics that do not liquefy, though they may be associated with other miracles (see Alfano and Amitrano 1951, 265–430).

Even so, the number of blood relics that fall within the guidelines specified above is impressive. Table 6, for instance, which is based mainly upon the exhaustive study of blood relics by Alfano and Amitrano (1951, 47–225) gives the location and date of the first reported liquefaction for seventeen such relics in the Naples area. Although many of these relics are believed to have continued to liquefy for centuries following their initial liquefaction, this cannot be established with any certainty. To take just one example, there is really no way to establish that the John the Baptist relic that was transferred to San Gregorio Armeno in 1828, when the convent of Santa Maria di Donnaromita was abolished (see Alfano and Amitrano 1951, 69–74), was really the same relic of John the Baptist that was liquefying at Donnaromita in the late sixteenth century. On the other hand, it probably doesn't matter. Since our concern is with the psychological appeal of the cults organized around liquefying blood relics, what matters is only that the blood relic of some particular saint is believed to have been liquefying regularly and predictably.

Furthermore, I assume that the most effective way to uncover the appeal of these cults is to concentrate, not on individual relics, but on the particular saints who are regularly associated with liquefying blood relics and on the

TABLE 6

Blood Relics in Naples Area that Liquefied Regularly and Predictably

	Successive Locations of Relic	*First Reported Liquefaction*
Januarius[a]	Cathedral, Naples	1389
John the Baptist	S. Arcangelo, Baiano; S. Gregorio Armeno, Naples	1554
Stephen	S. Gaudioso, Naples; S. Maria della Sapienza, Naples; S. Chiara, Naples	1561
Stephen	S. Gregorio Armeno, Naples	late 1500s
Patricia[a]	S. Patricia, Naples; S. Gregorio Armeno, Naples	1570
John the Baptist	S. Maria di Donnaromita, Naples; S. Gregorio Armeno	1577
Pantaleone	Cathedral, Ravello	1591
Ursula	Amalfi	1591
John the Baptist	S. Giovanni a Carbonara, Naples	1623
Lawrence[b]	S. Lorenzo Maggiore, Naples	1623
Pantaleone	S. Severo, Naples	1623
Januarius[a]	Capuchin church, Pozzuoli	late 1600s
Lawrence	Cathedral, Avellino	1709
Vitus	Carminello al Mercato, Naples	1725
Aloysius Gonzaga	Gesù Vecchio, Naples	1841
Alfonso Liguori	S. Maria della Mercede, Naples	1851
Lawrence[c]	S. Gregorio Armeno, Naples	1864

Sources: Mainly Alfrano and Amitrano (1951), but Thurston (1909; 1927b), Grant (1929), and Petito (1983) were also consulted.

[a] Relics that were still liquefying in the 1980s; see appendix C.

[b] This may not have been a blood relic since while some of the early reports describe it as a relic of "blood and fat" others describe it as a relic of "fat" only; see Alfano and Amitrano 1951, 141-2).

[c] Devotional histories usually try to equate this relic with an earlier relic of St Lawrence which was originally at S. Maria di Donnalbina in Naples and which is reported to have been liquefying since 1623 (see Alfano and Amitrano 1951, 140-1). But all the early reports describing the Donnalbina relic (which Alfano and Amitrano quote verbatim) consistently refer to it as a "pezzo di grasso," that is, a piece of fat, not blood.

cults that develop around these saints and their relics. In particular, I assume that the appeal of blood miracle cults is best explained by looking carefully at those blood miracle cults, organized around particular saints, that have proved to be the most popular with the people of Naples.

THE MOST POPULAR BLOOD MIRACLE CULTS

For the purpose of this analysis, I define a popular blood miracle cult to be one organized around some particular saint, one or more of whose blood relics (1) have been observed to liquefy in the twentieth century, (2) are reported to have liquefied regularly and recurrently for at least four hundred years, and (3) have been the focus of ritual activity for at least that long. If we apply those to the many individual relics discussed in Thurston's various articles and in the comprehensive work by Alfano and Amitrano (1951), we come to the conclusion that five saints in particular have been the focus of especially popular blood miracle cults. They are St Januarius, St John the Baptist, St Pantaleone, St Patricia, and St Stephen.

I have already described the liquefaction of the Januarius relic at the Tesoro. There are two other blood relics that are still liquefying and that are supposed to have been liquefying for at least four hundred years. They are (1) the relic of St Pantaleone's blood at Ravello, just above Amalfi, which liquefies continuously from 26 July to 11 September each year, a period that includes Pantaleone's feast day (27 August), and (2) a relic of St Patricia's blood in the convent church of San Gregorio Armeno in Naples, which liquefies every Tuesday during the year.[11] Alfano and Amitrano (1951) say that the following blood relics were liquefying in the Naples earlier in this century (though as far as I can tell they have now stopped liquefying) included (1) a relic of the blood of St John the Baptist at San Gregorio Armeno, which liquefied on 29 August (the feast of the Baptist's Decollation) and less often on 24 June (his feast day proper), and (2) a relic of St Stephen's blood at S. Chiara, which liquefied on 3 August (the Feast of the Invention of St Stephen, that is, the feast commemorating the discovery of his relics) and less often on 26 December (his feast day proper).

Each of these five saints, it turns out, is surrounded with traditions that seem to evoke castration imagery. Thus, I have already argued that in the case of the St Januarius cult at the Duomo, castration imagery is evoked by the cultic belief that this saint is supposed to have been beheaded. Castration imagery is evoked in a similar manner by the cults associated with St Pantaleone and St John the Baptist, if only because these two saints are *also* supposed to have been beheaded: pious tradition holds that Pantaleone was another early Christian bishop who was beheaded (*c*.304) for his faith, and the New Testament (Matthew, 14: 9–11) itself tells that St John the Baptist was beheaded.

The case of St Patricia is somewhat different. According to tradition,[12] Patricia was a niece of the Emperor Constantine who fled from a suitor selected for her in order to preserve a vow of virginity. A violent storm forced her party to land at Naples, where she fell ill and died a natural death a few months later. The blood that now liquefies, however, was not gathered at her death, but rather a year later. At that time a Roman aristocrat, having been cured of a painful illness after praying before the glass case containing Patricia's remains, secured permission to spend the night in prayer beside the case. Desiring to procure for himself a personal relic, he opened the case and removed a tooth from Patricia's skull. Blood immediately began flowing from the socket and continued flowing until the next day, when it was collected in two vials by church authorities. It is this blood that now liquefies.

Tradition holds that St Patricia's blood has been liquefying for at least twelve centuries. But as Thurston (1927b, 127) notes, this relic is not mentioned in a late-fifteenth-century report that discusses other blood relics in Naples and the surrounding area, though it is mentioned (for the first time) in a report published in 1624. This, plus the fact that St Patricia was not declared a patron saint of Naples until 1625, suggests that her relic first began liquefying in the early 1600s.

For Freud, teeth (like the head) were often phallic symbols, and in particular he argued that the extraction of a tooth was (like beheading) a symbolic castration (see Freud 1916–17, 156–7 and 164–5). Therefore it seems plausible that the bleeding caused by the extraction of a tooth, like the bleeding caused by beheading, also evokes castration imagery, even though this case involves a woman (St Patricia), not a man.

The final saint associated with a long-lived blood liquefaction cult is St Stephen, and at first glance there would seem to be no basis at all for associating St Stephen with castration or castration imagery. The core traditions in this case are presented in the New Testament (Acts 6–8), where we are told that Stephen became the first Christian martyr when he was stoned to death shortly after the Crucifixion for preaching that Christ was the Messiah. Nothing in this story suggests that any part of Stephen's body was severed from the rest. I will concede that the case of St Stephen is problematic for my argument. Still, if we examine the iconographic traditions surrounding Stephen, we do catch sight of something that seems relevant to the issue of castration imagery.

Since the New Testament tells us only that Stephen was stoned, I suspect that when most modern readers imagine the martyrdom of Stephen, they imagine his entire body being struck by stones. Medieval and Renaissance artists (and so too, presumably, their publics) had a different view of things.

In virtually all depictions of Stephen's martyrdom, the stones hurled at Stephen are shown striking only his head, or at most, his head and shoulders. This is way in depictions of Stephen that show him bleeding he is bleeding only from his head. However it arose, this tradition emphasizing the damage done to Stephen's head, and only to his head, during his stoning was strong enough to become the defining theme in his iconography. When Medieval and Renaissance artists depicted Stephen standing alone or in the company of other saints, they identified him by either placing a single stone on top of his head or by blood dripping off the top of his head.[13] If the head is a phallic symbol, then a bleeding or damaged head, of the sort emphasized in the iconography of St Stephen, would also seem to evoke castration imagery.

Again, I will concede that castration imagery is not evoked as clearly by the cultic beliefs about St Stephen as it is by the cultic beliefs surrounding Sts Januarius, Pantaleone, John the Baptist, and Patricia, where in each instance we find bleeding associated with a severed body part (a head or a tooth). But this means only that in four of the five longest-lived blood liquefaction cults (those associated with Sts Januarius, Pantaleone, John the Baptist, and Patricia), the case for the presence of castration imagery is fairly strong. Although in the case of the fifth cult, asociated with St Stephen, the case for castration imagery is not as strong, it is still plausible.

In summary then, a comparative analysis of the five longest-lived blood liquefaction cults reveals that at least four of the five (and maybe even all five) are surrounded by traditions that evoke castration imagery and that this imagery is most pronounced in the cult (the St Januarius cult at the Duomo in Naples) that has always been the most popular.[14] Thus the obvious question is why religious cults that evoke castration imagery should be so appealing to the people of Naples.

THE FATHER-INEFFECTIVE FAMILY

In the case of the blood-liquefaction cults of Naples, we have what we do not have for any of the other cults and devotions discussed in this book: studies by a perceptive psychoanalyst of the typical family environment in which the adherents of these cults are raised. There studies were conducted in the late 1950s and early 1960s by the late Anne Parsons (1931–64) and published posthumously in her *Belief, Magic and Anomie* (1969). Although Parsons mentioned the St Januarius cult only twice, and then only in passing, she did investigate the dynamics of family life among the Neapolitan working class. Her work easily establishes that this class is characterized by the widespread prevalence of the "father-ineffective" family.

By definition, a father-ineffective family is a family which there is an ideology of male dominance, the father is often absent from the home, and there is a *de facto* concentration of authority in the home in the hands of the mother. It is a family type that is almost always considered to be the result of the widespread economic marginality of males. The father-ineffective family is by no means restricted to Naples. It is widely prevalent in a great many of the European countries that border the northern shore of the Mediterranean and has attracted the attention of a great many Mediterranean scholars.

What is of interest to us here is that the dynamics of the father-ineffective family systematically affect the oedipal process in such a way as to produce a different outcome than the middle-class, northern-European family studied by Freud. In particular, the father-ineffective family seems more likely (1) to produce in sons a maternal (rather than a paternal) identification, (2) to intensify the son's desire for his mother, and (3) to intensify his castration anxiety.

IDENTIFICATION

There is considerable evidence that sons raised in father-ineffective families are more likely to develop an early identification with their mothers.[15] Almost universally, for instance, Mediterranean scholars have argued that an early maternal identification is responsible for the *machismo* complex typical of southern European countries (see the review of relevant literature in Saunders 1981). The machismo complex is an ideology of exaggerated masculinity that encourages men to be sexually aggressive, to dominate women sexually, and to brag about their genital attributes and sexual prowess to other men. The usual argument is that as a son raised in father-ineffective family matures, he will increasingly come to realize that his feminine identification (with his mother) conflicts with society's expectations, which hold that he should behave in a more masculine manner. The son will respond to the insecurity produced by this conflict by exaggerating his masculinity.

SEXUAL ATTACHMENT

Before discussing the effects of the father-ineffective family upon "sexual attachment," it is important to understand clearly what that term means in the psychoanalytic traditon, since the discrepancy between everyday usage and Freud's usage has often produced much misunderstanding.

Freud argued that we all experience a continuous buildup of sexual ("libidinous") energy, and that unless this energy is periodically released in some way, we experience tension and discomfort. Any activity that allows us to release this pent-up sexual energy is, by definition a sexual activity. The release of tension that accompanies sexual activity (so defined) inevitably produces a diffuse sense of physical pleasure. As a result, Freud tended to see any activity that produced a diffuse sense of physical pleasure as a sexual activity. Sexual intercourse in the commonly used sense of this term is a sexual activity in this sense, but so are a variety of other activities, like kissing, holding, touching, and caressing. Even the simple fact of being in the presence of someone you love can often produce a diffuse sense of physical pleasure, and so it too is a sexual activity in Freud's sense of the word.

Given this view of sexuality, it seems obvious that the young child will experience a variety of different sexual activities and will associate those activities with certain individuals more than others. The more the child associates a particular individual (say, the mother) with sexual activities, the more the child will invest that individual with sexual energy, a process that Freud labelled "cathexis." The more the child "cathects" a given individual, the more he or she will seek out additional sexual activities with that individual. It is when this occurs that we say the child has become sexually attached to that individual. The division of labour that prevails in most societies ensures that mothers, rather than fathers, are generally the ones who have primary responsibility for raising their children. This means that the mother is the parent who is more likely to hold, touch, and caress the children, which in turn means (for Freud) that the first and the strongest sexual attachment of both the son and the daughter will be to their mother.

It is this psychoanalytic perspective on sexuality that informs Parson's (1969) analysis of the father-ineffective family. Arguing that the greater interaction between a son and his mother in such a family (occasioned by the father's absence and the concentration of *de facto* authority in the mother), Parson suggests that the father-ineffective family should intensify the son's sexual attachment to the mother. The hypothesis that the absence of the father increases the son's sexual attachment to the mother has received substantial support from cross-cultural data (see for instance Stephens 1962; Carroll 1978).

CASTRATION ANXIETY

Finally, there are also good reasons for believing that the family-ineffective family intensifies the son's castration anxiety. Consider how and why castration anxiety develops. In the family situation described by Freud, both the father and the mother are present in the home fairly regularly. Therefore the son will eventually perceive that the father is a rival for the sexual favours of the mother; that is, the son will see that his father too wants to hold, touch, caress, share the same bed with, the mother, and so on.

In the eyes of the son, father is no ordinary rival, but rather a giant with enormous power. Facing such an omnipotent rival, the son will come to fear that his father will retaliate against him for daring to want what he (the father) also wants. When the son becomes aware of the anatomical difference between the sexes, he will suddenly know the likely form of this retaliation: someone will detach his penis, just as someone has detached the penises of his mother and sisters. This fear of penis detachment is what Freud called "castration anxiety." Driven by castration anxiety, the son will try to eliminate this apparent threat from his father by repressing his desire for his mother; that is, he will drive the sexual desire into his unconscious.

How would the structure of the father-ineffective family affect this process? Remember that the absence of the father in this situation does not mean that the father is completely absent for years at a time. On the contrary, although he might be absent during the day, or even for a period of several days or weeks, he does return regularly to the household. On these occasions, then, the son will still see the father as a rival, and, more important, will still believe that the father sees him as a rival.

But the special nature of the father-ineffective family will also intensify the castration anxiety that develops in the son as a result of this rivalry. The simple fact that the son's desire for the mother is stronger in this situation should in itself intensify the son's castration anxiety. Remember too that the son in the father-ineffective family has a father under the sway of the *machismo* ideology, which means that the father defines himself (and is likely to be defined by his son) as sexually aggressive. Such a father would almost certainly be regarded by the son as a more dangerous and hostile rival than the sort of father who would be found in the middle-class Viennese families studied by Freud. Consistent with all this is the finding, which emerged from the responses the TAT test that Parson (1969, 73–7) administered to her Neapolitan subjects that the father-son relationship in the father-ineffective family is characterized by a great deal of overt hostility. In any event, the intensification of the son's castration anxiety should have the effect of intensifying his repression of the desire for the mother.

In the end, then, the dynamics of the father-ineffective family create in sons an early feminine identification and a later commitment to the *machismo* ideology, *and* an especially strong, but strongly repressed, sexual desire for the mother.

EXPLANATION OF THE CULTS

I have already argued (in Carroll 1986a) that the strong but strongly repressed desire for the mother produced by the father-ineffective family gives rise to an intense devotion to the Virgin Mary. This is why the Mary cult has always been strongest in those parts of Europe (like southern Italy and Spain) where the father-ineffective family is most widespread. In particular, such an argument accounts for the traditional strength of the Mary cult in the Naples area, something that is evident in studies of local religion there (see for instance Tentori 1982).

I have also pointed out in my earlier work that Freud on several occasions (for instance, Freud 1919; 1924; 1930; 1932) discussed what the likely consequences of a strong but strongly repressed desire would be, consistently arguing that such a desire produces strong feelings of guilt and consequently strong desire for self-punishment. Guilt is produced, he argued, because the superego knows that there is a strong but forbidden desire in the unconscious. This guilt in turn produces a desire, usually unconscious, for expiation, and this desire to expiate guilt gives rise to the desire for self-punishment.

Furthermore, Freud (1924) even considered the particular case of concern here, involving a son with a strong but strongly repressed desire for the mother. He argued that in this particular case the resulting desire for self-punishment would usually become a desire for castration, since sons inevitably recognize that castration is the most fitting punishment for their incestuous desire. Freud of course was well aware that few males ever castrate themselves; his point was rather that this unconscious desire for castration often gives rise to less extreme forms of masochistic behaviour.

Some evidence that Freud's analysis is correct can be gleaned from the responses given by Parson's Neapolitan informants to the mother/son card in the TAT. According to Parsons the following responses were typical.

The son is asking for forgiveness of the mother, repenting of the evil he has done.

Maybe he [the son] did something very serious, probably he went away and so now he has come back to ask her forgiveness and the mother no longer wants to receive him.

The mother has a son she has not seen for many years ... He returns after having done many bad things, stealing and other things. He returns to the family to ask forgiveness. Who knows whether or not the mother will give it to him but I think she will.

The son is asking forgiveness for something ... A mother would always forgive her son, even if he were an assassin, even if he were Chessman.

The penitent son who returns to the mother and the mother cannot or does not know how to forgive him.[16]

The recurrent theme in these responses is guilt, that is, of wrongdoing being attributed to the son in the presence of his mother. Parsons tells us that these responses were more likely to be elicited from male respondents than from female respondents, and that only the male/son card (and not the father/son or the mother/daughter cards) elicited such attributions of guilt.

This attribution of guilt to the son (especially by male respondents) is exactly what Freud's theory leads us to expect if indeed the father-ineffective family does create in the son an especially strong but strongly repressed sexual desire for his mother. On the other hand, I find no clear support in Parson's data for the prediction that the son's excessive guilt should produce a desire for self-punishment, in particular, a desire for symbolic castration.

But evidence in support of this prediction is found, I have argued, in the excessive masochism that has always been a part of the ceremonies and rituals associated with the Mary cult in areas like southern Italy and Spain (for specific examples for this Marian masochism, see Carroll 1986a, 63–71).

The argument just summarized, which has proven useful in understanding the Mary cult, can also be used to provide a simple explanation for the popularity of the blood-liquefaction cults. We have already seen how the rituals and traditions surrounding these cults, at least the most popular of these cults, evoke castration imagery. If in fact the father-ineffective family, so prevalent among the Neapolitan working class, does produce in sons a strong sense of guilt and consequently a strong unconscious desire for castration as a way of expiating this guilt, then not only would Neapolitans (at least Neapolitan males) gravitate towards cults and devotions with a strongly masochistic emphasis, like the Mary cult, but they would also gravitate towards those cults, like the blook liquefaction cults, that invoke imagery suggestive of symbolic castration.

In summary, I am suggesting that the immense popularity of the various blood liquefaction cults in the Naples area derives from the fact that the rituals and beliefs surrounding these cults allows for the symbolic gratification of the unconscious desire for punishment and castration that is produced in Neapolitan sons by the unconscious guilt that results from the father-ineffective family.

This argument of course only explains why *males* would be attracted to blood miracle cults. What about females? In Carroll (1986a, 58–9) I argued that in the case of females the father-ineffective family (for a variety of reasons) would intensify the daughter's oedipal desire for the father, and reviewed some clinical evidence from Parsons (1969) in support of this conclusion. I then argued that identification with the Virgin Mary, an earthly woman impregnated by God the Father, allows the daughter to gratify this oedipal desire vicariously, and that for this reason females are attracted to participation in the Mary cult. But in the case of blood miracle cults, there does not seem to be any basis for saying that an intensification of the daughter's oedipal desire for the father would cause a cult which evokes castration imagery to be particularly appealing to females. I therefore see no reason for suggesting that blood miracle cults would be particularly appealing to females in areas (like Naples) where the father-ineffective family is prevalent. These considerations would seem then to lead to a simple prediction: blood miracle cults should be more appealing to Neapolitan males than to Neapolitan females.

At this point in history, when religion is thought of as being mainly a female activity, such a prediction might seem strange. But at least in Catholic areas, the domination of lay religious activities by women is very much a phenomenom of the nineteenth and early twentieth centuries.[17] Previously, the most important lay confraternities were male confraternities, and in countries like Italy and Spain especially, male confraternities were the ones most active in planning and organizing religious festivals. The suggestion, then, that over the centuries blood miracle cults might have been far more appealing to males than to females is more plausible than the modern experience of religion might suggest.

Nevertheless, I know of no specific historical evidence which shows that such cults were more popular with males, and I am perfectly willing to concede that my inability to point to such evidence constitutes a major weakness in my argument. It is to be hoped that, at some future date, evidence that bears on this prediction will be brought forward. But even if every prediction derivable from the argument cannot be tested, the argument still allows us to understand the key features of the blood miracle cults of Naples. Seeing these cults as being concerned with a desire for castration, for instance, allows us to understand the emphasis upon "decapitation" that seems associated with these cults, as well as the emphasis upon the "liquefaction of blood"; after all, the severing of a body part and the appearance of fresh blood are precisely the concepts that we would associate with literal castration. Just as importantly, the argument can help to explain one of the most puzzling of the historical patterns associated with the blood miracle cults of Naples, namely, a pattern of timing.

THE PROLIFERATION OF BLOOD-LIQUEFACTION CULTS

Before 1550, the only cult in the Naples areas organized around the recurrent liquefaction of a blood relic was the St Januarius cult at the Naples cathedral. As the final column in Table 6 makes clear, however, the next century or so saw the emergence of at least ten other cults of this sort, all scattered in and around the city of Naples. What accounts for this relatively sudden increase in the number of such cults?

This increase does correlate with the onset of the Reformation, but I can think of no theoretical basis for suggesting that the Reformation would have provoked such an increase. In the minds of those who remained faithful to the Church (and this would include most Neapolitan Catholics, since Protestantism made little or no headway with the common people of Naples), the Reformation – being an attack on Holy Mother Church by former members of the Church – might indeed reactivate unconscious memories of the phantasy attacks that very young children direct against their parents. In chapter 7 I will in fact argue that it was for this very reason that the Reformation led to an increase in stigmatization and to the emergence of the devotion to the Brown Scapular.

But under the hypothesis introduced in the last section, the appeal of blood-liquefaction cult derives from a sense of guilt and consequent desire for castration, which in turn derives from the dynamics of the father-ineffective family. I fail to see how the Reformation *per se* would affect any of this. On the contrary, given this hypothesis, the only obvious way to account for the sudden explosion of Neapolitan blood miracle cults in the late sixteenth and seventeenth centuries would be to assume that this period saw a dramatic increase in the prevalence of the father-ineffective family in the Neapolitan area. Is there any reason to believe this happened?

Quite apart from the issue of blood miracle cults, it turns out that the period from the middle of the sixteenth to the middle of the seventeenth century has always been considered by historians to have been a well-defined chapter in Neapolitan history. Although Naples came under the control of the king of Spain in 1503, the economy of Naples at first suffered little from Spanish rule. In the latter half of the sixteenth century, however, Spain's increasing financial difficulties at home led to an oppressive system of taxation in Naples that fell almost entirely upon the non-aristocratic classes. This situation was compounded by the fact that the collection of taxes was farmed out to tax collectors whose profits often exceeded the amounts remitted to the Spanish government.

Far worse than the direct taxes levied against the common people generally were the taxes levied against producers, notably the peasants who produced foodstuffs. These levies on food products were so excessive that large numbers of peasants were forced off the land, and migrated – as is always the case – to the cities notably Naples itself. The net effect was the pauperization of the countryside and the congregation in urban slums of large numbers of impoverished people. Confronted with the misery of this period, historians have always been driven to the use of colourful language:

But much more disastrous were the gabelles ... so that by far the greater burden of the taxation fell upon agriculture ... Peasants flocked to the more favored city and begged or starved in the streets ... The country was depopulated, land fell out of cultivation, and the result of course was perennial famine for country and city alike. (Vernon 1909, 162-3)

Large districts went out of cultivation; the peasants flocked to the cities to beg, or become brigands ... At the same time the coasts were harried by pirates.

Famine was endemic, and naturally culminated in outbreaks of plague, which were made worse by the criminal folly of the government in refusing to recognize the danger until precautions were too late. (Jamison *et al.* 1917, 218-2)

But during this time the blood-sucking policy of Spain and her Viceroys sapped the prosperity of the towns, encouraged brigandage in the countryside and piracy along the defenceless coast, and so ground down the inhabitants of Naples itself that the popular despair found vent at last (1647) in that most pathetic of insurrection, the rebellion of Masaniello. (Trevelyan 1956, 270–1)

As a result of the massive influx of the poor from the countryside, by the early seventeenth century Naples was one of the two largest cities in Europe (the other was Paris; see Mols 1974, 42), and the slums of Naples had already acquired the reputation they enjoy today (Minchinton 1974, 137).

All of this is relevant to the theoretical argument being advanced here because it means that during the late sixteenth and early seventeenth centuries Naples experienced precisely those economic changes that tend to produce the father-ineffective family. In the modern era, for instance, the widespread economic marginality of males in agricultural regions and the resulting migration of people to urban slums in which this marginality is maintained have been identified as important causes of the father-ineffective family in Spain and southern Italy (Gilmore and Gilmore 1979; Saunders 1981), in Mexico, Puerto Rico, and New York (Lewis 1965), in various Caribbean societies (Smith 1956; Clarke 1957), among blacks in the United States (Yorburg 1983) and blacks in Lesotho (Murray 1981).

Thus, although we have little direct information on family structure among the Neapolitan poor for the late sixteenth and early seventeenth centuries, it seems highly likely, given the known economic history of the period, that this period was characterized by a dramatic increase in the prevalence of the father-ineffective family in and around the city of Naples. This in turn would increase the number of sons raised in such families, and it is this increase – I argue – that accounts for the proliferation of blood-miracle cults during this same period.

WHY NAPLES?

On final puzzle remains. If indeed the father-ineffective family is found in so many places around the world (something established by the studies cited in the last section), and if in fact it is the father-ineffective family that generates support for a blood-miracle cult, then why haven't such cults spread throughout the Catholic world like, say, the Mary cult?

First of all, cults organized around blood relics that liquefy at least occasionally *have* appeared elsewhere. Alfano and Amitrano (1951) give several instances of liquefying blood relics that have been reported in other parts of Italy and in France and Spain. Nevertheless, the fact remains that the vast majority of all liquefying blood relics, especially those that have liquefied at predictable times for centuries, have been concentrated in the Naples area. I can think of only one reasonable explanation for this, and it has to do with the fact that these cults, unlike the Mary cult, are organized around a physical process.

I am not, remember, suggesting that a desire for symbolic castration *causes* the blood of St Januarius (or St Pantaleone or St John the Baptist or St Patricia or St Stephen) to liquefy. Excluding those cases of liquefaction that may be more apparent than real, I assume that the blood relics used in these cults do liquefy, and that this is the result of some set of physical processes. The fact that blood-liquefaction cults have not spread beyond Naples would be understandable then if the physical processes that produce these liquefactions is facilitated by some aspect of the Neapolitan climate (some combination of high seasonal temperatures and humidity, for instance) or the geographical location of Naples (see appendix B).

RELICS AND THEIR ASSOCIATIONS

Central to the interpretation developed here is the association between lique-fying blood relics and decapitation, and thus between these relics and castra-tion. If there is a physical process peculiar to the Naples region that induces the liquefaction of these relics, why does it affect primarily the relics of decapitated saints? Why, in other words, doesn't the same process affect the blood relics of non-decapitated saints. The answer, I suspect, is that liquefac-tion happens first, and only then comes to be associated with decapitation or some other tradition (like the extraction of a tooth) that evokes castration imagery. In at least one case, in fact, we know that this is exactly what happened.

In a report on the churches of Naples in 1560 written by Pietro de Stephano, we are told that the convent of S. Arcangalo a Baiano found among its posses-sions a small cruet of "blood" that was thought to be the blood of a martyr – but that they didn't know which martyr. A old priest suggested to the Abbess that she "let God decide the matter" by setting the cruet upon the altar on the feast days of various martyrs: "The Abbess ... followed this advice; and upon the feast of the decollation of St. John the Baptist, they solemnly sang First Vespers, as they had done for the other martyrs, and miracuously as they did so, the blood liquefied; this happened about six years ago; and the liquefaction has repeated itself on the same day, the feast of the decollation of St. John the Baptist, in each year following" (Alfano and Amitrano 1951, 54). De Stephano goes on to relate how he himself had witnessed this liquefaction on the saint's feast day (29 August) in 1558.

Even taken at face value, this account suggests that the liquefaction of this blood relic occurred before it was known to be associated with any particular saint, which lends support to the suggestion that all these cults are built around a physical process (producing liquefaction) that can occur independently of the beliefs surrounding the particular cult involved.

In this case then, it seems clear that a systematic attempt was made to "match up" the relic with one of a range of saints. Putting aside the suggestion that the entire process was really under Divine supervision, it seems obvious that this matching-up process allowed for considerable subjective bias. For instance, we know that most modern blood relics sometimes liquefy on days other than the feast day of the saint involved. We also know that in a substantial number of cases, it is not always clear whether the blood has indeed liquefied. Given this room for subjective interpretation, we might expect that during the process of matching up a liquefying relic with one of a range of different saints, there would be some psychological predilection to match up the relic with a saint who is surrounded by traditions that enhance the psychological appeal of the relic.

In the Naples area, given the prevalence of the father-ineffective family, and the resulting guilt and desire for symbolic castration that this type of family produces in sons, the psychological appeal of such a relic would be enhanced by associating it with a saint surrounded by traditions that evoke castration imagery, traditions for instance that associate the saint with decapitation or the extraction of a tooth. That, I suggest, is just what happened in the case of the St John the Baptist relic discussed above, and probably in the case of other blood relics as well.

CHAPTER FIVE

Heaven-Sent Wounds:
The Stigmata

The term "stigmata" has a range of meanings in the Catholic mystical tradition, but its most common meaning, and the one that will be used here, refers to visible wounds (or at least visible wound marks) corresponding to the wounds received by Jesus Christ during his Passion.[1] Most devotional accounts assert that the first person to "receive" the stigmata (and the implication is always that the stigmata have been given to the individual by some supernatural agency) was St Francis of Assisi. St Francis is supposed to have received the stigmata on Mt La Verna in 1224, two years before his death.

Whether St Francis was the first person to receive the stigmata has been a matter of debate among Catholic historians.[2] There is also some doubt as to whether the historical St Francis actually had the stigmata; even devotional accounts concede, for instance, that only two persons saw his stigmata during his lifetime. But historical priority aside, the fact remains that since the thirteenth century hundreds of Catholics have claimed to have received the stigmata and millions of Catholics have accepted these claims at face value.

This is not because the Church goes to great lengths to encourage a belief in the supernatural origin of the stigmata. On the contrary, the Church has always been very circumspect in this regard; only in the case of St Francis has the Church said that stigmata visible during a person's lifetime are of supernatural origin. In the case of Gemma Galgani (1878–1903), an Italian stigmatic canonized in 1940, the Church even went so far as to say that her stigmata were *not* in themselves evidence of saintliness. Yet despite such circumspection on the Church's part, stigmatics have long been objects of attention by ordinary Catholics, even in recent times. Therese Neumann and Padre Pio, for instance, two of this century's most well-known stigmatics, died in the 1960s, and Father Gino Burresi, perhaps the most well-known living stigmatic, received his stigmata as recently as 1969.

Some stigmatics develop many wounds corresponding to all the wounds acquired by Christ during his Passion. Consider the case of Marie-Julie Jahenny, a nineteenth century French girl:

> On the 21st March, 1873, she received the marks of the five wounds [in her feet, hands, and side]; the crown of thorns followed on Oct. 5th; on the 25th of November appeared an imprint on the left shoulder [interpreted as the bruise caused by carrying the cross] ... On Jan 12, 1874, her wrists showed marks corresponding to those which the cords must have produced when our Saviour's arms were bound ... By Jan. 14th stripes had appeared on her ankles, legs and forearms in memory of the scourging, and a few days afterwards there were two weals on her side. (Imbert-Gourbeyre 1894b, 27; translated by Thurston 1952, 63–4).

But the "core" set of wounds, that is, the wounds that appear on most of those people labelled as stigmatics, are wounds in the hands, feet, and side, which correspond to the wounds received by Christ when he was crucified. Henceforth, then, I will use the term "stigmata" to refer only these five basic wounds, unless otherwise noted.

ASSOCIATED CHARACTERISTICS

Stigmatization appears to be part of a cluster of characteristics that develop in association with one another. In compiling a list of those charactertistics, I am only summarizing what has already been established in greater detail by previous commentators like Imbert-Gourbeyre (1894a; 1894b), Biot (1962), Siwek (1953; 1967), and Thurston (1952, 32–129).

Sex of Stigmatics

The overwhelming majority of stigmatics are women. In Imbert-Gourbeyre's (1894a; 1894b) early study of 321 stigmatics, for instance, 280 (87 per cent) were women. Thurston (1952, 49n) objects to Imbert-Gourbeyre's sample on the grounds that it includes a number of people who experienced only the "invisible" stigmata, that is, people who experienced pain in their hands, feet, and side, but did not have any visible wounds. But even restricting ourselves to those twenty-three individuals whom Thurston (1952, 32–129) himself identifies as having had the visible stigmata, we still find that twenty-one (or 91 per cent) are female. The only male stigmatics who have been the subject of a significant amount of devotional literature are St Francis himself and Padre Pio (1887–1968).

Religion

Although some stigmatics have been Protestant,[3] the overwhelming majority have been Catholic. In part the explanation for this seems simple: stigmatization has for centuries been far more a part of the Catholic tradition than of the Protestant tradition, and so Catholics are routinely confronted with many more stigmatic "models" who can be imitated. It seems likely, however, that even in the Catholic tradition, stigmatization would eventually die out unless it were fed by some ongoing process, and so the correlation between the stigmata and Catholicism still needs to be explained.

Recurrent Bleeding

Usually, those people who have the stigmata are seen to bleed from one or more of those wounds. Such bleeding is almost always reccurent: that is, it starts and stops. Sometimes the bleeding is literally periodic: that is, it recurs at evenly spaced intervals. Many stigmatics for example, bleed on Fridays or during a twenty-four-hour period that lasts from Thursday night to Friday afternoon, periods traditionally associated with Christ's own Passion. Other stigmatics bleed on particular feast days or during liturgical seasons (like Lent) that commemorate the suffering of Christ. Others bleed in response to some recurrent activity, like the reception of Holy Communion.

Several things should be noted about this bleeding. First, in the typical case not all the wounds bleed all the time. St Francis, for example, never bled from his hands and his feet, only his side. Other stigmatics bleed sometimes from some of their wounds, sometimes from others. Second, I am using terms like blood and bleeding simply for convenience. In the vast majority of cases, the fluid seen on the wounds of the stigmatic was never subjected to chemical analysis.

Furthermore, I will not at all be concerned with those questions that have dominated previous discussions of the bleeding associated with the stigmata: whether the blood is real or whether it flows spontaneously or results from some mechanical process (such as a self-inflicted wound). On the contrary, if we again (as in the discussion of blood miracles) rule out supernatural causation, then the stigmata and the associated bleeding must ultimately have a psychological origin. What matters most is that the stigmatic believes she (or he) has wounds from which blood flows and that others believe this as well. It is of secondary importance to identify the precise physiological or mechanical processes that produce the wounds.

Pain

Virtually all stigmatics experience great pain. This pain is partly associated with the stigmata themselves; that is, they feel pain in the wounds that develop in their hands, feet, and side. But their experience of pain usually goes beyond this. Stigmatics almost always feel a wide variety of pains in various parts of their body, and this generalized pain is independent of the bleeding associated with their wounds.

Inedia

People who experience the stigmata also tend to experience inedia (living for long periods on little or no food). Stigmatics are by no means the only mystics to experience inedia; on the contrary, it is a condition that has been experienced by a great many Catholic mystics. Thurston (1952, 341–84), for instance, discusses inedia as a mystical phenomena in and of itself.[4] Nevertheless, the association between the stigmata and inedia is strong enough to have been noted by Catholic commentators like Imbert-Gourbeyre (1894b, 183–203) and Biot (1962, 58–70), and inedia is inevitably given special emphasis in biographies and commentaries dealing with particular stigmatics.

Here again my primary interest will not be the usual one, which in this case means that I will not at all be concerned with evaluating the validity of these claims about inedia. Siwek (1953, 222), a Catholic commentator who is willing to attribute all the other characteristics associated with stigmatization to hysteria, notes that in the case of inedia (at least extreme inedia) there can really only be two possibilities: either the stigmatic is faking (and taking some nourishment surreptitiously) or the phenomenon is of truly supernatural origin. I agree, and if we (again) rule out supernatural causation, that leaves only the "faking" hypothesis. In fact, careful analysis of particular cases usually turns up evidence of faking.

Veronica Giuliani (1660–1727), for example, was a well-known stigmatic who supposedly subsisted for several years on bread and water alone. But even devotional accounts make it clear the Giuliani was seen by several people eating food during these periods. It's just that the person seen was not *really* Giuliani; it was the Devil appearing as Giuliani. One nineteenth-century account tells us in all seriousness:

The Devil, despairing of being able to subdue her, conceived the idea of blackening her reputation, and of making her appear a sacrilegious hypocrite, by the following stratagem. He frequently assumed her form, and contrived to be caught [by some of the other nuns in the convent] in the act of eating greedily and surreptitiously, at improper hours, sometimes in the kitchen, sometimes in the refectory, and sometimes in the dispensary. (Salvatori 1874, 126)[5]

More recently, chemical analysis of urine samples obtained from Therese Neumann (1898–1962), another well-known stigmatic who supposedly went without food, proves that her inedia too was not quite what it seemed (Siwek 1953, 211–19).

But even granting that stigmatics fake their inedia, that still leaves us with the problem of explaining *why* they go to such great lengths to give the impression that they are not taking food.

Devotion to the Holy Eucharist

Most stigmatics have had an especially strong desire to receive Holy Communion as often as possible, even when they were living in periods of Catholic history when frequent communion was not the norm. Biot (1962, 62) suggests that inedia and devotion to the Eucharist are just the negative and positive aspects of the same phenomenon. In other words, in giving up nourishment from physical sources, the stigmatic comes to rely instead upon nourishment from a supernatural source.

Quite often the stigmatic's strong desire to receive Holy Communion leads to "Communions from a distance" (Imbert-Gourbeyre 1894b, 407–32; Biot 1962, 66–70). What happens in these cases is that a host "miraculously" appears on a stigmatic's tongue and is supposed to have come from some distant source, such as the tabernacle in the local church.

PREVIOUS EXPLANATIONS

By far the most common explanation of the stigmata (apart from those explanations that attribute it to a supernatural origin) is that it is a form of hysteria, or more precisely, what would today be called hysterical conversion, that is, a form of hysteria that affects a part of the body. This was Thurston's (1952, 110–29) conclusion, and in fact most modern Catholic commentators have been willing to grant a hysterical origin for most if not all of the symptoms associated with the stigmata (Biot 1962, 115–33; Siwek 1953). Certainly the fact that the overwhelming majority of those who experience stigmatization are women is powerful evidence in support of the hysteria hypothesis, since most of those who experience hysterical conversions are women. But even granting that the stigmata are a form of hysterical conversion, that hardly explains the process of stigmatization.

Suppose, for example, we found ourselves confronted with a patient with a paralyzed arm and concluded that the paralysis was the result of hysterical conversion. Would we consider this an explanation of the phenomena? Not really; it is at best a diagnosis. An explanation would presumably involve the identification of the precipitating conditions that led to the paralysis, and would include some account of why the patient's arm (rather than some other part of the body) was affected.

Even granting that stigmatization is a form of hysterical conversion, we still need to know what precipitating conditions make the stigmata more likely to appear in some people than in others, and we still need to explain the entire cluster of characteristics (inedia, recurrent bleeding, and so on) of which the stimata themselves are only a part.

In his various works on hysteria[6] (including those co-authored with Breuer) Freud advanced two central hypotheses. The first was that hysteria usually involved the somatic expression of opposing, but associated, wishes. Thus Freud (1900, 57) explained the vomiting of one of his female patients by suggesting, first, that she associated vomiting with morning sickness, and so the vomiting represented the vicarious fulfilment of her wish to be continually pregnant by a variety of men. But the fact that this wish was inconsistent with the patient's moral code had given rise to a strong defensive reaction that worked to negate the wish. By vomiting, the patient also felt that she would lose her figure and her good looks and so would be unable to attract men. The single hysterical symptom, then, vomiting, gratified the original wish as well as the demands of the defensive reaction against the wish.

Freud's second hypothesis (and the one that Breuer himself tended to de-emphasize) was that the conflicting desires that gave rise to hysteria were almost always sexual and, in particular, were sexual desires that had had their origin in the oedipal period.

Freud's first hypothesis – that hysterical conversion involves the somatic expression of associated but conflicting desires – is still widely accepted. His second hypothesis has not fared as well. Though most psychologists and psychoanalysts still seem willing to grant that hysteria has a sexual origin, there has been an increasing tendency to believe that the conflicting sexual desires that produce hysterical conversion originate in the pre-oedipal period. In particular, it now seems that oral sexuality is far more likely than phallic sexuality to be implicated in hysterical conversion. Equally important, recent investigators have increasingly argued that hysterical conversion often involves the somatic expression of aggressive as well as sexual impulses.[7]

In summary then, if stimatization is indeed a form of hysterical conversion (as so many commentators have suggested), then the modern literature on hysterical conversion would suggest that stigmatization is probably a process shaped by sexual or aggressive desires (or both) with roots in the pre-oedipal period. This is the possibility that I would like to investigate here. In doing this, I will be relying heavily upon the work of Melanie Klein,[8] since Kleinian theory offers a perspective on pre-oedipal processes that can account for most of the characteristics associated with stigmatization.

KLEINIAN THEORY

In Klein's view, one of the earliest and most important distinctions made by an infant is that between the "Good Breast" (the breast that provides warmth and, most of all, milk) and the "Bad Breast" (the breast that withholds milk, that is, that does not provide milk when the infant wants it). During the first six months or so of life, when the infant is in what Klein calls the "paranoid-schizoid" position, the infant attributes an independent existence to both the Good Breast and Bad Breast. These two images in turn give rise to the child's perception of the "Good Mother" and the "Bad Mother," each of which is also assumed to have an independent existence.

When the infant wants the Good Breast (or Good Mother) and doesn't get it, something that happens quite often during the first six months, the infant experiences frustration and rage. This in turn leads the infant to experience unconscious phantasies in which it attacks the Bad Breast and the Bad Mother. Since the infant at this stage of its development is overwhelmingly concerned with oral sexuality and orality in generally, these phantasy attacks will be of an oral-sadistic nature: that is, they will be phantasy attacks that involve cutting, lacerating, tearing, and so on of the surface of the Bad Breast and Bad Mother.

Increasingly over the first year of life the infant comes to realize that the Bad Breast and Good Breast (and the Bad Mother and the Good Mother) are simply different aspects of the same person. With this realization, the child enters what Klein calls the "depressive" position. This does not stop the phantasy attacks against the Bad Mother, but it does lead the child to fear that these phantasied attacks against the Bad Mother may have damaged the Good Mother as well. This gives rise to a very strong sense of guilt, which in turn leads to a strong desire to make reparation for the damage possibly done to the Good Mother.

The entire process that Klein is describing here is intensified at weaning, when the child is deprived of the Good Breast once and for all, and when the resulting feelings of deprivation, rage, guilt, and the consequent desire to make reparation to the Good Mother, are all especially strong. One of the most important of all the arguments in Kleinian theory is that the desire to make reparation to the Good Mother on account of the damage done to her during the course of these infantile phantasy attacks is one of the strongest influences on everyone's subsequent psychological development.[9].

Something else that occurs at weaning (in Klein's reconstruction), and something that will be very important to this analysis, is that the infant (whether a boy or a girl) turns to the father in the hope of finding a substitute for the oral gratification it has lost. What this means, then, is that when the father first becomes an object of sexual desire for the infant, he (the father) is very strongly associated in the infant's mind with oral sexuality. This, Klein argues, gives rise to a strong unconscious infantile desire to quite literally "incorporate the father through the mouth," just as the milk from the Good Breat was previously incorporated through the mouth.

Like Freud, Klein assumes that the infantile desires formed early in life remain forever in the unconscious, and under the right conditions can be activated and affect behaviour in later life. The basic hypothesis that I want to propose here is that the various phenomena associated with the stigmata can be explained in a fairly straightforward and parsimonious way on the assumption that stigmatization is a hysterical conversion shaped primarily by the three pre-oedipal desires just discussed, namely, (1) the sexual desire to incorporate the father as a substitute for the lost Good Breast, (2) the desire to make reparation for the oral-sadistic attacks made in fantasy against the mother, and (3) the desire for regular access to the milk from the Good Breast. In substantiating this hypothesis, I will concentrate on the biographies of six stagmatics: St Veronica Giuliani (1660–1727), Anne Catherine Emmerich (1724–1824), Louise Lateau (1850–83), St Gemma Galgani (1878–1903), Therese Neumann (1898–1962), and Padre Pio (1887–1968). I have chosen these six cases for several reasons. First, these six are among the stigmatics that seem to have been discussed most often in earlier reviews of the stigmata, like those by Biot (1962), Thurston (1952, 32–129, and Siwek (1953; 1967). Second, a substantial amount of biographical material is available in each of these six cases, in particular, material that bears on the stigmatic's early life. Third, many of these stigmatics have left accounts of their fantasies, in the form of visions and similar phenomena, and these accounts can easily be mined for information regarding unconscious processes. Fourth, these six stigmatics seem to be the ones mentioned most often in the devotional literature dealing with the stigmata. Finally, these six seem prototypical, in the sense that they embody most if not all of the characteristics and experiences usually asiocated with the stigmata. Table 7 shows the degree to which each of these six stigmatics has the characteristics mentioned earlier.

At one level, it seems obvious that stigmatics develop their wounds because they are imitating the Suffering Christ. Quite often, in fact, they are imitating some particular image of the Suffering Christ. For instance, whether the "spear wound" appears on the stigmatic's left side or right side seems in many cases to have been determined by the position of that wound on some image of Christ to which the stigmatic was particularly attached. Anne Catherine Emmerich and Gemma Galgani, in particular, are known to have developed wounds in imitation of the wounds found on a specific crucifix before which they often prayed (see Thurston 1952, 122–3; Germanus 1913, 68–9).

There is one recent twist to the stigmatization process that shows quite clearly that imitation is at work, and it has to do with the hand wounds. Until

TABLE 7

Degree to Which Six Stigmatics Conform to the Typical Stigmatization Pattern

	Sex	Religion	Recurrent Bleeding from One or More Wounds	Experience of Intense Pain	Inedia	Strong Devotion to Holy Eucharist
Veronica Giuliani	F	Catholic	x	x	x	x
Anne Catherine Emmerich	F	Catholic	x	x	x	x
Louise Lateau	F	Catholic	x	x	x	–
Gemma Galgani	F	Catholic	x	x	–[a]	x
Therese Neumann	F	Catholic	x	x	x	x
Padre Pio	M	Catholic	x	x	x[b]	–

Sources: Austin (1883, 212–25); Biot (1962); Carty (1953); Germanus (1913); Graef (1951); Molloy (1873); Salvatori (1874); Schmöger (1885a; 1885b); Siwek (1953; 1967); Thurston (1952, 32–129; 1955); von Lama (1935).

[a] Although Galgani seems to have had a normal appetite, Jesus is supposed to have granted her request that she lose her ability to taste food as a form of mortification; see Germanus (1913, 173–5).

[b] Though Padre Pio's biographers try to create the impression that he experienced inedia, a careful reading of these accounts suggests that, at the very least, it was not a very extreme form of inedia; see Carty (1953, 53–4).

quite recently, it was a centuries-old iconographic convention to portray Christ as being nailed to the cross with nails that were punched through the palms of his hands. Accordingly, all stigmatics, including the six just mentioned, developed wounds in the palms of their hands. In this century, however, mainly because of the image of Christ that appears on the Shroud of Turin, a number of investigators have suggested that the nails that pinned Christ to the cross must have been driven through his wrists.[10] Sure enough, one of the most recent stigmatics, Father Gino Burresi (who received the stigmata in 1969) developed bleeding wounds in his wrists, not his palms (Fox 1986, 125–6).

But even granting that imitation is implicated in the stigmata, we still need to explain why the stigmatic imitates the Suffering Christ. I want to suggest that in imitating the Suffering Christ the stigmatic is, first of all gratifying the sexual desire to incorporate the father that develops during the pre-oedipal period. This desire is gratified because stigmatics see stigmatization as a process that merges their bodies with the body of Christ.

Since any argument that tries to relate a religious phenomenon like stigmatization to something like a desire to incorporate the father will inevitably strike many readers as strange (and strained), let me hasten to remind my readers that in Klein's account of the pre-oedipal period, the desire to incorporate the father is expressed as a desire quite literally to "swallow the father," and that "swallowing a man's body" evokes imagery and associations strikingly consistent with the Catholic world-view.

Thus, according to Catholic doctrine, the bit of unleavened bread received during Holy Communion has become, through the process of transubstantiation, the actual body of Christ. This doctrine was rejected in part or in whole by the Protestant groups. Calvin, for instance, rejected it outright, denying that Christ was physically present in the Eucharist at all. Luther was willing to agree that Christ was in some way physically present, though he stopped short of saying that the material elements of the host actually became Christ's physical body.[11] But precisely because the doctrine of transubstantiation was so vigorously attacked by the Reformers, the Catholic Church has regarded a belief in that doctrine as the badge of the true Catholic and has always ensured that this doctrine is one of the very first to be instilled in the minds of young Catholics. The old *Baltimore Catechism*, for instance, put the matter simply and concisely:

Question 347. What happened when our Lord said: "This is My body ... This is My Blood"?
A. When our Lord said "This is My body," the entire substance of the bread was changed into His body; and when he said, "This is My blood," the entire substance of the wine was changed into his blood.

Question 353. Does this change of bread and wine into the body and blood of Christ continue to be made in the Church?
A: This change ... continues to be made in the Church ... through the ministry of His priests. (Schumacher 1945, 455 and 460)

This strong doctrinal insistence upon the equivalence of the Communion wafer and the real body of Christ has often led to Catholic folk beliefs quite unintended by Catholic theologians. Catholic theologians, for instance, have always been at pains to stress that even though the Eucharistic wafer does indeed become the Body of Christ, it nevertheless retains fully the "appearance" of unleavened bread. This however is a theological subtlety that is easily missed by the faithful, as is evident in the many Catholic traditions about hosts that bleed like a human body, that is, which exude real blood when cut.

Consider the following reports, all of which I have culled from the Folklore Archives at the University of California at Berkeley[12] and all of which were collected from people who went to parochial schools in the United States during the 1950s and early 1960s:

There was this little boy at St. Mark's ... years ago [who wanted] to find out if the Eucharist was really the body of Christ. So you know what he did? When he received Holy Communion, he didn't swallow it, but instead kept it up near the roof of his mouth, and when Mass was over, he went to the parking lot at St. Mark's ... and he took the Hold Eucharist out of his mouth and the moment he did, HORRIBLE torrents of BRIGHT red blood GUSHED from that terrible boy's mouth, and he DIED in an instant.

(collected in 1979 from a twenty-seven-year-
old man who had been raised in rural Illinois)

I remember hearing this story from a nun, my second grade teacher ... about a young girl who didn't swallow the wafer at all, but kept it on her tongue until she returned to her seat in church. She took the host out of her mouth and wrapped it in her handkerchief, but when she got home, the host had disappeared and in its place was a spot of blood.

(collected in 1980 from a thirty-one-year-
old woman who had been raised in Grenada Hills, California)

When I was in grade-school, one of the nuns told me this story ... a priest who was beginning to doubt his faith ... spilled some of the [consecrated] wine on the altar cloth ... [Later] he found a red stain on the altar cloth ... Probably every one thinks this not the least unusual, but the thing is that that very day, the church had run out of red altar wine, and had replaced the wine for the Consecration with white German wine. When the priest saw the red stain which was still wet, he realized that the wine ... [had] changed to Christ's blood ... His faith was renewed, and he never doubted again.

(collected in 1967 from a twenty-one-year-
old woman who had been raised in San Francisco)

Nor are such stories limited to children and those who supervise them. On the contrary, "bleeding hosts" have often been the focus of popular Catholic devotions over the centuries.[13]

Of course not all Catholics believe in bleeding hosts. My point is only that such stories represent an elaboration of a belief shared by all Catholics, namely, that in swallowing the communion wafter they are quite literally swallowing the actual body of Christ. This in turn means that the Catholic world-view makes "incorporation of a man's body through the mouth" a far more acceptable image to the conscious mind than is the case in other Christian traditions.

In summary then, my argument is that the stigmatic's desire to merge her or his body with Christ's reflects the gratification of the infantile desire to incorporate the father. Most stigmatics are Catholic because Catholicism, more so than other Christian religions, sees Communion as a literal swallowing of Christ's body. This makes it easier for the infantile desire to incorporate the father to be expressed in a range of fairly overt ways. One of these is the reception of Holy Communion itself; another is stigmatization.

Of course, if all this is correct, and both stigmatization and the reception of Holy Communion do gratify the same unconscious desire to incorporate the father, we would expect the two to be associated, and they are: we have already noted that stigmatics are known to have an especially strong desire to receive Holy Communion.

JESUS AS FATHER-FIGURE

At this point, many readers might object to my interpretation on the grounds that Catholics (and Christians generally) take Christ to be the *Son* of God. How then can I suggest that incorporating the body of Christ (in the Eucharist or during stigmatization) represent a desire to incorporate the *father*? Here we must remember that the psychological associations evoked in the Catholic mind by concepts like "Jesus Christ" and "God the Father" are shaped by more than just formal doctrines about the Trinity. For example, a great many Catholic attitudes are shaped by the New Testament, the Gospels in particular, and in these accounts "God the Father" is hardly ever mentioned. On the contrary, these accounts are overwhelmingly concerned with the life of Jesus Christ. More importantly, the events in the Gospels that are critical for salvation in the Catholic world-view (namely, the Incarnation, the Crucifixion, and the Resurrection) are events in which, on the face of it, Jesus is the central character. Likewise it is Jesus who is the focus of virtually all important Catholic liturgical practices. The Mass, for example, the most important of all Catholic rituals, is thought of as a symbolic re-enactment of the Crucifixion, and Holy Communion as the reception of the body and blood of Christ. Not of "God generally" or of "God the Father" but of Christ specifically.

All this may seem self-evident, but it leads to a conclusion easily ignored in the study of folk Catholicism, namely, that Catholics surround the figure of Jesus Christ with a strong aura of authority even though he is "only" the Son of God. In fact, it is my contention that the traditions preserved in the New Testament, together with Catholic liturgical practice, ensure that in a *de facto* sense the adult Christ is surrounded with a greater authority than any other male figure in the Catholic pantheon, *including* "God the Father."

But if Christ is the most authoritative male in the Catholic pantheon, then the conscious image of Christ can be used as a symbolic representation of the actual father, the first and most important of the authoritative males that every child encounters. The fact that the conscious image of Christ can be used as a symbolic representation of the father allows me to argue that the infantile desire to incorporate the father is gratified both by swallowing the Communion wafer and by merging one's body with Christ's in stigmatization.

WHY FEMALES?

Although the pre-oedipal processes described by Klein are the same for boys and girls, a difference develops during the oedipal period (and Klein's views on the oedipal period do not differ greatly from Freud's). Simply put, in the case of females, the dynamics of the oedipal period reinforce two of the desires that developed during the pre-oedipal period, namely, a girl's hostility towards her mother and her sexual desire for her father. In the case of males, however, exactly the reverse is true: the dynamics of the oedipal process undermine these two desires. Thus, for a boy the oedipal period sees an intensification of his sexual desire for his mother and an intensification of his hostility toward his father, all of which weakens his hostility towards his mother and his sexual desire for his father that had developed earlier.

In short, if stigmatization is in part the fulfilment of the pre-oedipal sexual desire to incorporate the father as a substitute for the lost Good Breast (and that is my hypothesis), then the fact that this desire is later (in the oedipal period) intensified in females but weakened in males would lead us to expect that most stigmatics should be female, as they are.

SUFFERING

So far we have really only explained why a Catholic with an especially strong pre-oedipal desire for his or her father would want to incorporate the body of Christ; we have not explained the stigmatic's emphasis upon the *Suffering* Christ in particular. The key here, I think, lies with Biot's (1962, 55) observation that the great pain associated with the stigmata is always accepted quite willingly. Phrased more actively, the stigmatic seems to *seek* pain. For instance, when Louise Lateau was asked what she most desired, she said, "The principal prayer that I made in the past was to suffer; that prayer I say now is that His Holy will be done in me, even if I have to suffer double" (quoted in Didry and Wallemacq 1931, 162). Similar remarks can be found in the accounts left by other stigmatics. Why should the stigmatic so willingly seek out pain? At the conscious level, there is no mystery about this. Most stigmatics themselves answer this question, and their answers usually fall into one or both of two categories.

First, many stigmatics see their suffering as expiation for sin, either their own sins or the sins of others. Veronica Giuliani, for example, tells us explicitly that the pain associated with her stigmata was expiation for her sins (Salvatori 1874, 146). She also tells us (p. 213) of a vision in which Jesus Christ made her the "mediatrix" between him and all sinners, so that through her suffering *all* sin might be expiated. Likewise, in discussing the sufferings of Louise Lateau, Didry and Wallemacq (1931, 162) show that both she and those around here clearly saw her suffering as an expiation for sin in the same way:

[God] wishes to find innocent souls eager to make reparation for the crimes committed around them, who for this end would suffer generously; heroic souls whose satisfactions should unite with those of the Divine Redeemer, to atone for the sins of the world ... To sacrifice oneself, to expiate faults not personally committed, is an act of charity renewing that of the garden of Olives and of Calvary ... Louse was one of those specially called [by Jesus] to follow this royal way of the Cross and of sacrifice.

Anne Catherine Emmerich and Padre Pio also saw at least some of their sufferings as expiation for sin (see Schmöger 1885b, 324; Carty 1953, 48–9). Gemma Galgani actually had a vision of Christ in which he told her that her sufferings, like his, were meant to atone for the sins of the world (Germanus 1913, 188).

The second attitude that stigmatics adopt towards their suffering is that through their suffering others may be relieved of suffering. This emphasis on vicarious suffering has been documented most clearly in the case of Therese Neumann. Graef (1951, 93–9) devotes an entire chapter to Neumann's "Sühneleiden," as her instances of vicarious suffering were called in Konnersreuth. In some of the more well-known examples of *Sühneleiden*, for example, Neumann developed (1) a paralysis of her throat muscles in order to relieve a young seminarian of a similar condition (and one that was supposedly preventing him from being ordained), (2) an intestinal illness in order to relieve her own father of a similar illness, (3) a burning thirst, a fever, and "incessant violent temptation" in order to relieve a dying young girl (who, we are told, had been seduced by a priest at the age of fourteen) of those same symptoms, and so on.

Anne Catherine Emmerich also believed her suffering relieved the suffering of others. Several years after receiving her stigmata, for example, she reflected upon what she claimed had been a lifelong desire to suffer vicariously for others: "I have always asked for the sufferings of others. I knew that God never sends afflictions without a design; there must be some debt to be paid off. And if these afflictions weigh heavily upon us at times, it is because ...

no one is willing to help the poor sufferer to pay off his debt. This I begged to be allowed to do" (Schmöger 1885a, 19).

In summary then, most stigmatics see their suffering as expiation for sin (either their own or those of others), as a means of relieving the suffering of others, or both. Under the Kleinian interpretation being developed here, this desire to experience pain in expiation for sin and to relieve others of pain can be seen as gratifying the infantile desire to make reparation for the phantasy attacks made against the mother. One immediate advantage of this interpretation is that it allows us to understand two central elements in the stigmatization process: the emphasis on "wounds" and the experience of inedia.

WOUNDING AND ORAL MORTIFICATIONS

If the stigmatic is really attempting to make reparation for her infantile phantasy attacks against her mother, we would expect that the nature of those attacks would affect the form of the reparation. Specifically, since those attacks are of an oral-sadistic nature, we might expect that the reparation offered would take a similar form – and it does.

Stigmatization involves, first and foremost, a literal wounding, that is, a tearing or puncturing of the stigmatics's skin. The wounds experienced by the stigmatic, in other words, are very much like the wounds that the infant, acting in accordance with its oral-sadistic impulses, wants to inflict upon the Bad Breast/Bad Mother. In developing precisely wounds of this sort on her or his own body, then, the stigmatic is making reparation for those early phantasy attacks in an especially fitting manner.

But though a willing acceptance of lacerations and woundings (as occurs in stigmatization) is one way to make reparation for the oral-sadistic attacks against the mother, we might also expect stigmatics to specifically mortify their mouth in some manner, since (in their phantasies) the mouth is the weapon that they use in these attacks. Some stigmatics do attempt fairly extreme oral mortifications. Bell (1985, 76–83), for example, has already called attention to the orality evident in the mortifications practised by Veronica Giuliani, who felt compelled to lick spiders from the walls, place a heavy stone on her tongue, and eat a variety of disgusting things, including cat vomit, leeches, dead mice, bugs, and worms.

Similarly, Anne Catherine Emmerich, in recalling her childhood, tells us of her compulsion to suck the pus out of abscesses in order to cure them: "When I was a child ... the neighbours used to come to me to bind up their wounds ... I was skillful at such things ... When I saw an abscess, I used to say to myself 'If you squeeze it, it will get worse; the matter [that is, the pus] must, however, come out in some way." Then I sucked it gently and it soon healed ... At first I felt disgust, but that only made me overcome myself, for disgust is not compassion" (Schmöger 1885a, 45). But in most cases, stigmatics engage in oral mortification simply by abstaining from food. What I am suggesting, in other words, is that the inedia characteristic of stigmatics is yet another way (in addition to their easy acceptance of wounding and laceration) of making reparation for the oral-sadistic attacks they made against their mother in their infantile phantasies.

Since inedia among Catholic mystics, especially female mystics, has been much discussed in recent years, I should point out that my interpretation of inedia here differs from the usual one. Bell (1985), for example, argues that inedia reflects a desire for autonomy. In his view, an emphasis on both celibacy and inedia was a way in which female mystics could prevent outside objects (= a penis and food) from penetrating their bodies. Certainly the biographical and autobiographical accounts reviewed by Bell, including those pertaining to Veronica Giuliani (who is the only important stigmatic discussed by Bell), do contain abundant evidence to support the notion that many female mystics have indeed been driven by a desire to assert their autonomy.

Bynum 1987, though restricting herself to medieval mystics, has made a similar argument. Though she is careful to make it clear that fasting had a differing meaning for medieval women than for modern women, she does argue that medieval fasting was a way in which women could gain control, not only over their own bodies, but also over others around them. Extreme fasting, Bynum suggests, was a practice that could be used to force fathers and husbands to let women escape from the household into the religious life. Here again, the lives of the female mystics that Bynum examines (none of whom were well-known stigmatics in the sense that that term is being used here) lend support to her argument.[14]

But if applied to the stigmatics being considered here, the sort of arguments developed by Bell and Bynum just do not ring true. The example of Veronica Giuliani notwithstanding, if there is one thing that most stigmatics do *not* gain after their stigmatization, it is autonomy. On the contrary, they usually became highly dependent upon others for their care and well-being. Anne Catherine Emmerich, Louise Lateau, and Therese Neumann, for instance, were so debilitated by their stigmata and associated illnesses that they were bedridden for long periods and had to be cared for by others. Padre Pio, though not bedridden, often needed help to care for and dress himself.

Just as importantly, the stigmatic is made the object of attention by all sorts of strangers, and the result is an almost constant intrusion by strangers into the stigmatic's private life. From Siwek's (1953) account of Therese Neumann, for instance, it seems clear that a substantial number of the pilgrims who journeyed to Konnersreuth actually ended up in Neumann's bedroom in order to be with her. A similar impression of the stigmatic's bedroom being invaded by large numbers of people is given by accounts of the lives of Anne Catherine Emmerich and Louise Lateau. Gemma Galgani's confessor (Germanus 1913, 182–3) tells us for a fact that onlookers often stayed near her to observe her thoughout the day and night.

Added to all this are the highly intrusive medical tests to which stigmatics are inevitably subjected. Gemma Galgani's biographers are fond of saying that she didn't like to be touched (something taken as a sign of her great modesty and chastity). Yet the reports of the priests and others who examined her (see Germanus 1913, 88–95) say that they not only saw but also touched the wounds in her hands and feet in order to verify the phenomenon. Her confessor even tells us that he himself quite often put a thermometer on her breast in order to validate the "temperature increase" that was regularly produced by her inflamed heart (Germanus 1913, 245). Anne Catherine Emmerich and Louise Lateau, in particular, were stigmatics subjected to several elaborate medical tests over a number of years.

This is not to say that arguments of the sort developed by Bell and Bynun are necessarily incorrect. After all, though almost all stigmatics experience inedia, the reverse is not true. There are many mystics who experience inedia without experiencing the stigmata, and in the case of these particular mystics, inedia may very well represent a drive for autonomy and control. What I am suggesting is only that when inedia develops in association with the stigmata, the autonomy argument makes little sense. In these cases, at least, it is easier to understand the patterns evident in the data if we view inedia as an oral mode of reparation for the oral-sadistic phantasy attacks made on the mother.

BLOOD AND MILK

Intimately associated with the child's desire for the oral incorporation of the father and its desire to make reparation for the phantasy attacks on its mother is its desire to re-establish the presence of the Good Breast, the breast that dispenses milk. This last infantile desire gives rise to what is perhaps the most striking phenomenon associated with the stigmata: recurrent bleeding. I am suggesting that a regular and recurrent "flow of blood" expresses the symbolic gratification of the infantile desire for a regular and recurrent flow of milk.

The notion that the blood flows from Christ's wounds conjures up breast-milk imagery is not novel. In her essay on the use of feminine metaphors to describe Jesus during the High Middle Ages, Bynum (1982, 132–3) points out that Christ's blood was indeed often likened to breast milk by medieval commentators. She argues that this symbolic equivalence was facilitated by the medieval belief that breast milk was literally processed blood. Quite apart from this, an unconscious association between a flow of blood from a wound and a flow of milk from the breast is easily established if only because each of these things involves the discharge of a bodily fluid.

The hypothesis that blood equals breast milk seems clearly to lead to a prediction about stigmatization that is not at all self-evident. If in fact blood is breast milk, then the wounds from which the stigmatic's blood flows are symbolic breasts. But which of the wounds associated with the stigmata is most easily seen as a symbolic breast? For two reasons, it seems likely that it would be the spear wound in the side, rather than the wounds in the hands or feet. First, since the spear wound is the only asymmetrical wound, it corresponds to the single breast from which the child nurses. Second, and most important, the spear wound is the wound that is closest to the breast. Bynum (1982, 133), in fact, points out that medieval writers did often call the spear wound in Christ's sides as a metaphorical breast when describing Jesus in feminine terms. For a painting that seems to invoke a great deal of breast-feeding imagery in its portrayal of Christ's spear wound, see Bynum (1987, 271–2 and plate 25).

If the bleeding wounds of the stigmatic are attempts to re-establish the presence of the Good Breast, we might therefore expect that the spear wound would be given pre-eminence. We might expect for instance that the spear wound would be the first of the five wounds to develop, or at least the first to start bleeding.

Neither Thurston, Biot, nor Siwek, nor any other commentator on the stigmata suggests that the spear wound is in any way central to the stigmatization process. Yet if we examine the biographies of the six stigmatics under consideration here, we find that:

1 Veronica Giuliani received her spear wound a full year before receiving the other four wounds (Salvatori 1874, 138–9). According to her own testimony and the results of an ecclesiastical investigation, even after she had received all five wounds, only the "spear wound" bled (Salvatori 1874, 151/153/166). Also relevant here is a purported memory that Giuliani recorded after she had received her stigmata. According to that memory, Giuliani's mother, upon her deathbed, had called each of her five daughters (including Giuliani) to her and "consigned" each to one of the five wounds of Christ Crucified. Giuliani, by her recollection, had been consigned to the spear wound (Salvatori 1874, 11).

2 Gemma Galgani's account of her initial stigmatization reports that she received all five wounds simultaneously. On the other hand, in discussing her wounds, Galgani's confessor gives the impression that the side wound gave off more blood than the others and certainly suggests that the pain associated with this particular wound was greater excessive than the pain associated with the others (Germanus 1913, 60–6).

3 The side wound was the first wound to appear on Louise Lateau, and it

bled immediately. The other wounds did not appear (and bleed) until over a week later (Molloy 1873, 40; Didry and Wallemacq 1931, 47).

4 The spear wound was the first of the five wounds to appear in Therese Neumann, and it bled for at least two weeks before any of the other wounds appeared. (Graef 1951, 23–5)

5 Although Padre Pio claimed to have received all five wounds simultaneously, the report of the first medical examination of his stigmatization states that only the spear wound showed any evidence of bleeding (Carty 1953, 17–18). In commenting upon Padre Pio's stigmata in general, Carty (1953, 23) also notes that the side wound "is the strangest of all [the five wounds], because it emits a great quantity of blood even though the wound seems more superficial."

Only in the case of Anne Catherine Emmerich can I find no evidence at all pointing to the pre-eminence of the "spear-wound" in the bleeding process. At one point in her recollections, for instance, Emmerich said that her side wound was received *after* the other four wounds (Schmöger 1885a, 276), while at another she said that they were all received simultaneously (Schmöger 1885a, 323). Neither account supports the argument I am making here.

Emmerich's case is somewhat complicated, however, by the fact that she consistently maintained that the first of her wounds to bleed was *not* one of the wounds associated with the stigmata, but rather a small wound in the shape of a cross that had appeared directly on her breast (Schmöger 1885a, 263). In other words, even in Emmerich's case, there is some emphasis on bleeding from the breast.

Quite apart from the fact that the spear wound is given pre-eminence in the case of most stigmatics, further support for the "blood equals breast milk" equation can be had by inspecting the fantasy material left by some stigmatics. Anne Catherine Emmerich, in particular, has left detailed accounts of her many visions, and in one of those accounts she describes a scene from the life of St Francis Borgia (1510–72):

I remember his [St Francis Borgia's] having scruples about daily Holy Communion and his praying before a picture of the Mother of God, where he received *a stream of blood* from the child Jesus and *another [stream] of milk* from Mary. He was told not to deprive himself of that on which he lived, daily Communion ... [Emmerich goes on to describe this reception of milk and blood, by St Frances Borgia and other saints, in detail] ... From Mary's breast, or from the region of the breasts, something like a little white vapor streamed out to them [the saints she is discussing] and was breathed in by them. It was like a stream of manna from her, while the Side of Jesus shone upon them a ray of rosy red light. (emphasis added; Schmöger 1885a, 558)

Notice that this passage not only associates milk from Mary's breast with

Jesus's blood, but also associates each of these concepts with Holy Communion *and* emphasizes the blood from Jesus's *side* wound (since the last sentence makes it clear that it was from this particular wound that the "rosy red light" emanated). All of this is entirely consistent with the argument being developed here.

Although Gemma Galgani never made such an explicit association between breast and breast milk, and side wound and blood, she came close. While looking at a crucifix, Galgani once began to yearn for the presence of Christ: "O Jesus, let me come to Thee, *I thirst for Thy life-giving Blood.* Wonderful to relate!" (emphasis added; Germanus 1913, 271). The image of Christ on the crucifix promptly became animated and beckoned her to his side, where he gave Galgani exactly what she had requested: "She in an instant was with Him; He pressed her to His Side and she, standing as if on a cloud and embracing Him with both arms, in blessed rapture drew from His Heart long draughts of love" (Germanus 1913, 271). I submit that the imagery involved in all of this, of the young Gemma Galgani gratifying her thirst for the blood of Christ by sucking at his side wound, is an only slightly disguised representation of the infant sucking at its mother's breast.

Finally, there is some evidence of a psychological association between stigmitization and breast milk in the case of Veronica Giuliani. For a five-year period, which included the three years of her visible stigmata, Giuliani believed she had been commanded by Jesus Christ (in a vision) to subsist only upon bread and water. Should she feel weakened by this regimen, Jesus told her, she should sustain herself by taking a few drops of a fluid that oozed from her left breast, and she did so. Moreover, she tells us that she regularly sensed the fluid inside her breast ("I also appeared to feel the effects of the fluid within my bosom"; see Salvatori 1874, 119). The fluid, which was collected and examined by her superiors, was found to be the colour and consistency of breast milk, though exuding a perfume-like fragrance (something taken to be a sign of its supernatural nature), and vials of the fluid came to be associated with miracles. Putting aside the allegedly supernatural character of the phenomena, I suggest that what we have here is clear evidence that during the period of her stigmata Veronica Giuliani was concerned with re-establishing the presence of the Good Breast, the breast that dispenses milk (to her).

In summary, the fact that the spear wound seems to be given pre-eminence in the bleeding process associated with stigmatization (something unnoticed by previous commentators, though easily derived from the argument presented here), together with the evidence linking the side wound and its blood to the concepts breast and breast milk in the fantasy material left by Emmerich, Galgani and Giuliani, suggests that the desire to re-establish the presence of the Good Breast is another of the infantile desires being gratified through stigmatization.

PREDISPOSING FACTORS

Although the infantile experiences described by Klein are universal, obviously only a few people, in particular only a small number of Catholics, develop the stigmata. It seems obvious then that there must be certain conditions that predispose some people to stigmatization. One such condition is almost certainly celibacy. The stigmata almost always develop in sexual mature individuals who have voluntarily embraced celibacy, and tends not to develop, say, in very young children or married Catholics. Thus, Veronica Giuliani and Anne Catherine Emmerich were nuns, Padre Pio was a Capuchin monk, and Louise Lateau, Gemma Galgani, and Therese Neumann were unmarried women who lived with their parents or guardians.

Freud (1907) argued that in individuals with particularly strong libidos, the excess libidinous energy that builds up as the result of voluntary renunciation of overt sexual intercourse would have two consequences: it would reactivate infantile sexual memories and would predispose these individuals to discharge this excess energy by participating in obsessive religious practices that bore some resemblance to these infantile sexual memories. In light of the argument developed in earlier sections, then, the stigmata can be seen as an obsessive religious practice that allows voluntarily celibate people to discharge excess sexual energy.

The fact that most stigmatics are celibate also accounts for what would otherwise be a loose end in this analysis. I have suggested, remember, that the stigmatic sees a regular flow of blood as a symbolic substitute for a regular flow of breast milk. But since most stigmatics are female, wouldn't this desire for a regular flow of breast milk be more easily gratified simply by nursing a child? Of course it would, but nursing a child is difficult if the person in question has renounced sexual intercourse and this renounced the ability to bear children herself.

Still, given the Kleinian argument that has been developed here, we must inevitably come to the conclusion that what would *most* predispose an individual to receive the stigmata would be an intensification of the pre-oedipal processes described by Klein. For instance, experiences that intensified the oral-sadistic phantasy attacks that the infant directs against the Bad Breast and the Bad Mother, and which therefore intensified the resulting guilt and the resulting desire to make reparation, should cause that person to be more prone to stigmatization in later life. Such experiences would presumably include things like infrequent nursing (that is, the experience of having only infrequent access to the Good Breast), and early and severe weaning.

There are of course no objective reports detailing how stigmatics were breast-fed as infants. On the other hand, several stigmatics claimed to be able to recall their infantile experiences in great detail. These are conscious fantasies that have been projected back in time rather than true memories. Still, if we grant that these fantasies have probably been shaped by unconscious memories of nursing experiences (memories which, remember, are never lost), then we would expect to find in these conscious fantasies some evidence of early deprivation, if early deprivation is indeed implicated in stigmatization.

Anne Catherine Emmerich was baptized on the day she was born, and in later life (after she had received the stigmata) she claimed that she could recall the events of that day in detail: "I felt myself a newborn babe in the arms of my godmother ... I felt shy and embarrassed. The three old women present, so also the nurse, were displeasing to me. My mother inspired very different sentiments, and I willingly took her breast" (Schmöger 1885a, 12). It is difficult to imagine a fantasy that would more clearly show evidence of the hated Bad Mother (the "three old women" and the "nurse" who were "displeasing") and the Good Mother who dispenses milk ("My mother inspired very different sentiments, and I willingly took her breast").

This emphasis on breasts and breast milk is evident in several other of the fantasies reported by Emmerich, even apart from the one concerning St Francis Borgia discussed earlier. Emmerich, for example, often reported visions in which she felt herself transported to different times and places in order to be in the company of saints. In one of these visions she was transported to ancient Rome and put in charge of two very young children, who were in fact St Agnes and St Emerentiania: "I had nothing to give them and in my perplexity, I laid them on my breast .. suddenly, to my surprise and alarm, I felt that they were really receiving nourishment from me ... [I handed them back to their nurses.] ... But now, to my great alarm, I noticed something strange about my breasts ... they had become swollen, full of nourishment, and I felt an oppression, a burning in them which gave me great anxiety" (Schmöger 1885b, 448. Emmerich then goes on to relate how on her way home (in the vision) several other "poor" children in the neighbourhood came and drained her breast as well, something that eventually relieved the "oppression" that she had felt in her breasts.

It was Thurston's (1955, 69n) view that remarks of this sort showed evidence of an "unhealthy imagination" and were therefore evidence against the supernatural origin of Emmerich's stigmata. Given the perspective in this book, however, such a fantasy can be seen as a fairly straightforward attempt to establish the presence of a Good Breast so swollen with milk that it actually causes pain.

Veronica Giuliani also reporting having clear memories of her infancy, and here again breast-feeding figures prominently. In one of her autobiographies she tells us that as an infant she voluntarily choose not to take milk from her mother's breast on Wednesdays, Fridays, and Saturdays (Salvatori 1874, 4; Bell 1985, 58–9). Since these are the traditional days for fasting in the Church, it seems likely that this "memory" was in part an attempt by the adult Giuliani to project a saintliness back onto her childhood. Still, the fact remains that one of her earliest memories involves not taking milk from her mother's breast. Giuliani also claimed that on the days when she refrained from the breast, her mother relieved her breast by breast-feeding some "poor" children in the neighbourhood. In Kleinian terms, the "not taking milk on certain days" element in this fantasy shows traces of an early infantile memory of not having access to the Good Breast as often as desired. The reference to her mother breast-feeding other children reflects Giuliani's infantile awareness of the fact that the Good Breast is unavailable, not because it has ceased to exist, but because it has been withheld (from her). It also seems consistent with the argument being developed here that the holy picture to which the young Giuliani was most devoted (she herself claimed her devotion to this picture began at the age of three) was a picture of the Virgin Mary breast-feeding the infant Jesus (Salvatori 1874, 7).

As well, we have an account of the first few months in the life of Louise Lateau (Molloy 1873, 35–8; Didry and Wallemacq 1931, 22–3), which was based on the recollections of Lateau and others in her village several years later. In April 1850, when Louise was only two and a half months old, her father died of smallpox. Both Louise and her mother had also contracted the disease, and the mother – we are told – became too ill to rise from her bed. The family was isolated in their hut for twelve days following the father's death. At first Louise's older sister Rosine, who was only three at the time, performed the necessary tasks for the household (which included her mother, Louise, and another younger sister) under her mother's supervision. Eventually, her mother became too ill to supervise Rosine, and the infant (Louise) was left completely unattended for something like two days. The food supply also ran out. The family was saved from starvation only because a neighbour forced his way into the hut, discovered the deplorable conditions, and brought food and help. One of the first things he did was to put fresh clothing on the infant, whose clothes had been saturated with feces and urine. We are also told explicitly (Didry and Wallemacq 1931, 31) that he obtained milk for her. This suggests that Louise's mother had been unable to nurse her child during her illness. We also know that Louise's mother remained ill and (bedridden) for the next eighteen months.

If taken as literal history, this story indicates that during the first few months of her life, Louise Lateau nearly starved to death, or – at the very least – was breast-fed irregularly. Given Klein's argument, this would almost certainly have intensified the hostility that the infant directs at the Bad Breast. On the other hand, if we take this report as a mixture of history and fantasy, it can be viewed as showing traces of an infantile memory of having been deprived of the mother's breast.

Finally, we come to Padre Pio. Since he was under instructions from Church authorities not to write anything publicly about his stigmata, and since he was a male, we might not expect to find him discussing breast-feeding in any explicit way. Yet he did. In one of the few authenticated letters sent privately by Padre Pio to one of his "spiritual children," he discusses this subject at length in a passage where he is drawing a metaphorical equivalence between the way God treats his children and the way a mother treats her newborn infant:

She [the mother] does not immediately bring it [the infant] to her bosom to nurse ... The mother is anxious not to injure the baby's health with milk not yet altogether purified from the heat of her maternity ... [also] the milk before she has recovered, would not be agreeable to the baby's palate, and so she is properly concerned that the baby, nauseated by the distasteful early milk not yet purified, might not afterwards be put off from normal nursing. (Carty 1953, 341–3)

Whatever the value of this passage as metaphor (or as a prescription for breast feeding), it does betray a concern with *an infant who does not nurse*, though Padre Pio (like Veronica Giuliani) projects the desire not to nurse onto the infant itself rather than (as Klein's reconstruction of infantile phantasies would have it) onto some image of the Bad Breast.

In summary, what we find in the fantasy material left by Giuliani, Emmerich, Lateau, and Padre Pio is some concern with (1) an infant who does not nurse, (2) establishing a plentiful flow of breast milk, or both.

CONCLUSION

The primary goal of this chapter has been to explain why stigmatization occurs and why it happens to some people and not to others. This explanation has been constructed by developing a psychoanalytic argument that sees stigmatization as the result of the intensification of three different infantile desires, notably (1) the desire to incorporate the father, (2) the desire to make reparation for the oral-sadistic attacks made in phantasy against the mother, and (3) the desire to re-establish the presence of the Good Breast. This argument has the advantage that it allows us to interrelate a wide range of observations, including the fact that stigmatics are usually female and Catholic, that they experience inedia, generalized pain, and recurrent bleeding, and that the spear wound seems to be given more emphasis than the other wounds of the stigmata.

Furthermore, the explanation developed in this chapter also provides a basis for understanding why the *idea* of stigmatization has always been so popular to ordinary Catholics. After all, if Klein is correct, the unconscious desires that give rise to stigmatization are desires that are found in the unconscious of us all, though in a less intense form. Stigmatization represents the direct gratification of those desires, but the same desires can be gratified vicariously, by identifying with the stigmatic or at least venerating the stigmatic. This, I suggest, is why stigmatics have always been so important in the Catholic mystical tradition.

Our analysis of the stigmata is not quite over. It turns out that stigmatics have been more common in certain historical periods than in others (the medieval period was *not* the period which produced most stigmatics), and this needs to be explained. It will be useful, however, to postpone that discussion until chapter 7.

CHAPTER SIX

The Forty Hours

It is no accident that Freud's first insight into the nature of unconscious processes came with his investigation of hysteria. What we observe in hysteria is the outcome of processes that are operative in us all but which in the hysteric have been intensified and exaggerated. The extreme nature of the phenomenon is the very thing that makes it easier to identify the underlying processes at work, and the same is true of stigmatization, itself a form of hysteria. This is one of the reasons that stigmatization has been included in this book. The study of stigmatization also provided a convenient context in which to introduce Kleinian theory. Nevertheless, acquiring the stigmata can hardly be called a "popular Catholic devotion."

True, as I have argued, in venerating those individuals with the stigmata, ordinary Catholics can gratify vicariously the unconscious desires that the stigmatic gratifies directly. This would explain the importance that has always been accorded to stigmatization in Catholic devotional literature. Nevertheless, if the desires that give rise to stigmatization are indeed found in us all, it seems reasonable to expect that there might be some widespread Catholic devotion that gratifies these same desires directly, though perhaps less flamboyantly. The analysis presented in the last chapter even gives us a clue as to what such devotions might look like.

Recall that one of the unconscious desires being gratified by stigmatization is the desire to incorporate the father, a desire that emerges when the child is forced to give up the breast. Stigmatics gratify this desire by convincing themselves that they have assimilated the body of the suffering Christ into their own, and the appearance of the stigmatic wounds validates this view. But since the desire to incorporate the father is conceptualized in oral terms it can also be gratified by eating a Eucharistic host, given the associations evoked by such a host in the Catholic tradition. It was this conclusion that allowed us to explain the intense attachment to the Eucharist that characterizes so many stigmatics.

But if devotion to the Eucharist gratifies, for the stigmatic, the desire to incorporate the father, it can gratify that same desire for ordinary Catholics. This suggests that if the cluster of desires that give rise to stigmatization are indeed being gratified less flamboyantly by some widespread Catholic devotion, then that devotion is likely to one in which veneration of the Eucharist host has a prominent place.

EUCHARISTIC DEVOTIONS

There are in fact a great many Eucharistic devotions in the Catholic tradition, and their history is fairly well documented.[1] The Eucharist, in the sense of the consecrated host, first emerged as an object of veneration in and of itself, apart from the act of Communion, during the thirteenth century. It was during this period, for example, that the practice of "elevating" the host at the moment of consecration was first introduced into the liturgy of the Mass.[2] This same period also saw the establishment of a special feast, the feast of Corpus Christi (called *fête Dieu* in France) dedicated to the Eucharistic host under the title of the "Blessed Sacrament."

Over the next few centuries, "exposure" of a Eucharistic host for public veneration became more and more common. An exposed Eucharistic host, for instance, was routinely carried aloft during the *Corpus Christi* procession.[3] In certain places, notably Germany and the Low Countries, it was also common for the Blessed Sacrament to remain exposed throughout the Mass. By the latter half of the fifteenth century, veneration of the Eucharist had become especially popular in Italy, as witnessed by the proliferation of confraternities dedicated to the Blessed Sacrament that were established in cities like Spoleto, Parma, Perugia, Orvieto, Genoa, Bologna, Ravenna, and Milan (Beringer 1925b, 87). In 1501 the first such confraternity was established in Rome itself, usually a sign that the devotion involved was on the verge of being promulgated by the papacy.

In retrospect, however, it is clear that one particular Eucharistic devotion came to have more of a transnational appeal than any other. This was the Forty Hours devotion. I now want to demonstrate that although the Forty Hours devotion and stigmatization seem to have little in common, they both gratify more or less the same cluster of unconscious desires.

THE FORTY HOURS

The Forty Hours, often called by the Italian *"Quarant'Ore"* even in English publications, is a devotion in which the Blessed Sacrament is exposed continuously in a church for some long period of time. What this means in practice is that a single consecrated host is placed in a receptacle that allows it to be seen, and this receptacle itself is then placed in a central location in the church, usually on the main altar. One of the few requirements of the devotion is that there always be several people present in the church and watching the Blessed Sacrament during the time of its exposition.

As in the case of the rosary (see chapter 1), the modern form of the Forty Hours reflects the merging of several different and independent traditions. As a result, several different individuals and religious orders have been credited with having introduced this devotion. Earlier Catholic commentators like Thurston (1904c, 110–34) were much concerned with sorting through these various claims and establishing priority. Recent scholarship (for example, Cargnoni 1986) suggests simply that several different people independently introduced devotions that approximated the final form of the Forty Hours. On one point all commentators have always been agreed: the early history of the devotions is closely tied to the city of Milan in northern Italy.[4]

Though something like the Forty Hours was being preached in Milan as early as 1527, its emergence as a widely popular devotion can only be traced back to 1537. Milan in that year was in imminent danger of being invaded by a French army, and the Forty Hours was proposed by various preachers as a means by which Milan might be spared the inevitable devastation that such an invasion would produce. Every church in the city staged the devotion, so that as soon the Forty Hours ended at one church it began at another. A change in the political situation ensured that the invasion did not take place, something that the Milanese quite naturally attributed to the efficacy of the new devotion. As a consequence Milan committed itself to re-enacting the formula of 1537 annually – with every church in the city performing the Forty Hours devotion in succession. Records of the archdiocese of Milan show that by 1575 the new devotion had spread from the city itself to the surrounding countryside (Thurston 1904, 135).

These same archdiocesan regulations are also some evidence of the great appeal of the new devotion to the laity. These regulations required, for example, that a committee composed mainly of laymen (though headed by a cleric) be established in every parish and that this committee be put in charge of all adminstrative details relating to the Forty Hours. It was this committee that divided the period of the devotion into temporal segments, assigned each segment to some particular set of parishioners, notified the confraternities and other associations participating of the times to which their members had been assigned, and so on. Although the Milan regulations required only that at least ten lay persons and one cleric be present during the exposition, attempts were made to secure as broad a representation of the community as possible. One of the instructions given by St Charles Borromeo, who was Archbishop of Milan from 1595 to 1631 and who did much to popularize the Forty Hours, says, "Let there be always a good number of persons present, especially the parishioners, when the devotion is held in a parish church, all the families and persons of the parish being divided according to hours, but without assigning any of the night hours to women" (quoted in Thurston 1904, 138). While granting that Borromeo's suggestion that *all* the families in a given parish might want to participate is a little optimistic, the evidence from the period does suggest that a great many families in each parish did participate. Within a decade of the public celebration of the Forty Hours in Milan in 1537, the devotion was being practised in a number of other Italian cities, including Pavia, Gubbio, Bologna, and Siena. It was practised for the first time in Rome itself in 1548, and from there quickly spread through the rest of Italy. This is not to say that all communities followed the Milanese pattern of rotating the Forty Devotion among a number of churches. In some places the devotion was practised only in certain churches, in others, in several churches simultaneously. What was spreading then, was simply the practice of venerating an exposed Blessed Sacrament in a church for a considerable length of time.

The Forty Hours first appeared in cities in both France and Spain during the 1570s. By the early 1600s it had spread to the Low Countries, and by the 1620s to the German Catholic states. Though there appears to have been a general decline in the popularity of the devotion during the eighteenth century, its popularity increased again during the nineteenth. In the late nineteenth and early twentieth centuries, it was found in all parts of the Catholic world.

OF MONSTRANCES AND MOTHERS

Given the theoretical argument I have developed so far, the infantile desire to "incorporate the father through the mouth" could in principle be gratified by any Eucharistic devotion. To understand why the Forty Hours devotion in particular achieved such a great popularity, we have to look to the things that most distinguish it from other Eucharistic devotions – and this brings us back to a familiar Kleinian concept: reparation.

Before the sixteenth century, the devotional literature that dealt with Eucharistic devotions (like the *Corpus Christi* procession, for instance) tended to portray the Eucharistic host as a "powerful relic" or as "spiritual nourishment" or both (see the discussion in Zika 1988). Nothing in the pre-sixteenth-century traditions associated the Eucharistic host with the idea of reparation. But in the sixteenth century that changed, and the change occurred precisely in connection with the Forty Hours. In 1537, for instance, the Milanese preachers who promulgated the new devotion argued that the threatened French invasion was punishment for the sins of the Milanese people, and that those sins could be expiated by making reparation to the Blessed Sacrament through the Forty Hours devotion. In 1539 Pope Paul III, when attaching indulgences to the Milanese devotion, generalized this emphasis by suggesting that the Forty Hours could be a means of "appease[ing] the anger of God provoked by the offences of Christians" (Thurston 1904c, 129); that is, it could be used as a means of expiating the sins of all Christians.

The association of the Forty Hours devotion with expiation was most firmly established in the latter half of the sixteenth century, when the Jesuits began actively promulgating this devotion as a way of expiating the sinful excesses committed during the Carnival season that immediately precedes Lent. Similarly, when Pope Clement VIII organized the Forty Hours in the city of Rome in 1592, he explicitly stated that the practice of the devotion could expiate the "sins of men" and so stop the punishments being sent by God because of those sins, punishments that included (in Clement's mind) a Turkish invasion, the spread of Protestantism, problems faced by a good Catholic monarch like the King of France, and so on.[5] In other words, though the particular sins being expiated through the devotion might vary depending upon who was promulgating it, the Forty Hours devotion has always been seen as a means of making reparation for sin of some kind.[6]

In the last chapter, I argued that the emphasis upon reparation that stigmatics associate with their suffering gratifies the unconscious desire to make reparation for the infantile attacks made in phantasy against the mother's breast, and I think that it means the same thing here. But if this is correct, we should find that the Forty Hours has been shaped by the memories of the paranoid-schizoid positions (just as stigmatization was shaped by those memories). Has it? To answer this question it will be useful to isolate the additional characteristics, apart from an emphasis on reparation, that most distinguish the Forty Hours from other, less popular Eucharistic devotions.

A CONSIDERABLE AMOUNT OF WATCHING

At first glance, one of the distinguishing features of the Forty Hours might seem to be an association with the number forty. But this would be a bit misleading, since there never appears to have been any great significance attached to forty hours as a precise period. Certainly, the number forty does not seem to have evoked a consistent set of associations in the minds of those promulgating the devotion. When the devotions was first instituted at Milan, for instance, it was said that the forty hours recalled the forty hours that Christ's body rested in the tomb before the Resurrection. Later popularizers of the devotion, however, suggested that the forty referred to the forty days that Christ spent in the wilderness or to the forty days that he spent on earth after the Resurrection. More recent promulgators (Beringer 1925a, 347; Corblet 1886, 451) have tended to endorse all three interpretations simultaneously.

Moreover, although the actual practice of the devotion has in some places been tied closely to a precise period of forty hours, in other places it has not. In France during the early nineteenth century, for instance, devotees prayed in front of the exposed Blessed Sacrament for "thirteen or fourteen" hours for each of three consecutive days (Bergier 1863, 425–6). In this case, obviously, the duration of the devotion would indeed have been close to forty hours. But Fortescue (1943, 349n) notes that in places where the devotion was spread over three days and a Mass said each day, the time between the first and last Mass was usually more like forty-eight hours.

Generally, it seems that the concern is not so much that the devotion last precisely forty hours, but rather that it last simply for a "considerable" period of time, certainly a period of time that goes beyond one full day. Furthermore, the intent has always been that for this considerable period of time the exposed Blessed Sacrament be the undisputed centre of attention. Thus, until quite recently not even the celebration of the Mass, supposedly the central act in Catholic worship, was allowed to diminish the necessity of watching the Blessed Sacrament for the duration of the Forty Hours. Only in 1967, in fact, did the Congregation of Rites declare that the exposition of the Blessed Sacrament during the Forty Hours was to be interrupted during Mass; even then, the Congregation specified that the faithful be properly prepared before the old practice was changed (see Cargoni 1986, columns 2722–3).

A final characteristic of the Forty Hours is its strong visual emphasis. Devotees, in other words practitioners, are not just supposed to *pray* before the Blessed Sacrament; they are supposed to watch it. This is why those present during the devotion are usually described as "watchers" in the devotional literature.

In summary, then, the distinguishing feature of the Forty Hours seems to be its emphasis on staring exclusively at an exposed Blessed Sacrament for a considerable length of time. The simplest and most prosaic way to explain this would be to argue that something about the appearance of what was being seen was particularly appealing to the practitioners of the devotion. What in fact did they see, in a concrete and literal sense, when they looked upon an exposed Blessed Sacrament?

EXPOSITION OF THE EUCHARIST

In this context, the term "Blessed Sacrament" refers to a Eucharistic host, that is, to a piece of unleavened bread (traditionally circular) that has been consecrated by a priest and that as a result has become the body and blood of Jesus Christ. During Holy Communion small consecrated hosts of this sort are distributed to individual communicants. To say that the Blessed Sacrament is "exposed" usually means only that a single consecrated host (often larger than the Communion hosts) is displayed in such a manner so that it can be seen by the faithful.

The usual way of exposing a host (apart from simply holding it aloft) is to insert it into a special type of receptacle. Such a receptacle, similar in function to a reliquary, was originally called an *ostensorium*, and in more recent times, a monstrance.[7] Monstrances first came into use in the fourteenth century, just after the Eucharist host itself had started to become an object of special veneration.

Most early monstrances consisted of a glass (or crystal) cylinder set vertically upon a base of the sort used in the construction of the chalice and surmounted by a peaked metal crown. The consecrated host was set into a special lunette holder at the bottom of the glass cylinder. The overall effect was quite architectural; these monstrances in fact looked very much like towers.[8] In a somewhat less common type of monstrance, the glass cylinder was replaced by a four-lobed, or "cloverleaf," window through which the host could be viewed.

A third type of monstrance, and the type that came into increasing use during the late fifteenth century, was the "sun" or "sunburst" type. In such monstrances a round glass window is set dead-centre in the midst of a circular field of some sort. Sometimes the circular field is a solid disc; sometimes it is defined by "rays" radiating out from the glass window at the centre. The host, naturally enough, is viewed through that centre window. As with earlier versions, the whole arrangement is set upon a chalice-like base.

By the beginning of the sixteenth century, that is in the period immediately preceding the emergence of the Forty Hours as a popular devotion, the sunburst monstrance had by all accounts become the most common type of monstrance in use and so this was the type of monstrance used in the Forty Hours devotion. True, during the sixteenth century the monstrance used in the Forty Hours was often draped with a veil that obscured it. But such a veil seems to have been quickly disposed of, and by the end of that century monstrances were being seen directly (McKenna 1933, 188–91). Thus, when the practitioners of the Forty Hours stared for hours at an exposed Blessed Sacrament, they were staring at a circular host in a sunburst monstrance.

In a great many cases, dating at least from the early seventeenth century, we even have representations of the entire scene, monstrance and all, that confronted the practitioners of the Forty Hours. Thus, the Forty Hours devotion in some of the churches in major European cities made use of elaborate theatrical backdrops called *apparati*. These *apparati* usually involved several different layers (flats), were well lit, and portrayed biblical or allegorical scenes. A presentation of a Forty Hours devotion using the most elaborate of the *apparati* was an important theatrical and artistic event, and was well advertised. Weil (1974), gives the titles of seventy-nine different pamphlets published between 1608 and 1825 that advertised the presentation of the Forty Hours using *apparati* at churches in the city of Rome alone. More important, (for our purposes) sketches or paintings of the *apparati* themselves, often executed by well-known artists, have also survived, and Weil reproduces twenty of these *apparati*, each of which was actually used in a major European city.

It can easily be seen from these paintings and drawings that the monstrance used in the devotion was almost invariably a sunburst monstrance.

If then there was something appealing about staring at an exposed Blessed Sacrament, this really means that there was something appealing about staring at the Blessed Sacrament in a sunburst monstrance. But what? Think carefully about the design of such a monstrance: a circular window, surrounded by a (usually larger) circular field of contrasting colour and texture. The overall effect is of a structure defined by concentric circles with contrasting fields.

Moreover, in the *apparati* reproduced by Weil the concentricity of the monstrance itself was often generalized to the entire scene. This was done in several steps. First, both lighting and placement could be used to ensure that the already concentric monstrance would be the focal point of the entire composition. In Weil's (1974, 219) words,

These [*apparati*] were illuminated by thousands of oil lamps and candles placed behind the flats so that neither the lamps nor the workmen who tended them could be seen by the viewer ... the monstrance containing the Eucharist was placed at the deepest point of the theatre where it was bathed in the light of all the hidden lamps as well as others placed behind the monstrance. The Eucharist glowed as if it were the source of illumination for the entire scene.

Having used position and lighting to make the concentric monstrance the focal point of the scene, the designer would then allow the concentricity of the monstrance to "radiate" outward by surrounding the monstrance with concentric designs. The drawings and paintings reproduced by Weil show that the monstrance was often surrounded by ever-widening circles of clouds, angels, rays of light, and so on.

In most parish churches, of course, such elaborate displays were not used. Even so, the concentricity evident in the design of a sunburst was still emphasized, if only by ensuring that nothing would detract from that design. According to the Clementine Instruction,[9] which were regulations issued by Clement IV in 1705 and which for all practical purposes have regulated the Forty Hours in most parish churches since that date, the monstrance must be exposed at the high altar of the church, and all other images and relics normally on the altar must be removed. As well, any paintings on or near the altar are to be covered and the monstrance surrounded by candles so that it is well lit.

The Forty Hours devotion, in short, is centred (in a very literal way) on the visual image of a concentric monstrance. If such an image were to evoke infantile memories, what memories might those be? I can think of only two things that figure prominently in infantile experience and that exhibit the same design, namely, concentric circles enclosing contrasting fields, as a sunburst monstrance. The first is the human eye, with its dark pupil set into the centre of the iris. The second is the mother's breast, which displays a nipple set into a dark aureole, which itself is set in the centre of a much lighter circular field that is defined by the structure of the breast proper. It is this last association that explains the appeal of the Forty Hours.

I am not suggesting that there is any conscious association between the exposed Blessed Sacrament and mother's breast. What I am suggesting is that the concentricity of both the sunburst monstrance (and, often, the *apparati* that surrounded it) and the concentricity of the mother's breast establishes an unconscious association between the two things.

Putting everything together, my argument is that because the Forty Hours is a devotion that (1) makes reparation for sin and (2) requires long visual focus upon a concentric monstrance whose design evokes infantile memories of the mother's breast, it is a devotion that is perfectly suited to gratifying the infantile unconscious desire to make reparation for phantasy attacks against the mother's breast which develops in children during the paranoid-schizoid position.

CONCLUSION

I am arguing that the Forty Hours devotion became the most popular of all Eucharistic devotions in the Catholic world because it gratifies much the same cluster of unconscious desires that are gratified in an extreme way by stigmatization. First, because it concentrates on the Eucharist, the consecrated host that is the body of Christ, it gratifies the infantile desire to incorporate the father through the mouth. Second, because it is a devotion so consciously tied to the idea of reparation and because it uses a concentric monstrance, it can gratify the infantile desire to make reparation for the phantasy attacks against the mother's breast. Other Eucharistic devotions may gratify the first desire, and so achieve some measure of popularity, but (not being associated with reparation) they do not gratify the second.

As with all the explanations offered in this book I see no reason to suggest that this one should be offered to the exclusion of others. Klauser (1969, 137), for instance, explains the post-Reformation popularity of Eucharistic devotions in general by suggesting that (1) all Reformation leaders saw veneration of the Blessed Sacrament as tantamount to idolatry and so (2) veneration of the Eucharist was a way in which Catholics could make a "warlike confession of faith." The argument is reasonable, and I suspect that Protestant attacks on the Eucharist did indeed induce a Eucharistic counter-reaction of the sort that Klauser is proposing. But nothing in this sort of argument explains why the Forty Hours came to be more popular than other Eucharistic devotions. By contrast, this is precisely what the psychoanalytic argument developed here can explain.

The argument presented here can also explain why no popular devotion resembling the Forty Hours developed *before* the early sixteenth century, even though the Eucharistic host had been the focus of a few Church-approved devotions since the thirteenth century. After all, it was only in the late fifteenth century that the increasing use of the sunburst monstrances made it likely that staring at an exposed Blessed Sacrament would evoke infantile memories of the mother's breast. More important, it was only in Milan in the 1520s and 1530s that veneration of the Eucharist was clearly and unambiguously tied to reparation, an element that (if my analysis is correct) is so important for understanding the appeal of the Forty Hours. In other words, only in the early part of the sixteenth century did the three elements that make the Forty Hours so appealing – the veneration of the Eucharist, the use of a concentric monstrance, and the emphasis upon reparation – come to be juxtaposed within a single devotion.

CHAPTER SEVEN

The Brown Scapular:
Ticket to Heaven

A scapular consists of two small rectangular pieces of cloth held together by two strings. It is worn over the shoulders so that one of the rectangles falls over the wearer's chest and the other over the wearer's back. Over the centuries the Church has associated seventeen different scapulars with various indulgences. Although nearly half are associated with the Virgin Mary under one of her many titles, there are also scapulars associated with Christ and with particular saints; see Table 8. The oldest scapular, however, and the one that has proved the most popular of all with lay Catholics, is the Brown Scapular of Our Lady of Mount Carmel.

What is particularly striking about the Brown Scapular is that it has long been associated with a belief that will strike many people, including many Catholics, as scandalous. Simply put, this belief is that the simple fact of *wearing* the Brown Scapular at the moment of death is a sure guarantee of achieving Salvation. The Brown Scapular, in other words, is literally a ticket to Heaven and a sure means of avoiding the pain of Hell. Many readers, I suspect, will see in the Brown Scapular one of the last of the many abuses relating to relics, indulgences, and so on that so infuriated Reformation-era critics of the Church, including both hostile critics like Luther and more friendly critics like Erasmus. All the more surprising then that the historical evidence (as we shall see) suggests that the Brown Scapular did not come into widespread use among lay Catholics until after the Reformation had begun.

Two questions need to be answered: what accounts for the great popularity of the Brown Scapular, and why should this devotion have arisen in precisely that historical period when the Church, under the influence of the Counter-Reformation, was purging itself of a great many popular devotions that seemed, like devotion to the Brown Scapular itself, to verge on the magical?

THE SCAPULAR TRADITION
AT FACE VALUE

In devotional accounts (see for instance Haffert 1942, Pacquin 1949, Connors

1949, Lynch 1950), the Brown Scapular, like the Rosary, was introduced to humankind by the Virgin Mary herself during an apparition. In this case, Mary appeared to St Simon Stock on Sunday, 16 July 1251 while Stock was living in Cambridge, England. The date here is significant: 16 July is the traditional feast day of Our Lady of Mount Carmel, the patroness of the Carmelite order, and in 1251 Simon Stock was the Prior-General of that order. The Carmelites, who had originated near Mount Carmel in Palestine, were at this time trying to establish themselves in the West and were meeting a great deal of resistance both from the secular clergy and from other monastic orders. That Mary should appear to this Carmelite leader on 16 July was obviously intended as a sign of divine encouragement to this beleaguered order of monks.

But Mary did more than simply give encouragement to Simon Stock and, more generally, to the Carmelites. She presented Stock with the Brown scapular, and told him, "THIS SHALL BE FOR YOU AND FOR ALL CARMELITES THE PRIVILEGE, THAT WHOEVER DIES CLOTHED IN THIS SHALL NOT SUFFER ETERNAL FIRE." The promise is clearly that those who die wearing the Brown Scapular will avoid Hell and so be assured of getting to Heaven.

But that was not the end of Mary's intervention in connection with the Brown Scapular. In 1322, Pope John XXII published a bull in which he described how the Virgin had appeared to him and told him that those who died wearing the Brown Scapular would win a early release from Purgatory. More specifically, Mary promised that in the case of such a person she herself would descend into Purgatory on the Saturday after that person's death and set that person's soul free, that is, take the soul to Heaven. Because of the emphasis on "Saturday" in this promise, the promise itself became known as the Sabbatine Privilege.[1]

A MORE CRITICAL VIEW

Virtually every aspect of the devotional account just given has generated enormous controversy over the past three centuries. In trying to establish a more historically accurate account of the scapular tradition, I have relied both on the work by modern Carmelite scholars like Zimmerman (1904a; 1904b; 1904c; 1927), Rushe (1911), Xiberta (1949), and Ceroke (1964), and on the somewhat more critical commentaries by Jesuit scholars like Hilgers (1913a; 1913b) and Thurston (1904b; 1911a; 1911b; 1927d; 1927e).

The first documentary reference to the vision of St Simon Stock appears in a collection of Carmelite documents (called the *Catalogus Sanctorum*) published at Venice in 1507, over 250 years after the alleged apparition took place. More important perhaps, an examination of the early accounts of this apparition, including this first account, makes it clear that what Mary is supposed to have handed Simon Stock is something quite different from what is today called the Brown Scapular. In that first (1507) version of the story we

TABLE 8

Scapulars Approved by the Church

Scapular	Prescribed Colour of Cloth Rectangles
Approved before Nineteenth Century	
Scapular of the Most Blessed Trinity	white
Scapular of Our Lady of Ransom	white
Scapular of Our Lady of Mount Carmel	brown
Black Scapular of the Seven Dolours of Mary	black
Blue Scapular of the Immaculate Conception	blue
Approved in Nineteenth and Twentieth Centuries	
Scapular of the Most Precious Blood	red
Black Scapular of the Passion	black
Red Scapular of the Passion	red
Scapular of the Blessed Virgin Mary, under the title "Help of the Sick"	black
Scapular of the Immaculate Heart of Mary	white
Scapular of St Michael the Archangel	blue and black
Scapular of St Benedict	black
Scapular of the Mother of Good Counsel	white
Scapular of St Joseph	violet
Scapular of the Most Sacred Heart of Jesus	white
Scapular of the Sacred Heart (called *la sauvegarde*[a])	white
Scapular of the Sacred Heart of Jesus and Mary	white
Scapular of St Dominic	white
Scapular of St John of God	black
Scapular of the Holy Face	white

Sources: Hilgers, 1913b; Magennis, 1923; Beringer, 1925a; 1925b

[a] Though this particular scapular of the Sacred Heart was not associated with papal indulgences until the nineteenth century, it was used widely, at least in France, from the mid-eighteenth century forwards; see the discussion of these *sauvegardes* in chapter 8.

are told: "The Blessed Virgin appeared to [Simon Stock] with a multitude of angels, holding in her hands the *Scapular of the Order* [emphasis added]. She said, 'This will be for you and for all Carmelites the privilege that he who dies in this will not suffer eternal fire'" (Ceroke 1964, 97). For both Hilgers and Thurston, the reference here is clearly to something that was piece of clothing worn by Carmelite monks. Hilgers (1913b) in particular goes to great lengths to demonstrate that in the Middle Ages the word *scapula* was applied to a piece of clothing worn by the monks of several different monastic orders on top of their tunics. Such a *scapula* was about the width of a man's body, and slightly less than double a man's height. A hole was cut in the middle for the head, and when worn, it hung over the shoulders, front and back, not quite reaching the ground.

Similar remarks apply to the scapular that was originally associated with the Sabbatine Privilege. The bull supposedly issued by John XXII is now generally regarded as apocryphal, and the earliest accounts of the Sabbatine Privilege date from the late fifteenth century. Here again, in those early accounts the *scapula* being discussed was almost certainly part of a monk's habit.

Originally the monastic *scapula* was little more than an apron to be used while engaged in manual labour. With time, it came to be regarded as a essential part of monastic garb. As early as 1257, Carmelite monks were required to wear their *scapula* when sleeping. Concomitant with this shift (from a working garment to an essential part of a monk's habit) came a decrease in both the length and the width. Among the Carmelites the "sleeping" *scapula* eventually shrank to about twenty inches in length and ten inches in width. Such middle-sized scapulars also came to be worn by the various lay people who entered the "Third Orders" associated with the monastic groups, including the Carmelites.

There seems little doubt that the design of the various small scapulars that have sprung up over the last few centuries is derived from the design of the *scapula* that was originally part of monastic garb, and further, that the small size of these modern scapulars is just the result of the reduction in the size of these *scapula* over the centuries.

Still, the important point – at least given our concerns here – is that the reference to the "Scapular of the Order" in the early descriptions of St Simon Stock's apparition, and the similar references in early accounts of the Sabbatine Privilege, are to the *scapula* of the Carmelite monks and *not* to what is now called the Brown Scapular of Our Lady of Mount Carmel. This conclusion is hardly controversial. Even modern Carmelite scholars (Zimmerman 1904b; 206–15; 1927, 324–6) have generally been willing to concede that the early scapular tradition was concerned with Carmelite garb and not with the small string scapular that later became so popular. In other words, the original "scapular promise" seems to have been a promise that those who died in the clothing of a Carmelite monk would not go to Hell and would not suffer in Purgatory. This, as Thurston (1927b, 51–2) notes, allows us to relate the original scapular tradition to other, more well-documented traditions.

There are in fact several documentary references in the medieval period to claims made on the behalf of the efficacy of particular monastic habits. As early as 1229 for instance, it was claimed that the Devil would have no power over a man who died in the habit of the Cistercian monks. During the fourteenth and fifteenth centuries there are several references (often critical) to the claim that anyone who died in the Franciscan habit would be saved from Hell. The original scapular tradition, then, was probably nothing more than the claim that the Carmelite habit, like that of the Franciscans and the Cistercians and others, would serve its wearer as a protection against Hell and Purgatory.[2]

But none of this tells us when a devotion to the *small* scapular, now called the Brown Scapular of Our Lady of Mount Carmel, become widespread among ordinary lay Catholics. In this regard, even a staunch Carmelite defender of the Scapular Devotion like Ceroke (1964, 104) is willing to concede that the Brown Scapular did not become a widely popular devotion until the late fifteenth century. If he is correct, of course, this would mean that devotion to the Brown Scapular would have arisen at about the same time as devotion to the Rosary (see chapter 1). Thurston (1927a, 488), by contrast, was of the opinion that there was no evidence of any widespread devotion to the Brown Scapular until the beginning of the seventeenth century, since it is only during this period that we encounter a substantial number of documentary references to the Brown Scapular.

In this particular case Thurston was probably a little too conservative. The Church made 16 July, the traditional feast day of Our Lady of Mount Carmel, into "the scapular feast" as early as 1609 (Zimmerman 1913, 355). It is not likely to have done this if devotion to the Brown Scapular was only just beginning. Furthermore, even Thurston (1927b, 45–6) admits that at least two Carmelite documents of the late sixteenth century contain woodcuts that show Mary handing Simon Stock what is clearly a "string scapular" (that is, a small scapular). All in all then, I doubt that Thurston would disagree vehemently with Hilgers' (1913b, 511) conclusion that devotion to the Brown Scapular became widespread during the later part of the sixteenth century.

Given the long history of the Church, the difference between the late fifteenth century (Ceroke's conclusion) and the late sixteenth century (Hilgers' conclusion) does not seem very important. Unfortunately, it *is* important if only because the period that separates these two conclusions was itself so important in the history of the Church. It was during this period, remember, that the Reformation began: in 1517 Martin Luther (1483–1546) posted his ninety-five theses on the door of the church at Wittenberg in Saxony; in 1523–4 Uldrich Zwingli (1484–1531) introduced the ecclesiastical reforms at Zurich that provoked his break with the Church; and in 1541 John Calvin (1509–64) returned to Geneva, where he established his theocratic government. Likewise, in 1543 the Church itself convened the Council of Trent in response to the rise of Protestantism, and this Council introduced a number of internal reforms that greatly changed Catholic life. By the closing decades of the sixteenth century, Protestantism – of one form or another – had made significant inroads into France and Poland and had become the official state religion in parts of Switzerland and Germany, in the Scandinavian states, and of course in

England and Scotland. The difference between the conclusions reached by Ceroke and Hilgers, then, is the difference between considering the Brown Scapular a pre-Reformation devotion or a post-Reformation devotion.

In trying to pinpoint the historical origins of the Scapular devotion more precisely, it seems worth mentioning that Ceroke (1964, 105–6), a Carmelite scholar who had access to a great many of the original documents relating to the Scapular tradition, very explicitly mentions Thurston's claim that there are no documentary references to the "string scapular" before the late sixteenth century, and produces no evidence to contradict this statement. On the contrary, Ceroke seems to concede Thurston's point by saying the absence of any evidence of a lay devotion to the Brown Scapular before the sixteenth century does not in itself undermine the credibility of the tradition concerning Mary's vision to Simon Stock (which is what Ceroke is mainly concerned with defending) since Mary's original promise was directed only to Carmelites.

But perhaps the strongest evidence in favour of a post-Reformation origin for the Brown Scapular is, as Thurston (1927a; 1927b) points out, the fact that we find no references to the Brown Scapular in the sources where we would expect such references to be. There is, for example, not a single reference to the Brown Scapular in the writings of Erasmus (1466–1536). Since Erasmus satirized the Franciscan claim that their habit would protect its wearer from Hell and often singled out the Carmelites for criticism[3] (partly because some of the severest criticism directed at Erasmus came from Carmelite sources), it seems unlikely that he would have ignored a Carmelite-sponsored devotion like the Brown Scapular if such a devotion had been widespread at the time. Nor is there any reference to the Brown Scapular in the collected works of Martin Luther, even though Luther routinely criticized other Catholic devotions that claimed to reduce the time spent in Purgatory.[4]

Particularly damaging to Ceroke's suggestion that the Brown Scapular was a popular devotion by the beginning of the sixteenth century is the fact that there is no mention of Brown Scapular in the writings of St John of the Cross (1542–91), one of the most influential Carmelite mystics of the period and someone who almost certainly would have mentioned a popular devotion so closely tied to the Carmelite order if such a popular devotion had existed. St Teresa of Avila (1515–82), another Carmelite mystic and someone closely associated with St John of the Cross,[5] did mention receiving "some scapulars" in one of her letters (Zimmerman 1927, 329–30). But this letter was written in 1581, a year before her death, and there is no mention of the Brown Scapular in Teresa's autobiography (St Teresa 1911).

This absence of references to the Brown Scapular throughout most of the sixteenth century stands in marked contrast to the plenitude of references to, say, the Rosary. For example, after pointing to those catalogues (already mentioned in chapter 1) from the early sixteenth century that list the titles of books concerned with the Rosary, Thurston (1927b, 55) also directs our attention to the range of devotional articles prohibited by the anti-Catholic legislation passed during the reign of Queen Elizabeth (1558–1603). One part of this legislation reads: "Bringing into this country ... [any] things ... called by the name of *Agnus Dei*[6], or any crosses, pictures, beads, or such like vain and superstitious things ... shall incur the dangers, pains, forfeitures [established by this statute]." By looking at what was prohibited we can gain a sense of what objects were seen to be most associated with Catholic devotion, and while the Rosary ("beads") would seem to be one such object, the Brown Scapular is not.

Finally, the Rosary is mentioned by some of the very people who do not mention the Brown Scapular. There are for example twenty different entries listed under "Rosary" in the Index to the Collected Works of Martin Luther (Lundeen 1986). Most of these are references to passages where Luther mentions the Rosary only in passing, but in at least one case (see Spitz 1960, 24–5) Luther did discuss (and ridicule) the various forms of the Rosary that existed in his day. Similarly St Teresa of Avila (1911, 262) says in her autobiography that she prayed the Rosary regularly.

What then are we to conclude? Simply this: that the remarks of Carmelite scholars like Ceroke notwithstanding, the evidence very strongly supports the assertion that the wearing of the (small) Brown Scapular did not begin to become a popular devotion until the *end* of the sixteenth century. It was therefore very much a post-Reformation phenomenon.

I have gone to such lengths to establish the precise period in which the Brown Scapular became popular because I think that the fact that it developed after the Reformation had begun is an important clue to understanding the appeal of this devotion. More specifically, we are now in a position to consider the possibility that devotion to the Brown Scapular, at least initially, was some sort of Catholic response to the Reformation.

FOLK BELIEF AND CHURCH POLICY

It is important to emphasize that a belief in the "Scapular Promise," that is, the belief that simply wearing the Brown Scapular is a protection against Hell and Purgatory, has not been actively encouraged by the Church. Apart, possibly, from remarks by a few overzealous devotees, most pronouncements from the Church hierarchy and the clerical commentators have consistently stressed that simply wearing the Brown Scapular is *not* enough to merit salvation.

With regard to the first part of the Scapular Promise (concerning the Scapular's efficacy in enabling the wearer to avoid Hell) the Church has traditionally argued only that if people adhere to the Catholic faith and wear the Brown Scapular as evidence of their veneration of Mary and their recognition of Mary's great ability to intercede on behalf of human beings, they may securely hope that Mary will procure for them "the necessary graces for ... perseverance in good" (Hilgers 1913b, 511). In other words, by wearing the Brown Scapular and thereby venerating Mary, Mary will help you to avoid sin and so, by extension, avoid Hell.

With regard to the Sabbatine Privilege (and the Brown Scapular's efficacy in winning an early release from Purgatory), the official position of the Church has been that if believing Catholics (1) wear the Brown Scapular as evidence of their veneration of Mary and their trust in Mary's abilities as intercessor, (2) lead "chaste" lives, and (3) fulfil certain ritual obligations, they can reasonably expect Mary to intercede on their behalf to win them an early release from Purgatory. The Church has also been willing to concede that the effect of Mary's intercession might be especially felt on Saturdays (see Hilgers 1913a).

But such circumspect pronouncements notwithstanding, the pious belief that simply wearing the Brown Scapular is sufficient to achieve salvation has persisted. The best evidence for this lies in the fact that so many modern Catholic commentators feel compelled to deny the assertion that the Brown Scapular is a magic amulet that will guarantee salvation for its wearer (see for example the statements by Hilgers 1913b, 511; Magennis 1923, 67; Lynch 1950, 58–60; Ceroke 1964, 50). On occasion Church spokesmen have candidly admitted the existence of these pious beliefs about the Brown Scapular. When a reader wrote to the *Irish Ecclesiastical Record* (a Catholic journal published with episcopal approval) to protest an earlier reference in that journal to "a fable" like the Sabbatine Privilege, P. Morrisroe (1911, 98) – who regularly answered questions concerning Church liturgy for this journal – responded: "The legend of the origin of the Brown Scapular may not stand the test of the iconoclastic criticism which Father Thurston[7] has ably brought to bear upon [it] ... but it is true to say that the Sabbatine Privilege is still "piously believed" in by the faithful generally ... Further the Congregation of Rites has encouraged and continues to encourage, apparently, this pious belief."

I have been unable to track down the specific action on the part of the "Congregation of Rites" to which Morrisroe is referring in the last sentence, but I suspect that it refers to one of the many official pronouncements from the Church to the effect that although the Sabbatine Privilege is not in and of itself correct, it is permissible to preach of its contents.

Moreover, these pious beliefs about the Brown Scapular have often found their way into quasi-official Catholic publications, even in relatively recent times. Consider for instance the following passage from a religion textbook for seniors that was widely used in Catholic high schools throughout North America in the late 1950s and early 1960s. The passage appears in a section entitled "Assisting dying Catholics":

See to it also that the sick person is wearing a scapular or a blessed scapular medal[8]. In the previous unit you may have learned about the numerous blessings and indulgences granted for wearing the scapular. Provide for your own death by wearing one always. Be faithful to the Mother of God and resolve never to set aside the badge of her protection. At the hour of death he who is clothed in the scapular may hope to be saved from eternal flames, and can look forward to a speedy release from purgatory. This is the promise given to St. Simon Stock by our Lady of Mt. Carmel.[9] (Elwell *et al.* 1960, 138)

The last line here makes it clear that the particular scapular being discussed is the Brown Scapular.

Like so many other Marian devotions in the Roman Catholic Church, devotion to the Brown Scapular has declined dramatically since Vatican II. Even so, organizations like the Blue Army of Our Lady of Fatima are still promoting devotion to the Brown Scapular and the Rosary throughout the world (see, for instance, Fox 1985). Various forms of the Brown Scapular can still be purchased in almost all stores selling Catholic religious articles, and I have often come across such scapulars being sold at church bazaars.

PSYCHOLOGICAL ASSOCIATIONS

One of the strongest associations evoked by the Brown Scapular in the mind of most Catholics would of course be an association with the Virgin Mary, simply because Mary is supposed to have introduced the Brown Scapular during an earthly apparition. One modern Catholic commentator (Smet 1967, 120) has even suggested that this devotion is among the most popular of all Marian devotions in the history of the Church. My own impression is that over the centuries it has been second in popularity, among Marian devotions, only to the Rosary. Another distinguishing feature of the Brown Scapular is that at least until this century it had to be made of wool. Since the wearing of wool next to the skin is somewhat uncomfortable (something explicitly recognized by the organizations that promote the use of a wool Brown Scapular; see Carroll 1986a, 70–1), discomfort would be another association evoked by the Brown Scapular.

On the other hand, neither of these associations – with Mary and with discomfort – is unique to the Brown Scapular. Until the proliferation of scapulars in the late nineteenth century, most scapulars were Marian scapulars (see Table 8), and all of them were required to be made of wool. If we want to find out why the Brown Scapular in particular became so popular, we must look to what distinguishes it from other scapulars.

The most obvious physical characteristic that distinguishes the Brown Scapular is of course its colour, the fact that it is indeed brown. Other scapulars (see Table 8) may be white, black, blue, purple, or red, but they are not brown. By contrast, while it is permissible to make the Scapular of Our Lady of Mount Carmel from either brown or black wool, in fact such scapulars are almost always brown. In one sense, of course, the Brown

Scapular is brown simply because the *scapula* that was part of the Carmelite habit was probably brown. But whatever the historical circumstances that led to the use of this colour initially, it is difficult to escape the conclusion that the brownness of the Brown Scapular is somehow tied up with the fact that this scapular has become more popular than any other.

I might add here that the Church's regulations governing the construction of scapulars work to ensure that the brownness of the Brown Scapular is in no way obscured. Thus it has been customary, especially in recent times, to sew a cloth picture of some sort onto one or both of the brown rectangles of this scapular. There is no official picture that must be sewn on, but a depiction of Mary and St Simon Stock is common. Nevertheless, Church regulations specify that nothing can be sewn onto a scapular that obscures its essential colour ("Covering of Scapulars" 1911, 94–5; Beringer 1925a, 488). In the case of the Brown Scapular, then, this means that its brownness is always one of its dominant physical features.

Apart from brownness, another association that seems to be evoked by the Brown Scapular (and not by other scapulars) is punishment. Remember that the promise given to Simon Stock was not that those who die wearing the Brown Scapular "will go to Heaven," but that they "will not suffer eternal fire." Likewise, the emphasis in the Sabbatine Privilege was upon "avoiding the fires of Purgatory." To the Catholic theologian, of course, avoiding Hell and Purgatory and going to Heaven are equivalent. But if we concern ourselves less with theology and more with psychological associations, the explicit mention of punishment in these two original legends cannot be overlooked. This seems especially true given that the assocation with punishment is emphasized in many other ways as well.

For instance, apart from an image of Our Lady of Mount Carmel with Simon Stock, the most common thing likely to be affixed to one of the rectangles of the scapular is some version of the promise that Mary supposedly made to Simon Stock. The usual paraphrase of this message seems to be: "Whoever dies wearing this holy scapular will not suffer eternal fire." This message, I must emphasize, usually appears alone, without the circumspect pronouncements with which the Church hierarchy surrounds the original promise. The fact that this message is printed on the Scapular itself reinforces the conclusion that the imagery of punishment is central to the Brown Scapular's appeal.

The close association of the Brown Scapular with punishment can also be seen by examining depictions of Our Lady of Mount Carmel. But here we must be careful, since several different iconographic traditions are associated with such depictions, some of which have always enjoyed more favour with lay Catholics than with the Church hierarchy. As a way of introducing the issues here, let me relate a personal experience.

Having been born in the North Beach area of San Francisco, and having a number of family ties to that area, I have always had a special affection for the Church of Sts Peter and Paul, which dominates this neighbourhood. Sts Peter and Paul was established just before the turn of the century as an "Italian national church"; that is, it had no parish boundaries and was expected to serve the Italians of San Francisco, most of whom were concentrated in this district. To either side of the main altar, and along the two sides of the church, there are half a dozen or so side altars, each associated with some particular devotion. One of these side altars is dedicated to our Lady of Mount Carmel. The statue at this altar portrays a stately Mary dressed in the brown robes and light-coloured cloak of the Carmelite order. She is holding the Infant Christ in her left arm and a scapular in her right. This is the portrayal of Our Lady of Mount Carmel that has always been favoured by the official Church.

But at the back of the church are three rooms into which are crowded the statues and pictures belonging to the folk Catholicism of the Italians and Italian-Americans who once flocked to Sts Peter and Paul. Whereas the side altars in the main body of the church are associated with transnational devotions which have long been endorsed by Church authorities, most of the pictures and statues in these three rooms reflect purely regional Italian traditions. In fact there are nearly two dozen pictures and statues in these rooms, and all are carefully labelled and identified – with one striking exception.

That one exception is a magnificent plaster statue that portrays Mary, with the infant Christ in her arm, sitting slightly above a dozen or so people writhing in a graphically portrayed sea of flames. This too is a representation of Our Lady of Mount Carmel, and its shows her descending into Purgatory to free souls (at least some souls) in accordance with the Sabbatine Privilege. From the position of Mary's outstretched right hand it appears that at one time she must have held a scapular, though this is now missing. But it is the tortured faces of those people ensnared by flames, faces whose agony is evident and finely portrayed that commands the immediate attention of anyone who looks on this statue. This is the portrayal of Our Lady of Mount Carmel that has always enjoyed more favour with the laity than with the hierarchy.

Pope Gregory XIII issued a decree dated 1577 (but which first appeared only in 1613) that expressed the ambivalence that the Church has always had towards the Sabbatine Privilege: he did not endorse the Privilege *per se*, though he did allow the Carmelites to preach of its contents. But in this same decree Gregory expressly forbade the painting of pictures that represented the Virgin Mary descending into Purgatory to free souls (Hilgers 1913a, 290). This papal prohibition notwithstanding, images of Our Lady of Mount Carmel descending into Purgatory became the object of popular devotion in many places.

In his study of devotional images (mainly small statues and panels intended for altar screens) used in Hispanic New Mexico during the early 1900s, Wroth (1982) reproduces photographs of 202 of those images. Eight of them are of Our Lady of Mount Carmel. Indeed, at least in Wroth's sample, there are more images of Our Lady of Mount Carmel than of Mary under any other title (though images of Our Lady of Guadalupe come a close second). Most of these eight images of Our Lady of Mount Carmel (see plates 50, 55, 84, 167 and 172 in Wroth's book) are variants of the image approved by Church (Mary holding the Christ Child, with each holding out a Brown Scapular). But three (see plates 25, 78, 79) show Mary hovering above some tormented souls in Purgatory.

Similarly, in my own wanderings around Naples and the surrounding area in connection with blood relics (see appendix C) I never once saw an image depicting Mary descending into Purgatory in a church (and I was very consciously looking for such images). I did however see this scene portrayed in several neighbourhood shrines and ceramic wall murals (which by my guess date from the early part of this century).

Even today, in North America, though "Our Lady of Mount Carmel descending into Purgatory" may have been banished to unlabelled obscurity in a back room at Sts Peter and Paul in San Francisco, it is still possible to purchase a Holy Card portraying this scene from stores selling Catholic religious goods. In the Holy Cards of this sort that I have seen, the viewer's attention is most immediately commanded by the graphic portrayal of the souls suffering in agony in a sea of flames.

In summary then, whether we look at the origin legends surrounding the Brown Scapular, at the message most often printed on this scapular, or at popular portrayals of Our Lady of Mount Carmel over the centuries, we come to the same conclusion: some of the strongest images likely to be evoked in the Roman Catholic mind by the Brown Scapular are images associated with punishment.

THE EXPLANATION

I do not think it too daring to suggest that a soft, brown piece of cloth evokes anal imagery, and that such a piece of cloth can be regarded as symbolic excrement. If the reader is willing to grant the reasonableness of this equation, then wearing a soft brown cloth next to the body in order to avoid punishment becomes smearing excrement on ones self to avoid punishment. Though such an interpretation would almost certainly distress devotees of the Brown Scapular, it is an interpretation that puts us on familiar theoretical ground, since it meshes well with theoretical conclusions that Melanie Klein reached in her clinical work with young children.

Remember Klein's argument: when children enter the depressive position during the first year of life, they increasingly come to see that the "Bad Mother" and the "Good Mother" are just two different aspects of the same person. The continuing attacks on the "Bad Mother," then, inevitably give rise to the belief that the "Good Mother" may have been damaged. This in turn gives rise to guilt and the desire to make reparation.

But Klein also argues that these processes occur simultaneously with the child's development though the oral, anal, and genital stages described by Freud. This means that the child's choice of phantasy weapons is determined by the sexual stage at which the child finds himself or herself (see, for instance, the discussion in Klein 1945). During the oral stage, the child makes oral phantasy attacks, that is, attacks that involve biting, ripping, tearing, puncturing, and so on. The discussion in chapter 5, remember, suggested that the infantile memory of these oral attacks on the mother shaped the process that gave rise to stigmatization. Similarly, when children pass into the anal stage, they quite commonly use feces in their phantasy attacks. Her own research with children led Klein to conclude that although feces are first used as "bombs" in these phantasy attacks, children soon begin to make phantasy attacks in which they smear the mother (and sometimes the father) with feces (see, for instance, Klein 1925, 114; 1927, 172; 1952, 63–4).

In a related argument, Klein suggested that the reparations made by children generally bore some resemblance to the phantasy attacks that created the desire to make reparation. That is why reparation for oral attacks involve oral reparations (see chapter 5). Likewise, phantasy attacks that involve smearing the mother (or father) with feces give rise to phantasy reparations that involve smearing feces on himself or herself (Klein 1936, 294–5).

But if a Brown Scapular is indeed symbolic feces, then Klein's analysis (just reviewed) suggests an obvious hypothesis that would explain the appeal of this particular scapular: the wearing of the Brown Scapular is the symbolic gratification of the infantile desire to make reparation for the fecal attacks directed in phantasy against the mother.

Such a hypothesis allows us to account not simply for the insistence upon brownness that is so much a part of the devotion, but also for the association with punishment. Under this interpretation, in other words, the punishment associated with the Brown Scapular represents both the punishment that the child initially wants to inflict upon the mother, and the punishment that the child later wants to inflict upon itself in reparation. Similarly, the association of the Brown Scapular with the Virgin Mary, the "Mother of God," derives – under this argument – from the fact that this devotion gratifies the infantile desire to make reparation for phantasy attacks against the mother.

My final argument then is that because of the Brown Scapular's association with brownness, with punishment, and with the Mother of God, wearing the Brown Scapular enables the practice of this devotion to gratify the infantile desire to make reparation for the fecal attacks directed in phantasy against the real mother. One advantage of this interpretation is that it explains why popular devotion to the Brown Scapular arose so quickly following the onset of the Reformation.

A REFORMATION RESPONSE

Remember that to most of those who remained Catholic the Reformation was (and probably still is) an attack upon the one true Church. But because the image of the Church as *Mater Ecclesia*, "Holy Mother Church," had been entrenched in Catholic thinking since Patristic times, the Protestant attack on "Holy Mother Church" would almost certainly have reawakened in a great many Catholics their infantile memory of having made phantasy attacks against their mother.

That infantile memories of this sort would have been reawakened by the Reformation seems especially likely given the backgrounds of the most prominent Protestant leaders. After all, during the Reformation of the Church was *not* being attacked by "external enemies" like the Turks (or later, the Communists). Rather it was being attacked by people who have been Catholics themselves, and moreover, had been active in the Church hierarchy. Thus Luther was an ordained priest of the Augustinian Order and Zwingli an ordained secular priest. Calvin was not an ordained priest, but he had been a popular lay preacher before he broke with Rome. In a very real sense, then, what happened during the Reformation was that Holy Mother Church was being attacked by men who had been once her own true "sons."

But if this attack on "Holy Mother Church" by her former sons did reactivate infantile memories of the fecal attacks made in phantasy against the mother, it would also have reactivated the infantile memories of the desire to make reparation for these fecal attacks. A devotion that required the wearing of two pieces of soft, brown cloth next to the body (so easily regarded as a symbolic smearing of oneself with feces) would be ideally suited to gratify this reawakened desire to make reparation. On the other hand, the association of the Brown Scapular with anality was not so clear-cut as to violate the general repression of overt anality that is a feature of Western culture.

A PUZZLE: THE BROWN SCAPULAR AND THE STIGMATA

Though the explanation developed to this point allows us to understand why the Brown Scapular became a popular devotion only after the onset of the Reformation, it also raises a theoretical puzzle: granting that the Reformation attack on the Church might indeed have reawakened infantile memories of the phantasy attacks on the mother, why should it have reawakened only infantile memories of the *anal* attacks on the mother? Why not, say, infantile memories of the *oral* attacks launched in phantasy against the mother?

In fact, the only theoretically justifiable position is that the Reformation *would* have reactivated infantile memories of all the phantasy attacks against the mother, including both oral and anal attacks. But this in turn suggests that we should be able to find among Catholics in the post-Reformation period some evidence of a desire to make reparation for the oral attacks against the mother just as the emergence of devotion to the Brown Scapular is evidence of a desire to make reparation for the anal attacks against the mother. I think we do, and it concerns the stigmata.

Chapter 5 has already established that stigmatization *per se* is by no means a post-Reformation phenomenon. St Francis, remember, is supposed to have received his stigmata in 1224. Still, the argument presented there, when merged with the argument developed here, would seem to lead to a fairly straightforward prediction: if the Protestant attack on the Church did reactivate the infantile desire to make reparation for *all* the attacks launched in phantasy against the mother, the Reformation should have provoked a sharp increase in stigmatization, since stigmatization gratifies the desire to make reparation for oral attacks against the mother, just as the use of the Brown Scapular gratifies the desire to make reparation for the anal attacks against the mother. Although I know of no commentator who has previously called attention to such a pattern, the pattern is there.

Virtually all well-known stigmatics apart from St Francis himself (including the six stigmatics discussed in chapter 5) lived after the Reformation. In his overview of several dozen stigmatics, Austin (1883) starts with St Francis and does list a dozen or so people who experienced the stigmata in the pre-Reformation period. But his description of these cases makes it clear that these were invariably people who received only the "invisible" stigmata or who experienced, say, only "bloody sweats" or a "crown of thorns." If we restrict our attention to people who received the full stigmata, that is, wounds corresponding to the five wounds of the crucified Christ, then Austin's next case (after St Francis) is Veronica Giuliani, who received her stigmata in the late seventeenth century.

I have already noted that Imbert-Gourbeyre's (1894a) sample of 321 stigmatics is difficult to assess because he included a great many people whose stigmata was either invisible or partial, and unfortunately he does not provide the sort of detailed description of each stigmatic that would allow us to delete such cases from his sample. Still, if the Reformation did provoke a dramatic increase in stigmatization, we should still be able to find some traces of it in the Imbert-Gourbeyre sample, and we do. Table 9 arranges his 321 cases by the century in which the particular stigmatic first developed his or her stigmata.

The data in the table show that the sixteenth century did indeed witness a dramatic upsurge in the number of stigmatics. That this pattern is not a methodological artifact, one that results from an increase in the population or from the fact that we are more likely to know about later stigmatics, is seen in the fact that this upsurge drops off in the eighteenth and nineteenth centuries, when instances of stigmatization go back to pre-Reformation levels. In short, what Imbert-Gourbeyre's data, incomplete though they are, indicate is that the Reformation did provoke an upsurge in stigmatization, and that this upsurge lasted little more than a century.

That the Reformation induced a change in the Catholic Church is by no means a novel suggestion. Even so, not one of the Catholic commentators who

TABLE 9
Imbert-Gourbeyre's Sample of Stigmatics, Arranged by Century

Century	Stigmatics Developing Stigmata Number	Percentage
Thirteenth	32	10
Fourteenth	22	7
Fifteenth	25	8
Sixteenth	69	21
Seventeenth	114	36
Eighteenth	30	9
Nineteenth	29	9
	321	100

Source: Imbert-Gourbeyre (1894a)

have discussed the Brown Scapular, and this includes critical commentators like Thurston and Hilgers, thought to relate this devotion to psychological changes induced by the Reformation. Nor has any commentator, as far as I know, suggested that the Reformation induced an increase in stigmatization, though it seems to have done just that. Here again, then, the psycho-analytic approach allows us to discover quite clear patterns that have been previously overlooked.

CAR(A)MELIZING OUR THOUGHTS

A recurrent theme in this book is that the underlying appeal of various Catholic devotions is best discovered, *not* by examining theological commentaries on these devotions, but rather by searching for the psychological associations that these devotions would evoke in the Catholic mind. This often means concentrating on precisely the characteristics – like the brownness of the Brown Scapular – that would strike the theologian as being relatively unimportant and peripheral. In this chapter, I have so far examined the brownness of the Brown Scapular and its association with punishment and the Mother of God, and have argued that devotion to the Brown Scapular gratifies the infantile desire to make reparation for fecal attacks against the mother. There is one last element that seems strongly associated with the Brown Scapular, and I now want to show that it too can be accounted for by this same hypothesis.

The Brown Scapular is associated not just with the Virgin Mary, but with the Virgin Mary under the very specific title "Our Lady of Mount Carmel." The proximate cause of this association is simply that this devotion was (and is) promulgated by the Carmelite Order, which was founded near Mount

Carmel in Palestine and whose patroness is Our Lady of Mount Carmel. But this hardly explains why the scapular promulgated by this particular order of monks became more popular than the scapulars promulgated by other groups in the Church.

A clue as to what is involved here, I think, can be had by trying a simple experiment, one that I have tried often with my own students: just ask someone what associations are evoked by the word "Carmel." In a significant number of cases, I predict, "Carmel" will evoke "caramel." There is of course no etymological association between "Carmel" and "caramel"; the words just sound the same. On the other hand, Freud himself very often found that psychological associations were derived from purely phonetic similarities (see in particular, his work on jokes; Freud 1905), and this same idea has proved useful in more recent psychoanalytic work (Carroll 1986b).

But if "Carmel" does evoke "caramel," we must remember that "caramel" is a thick, brown viscous substance formed when sugar is slowly heated. It is also a term often applied to the soft brown candy made from caramel. But thick brown viscous substance and soft brown candy are concepts that easily evoke anal imagery. In the end, then, I am suggesting that the word "Carmel" itself, because of the phonetic similarity with "caramel," evokes anal imagery just as the brownness of the Brown Scapular also evokes anal imagery. The association of the Brown Scapular with Our Lady of Mount Carmel thus becomes one more reason why wearing this scapular is a particular appropriate way of gratifying the infantile desire to make reparation for the fecal attacks launched in phantasy against the mother.

This argument would of course collapse if the phonetic similarity between "Carmel" and "caramel" existed only in English. But as Table 10 indicates, the phonetic similarity of the words corresponding to "Carmel," Carmelite," and "caramel" exists in all the languages that predominate in the Catholic areas of Europe.

I am not suggesting that the anal imagery evoked by "Carmel" equals "caramel" *caused* the scapular to be associated with Mount Carmel. I repeat: the scapular is dedicated to Our Lady of Mount Carmel because it was a devotion popularized by the Carmelite monks. On the other hand, I believe that the association of the Brown Scapular with Mount Carmel (and the resulting association with "caramel" and "feces") made it easier for the wearing of the scapular to represent reparation for the fecal attacks against the mother. The association with Mount Carmel and the Carmelites, then, is just one more element that ensured that the Brown Scapular would become much more popular than all the other scapulars dedicated to Mary.

TABLE 10

Similarities between "Carmel," "Carmelite," and "Caramel" in Various European Languages

	"Carmel" *(Mountain in Palestine)*	*"Carmelite"* *(Monastic order)*	*"Caramel"* *(Sugar)*
Medieval			
Latin	Carmelo	Carmelita	?
Italian	Carmine, Carmelo	Carmelita, Carmelitano	caramella
Spanish	Carmen, Carmelo	Carmelita	caramelo
Portuguese	Carmelo	Carmelita	caramelo, carmelo
German	Karmel	Karmelito	Karamel
French	Carmel	carme, carmélite	caramel

CHAPTER EIGHT

The Sacred Heart of Jesus

As should be obvious by now, this book owes much to Herbert Thurston. Thurston was a rationalist who spent virtually his entire adult life subjecting pious Catholic beliefs and devotions to critical analysis in an effort to sift historical fact from religious fancy. His arguments were almost always concise, well documented and – to my mind – convincing. But Thurston was not just a rationalist. He was also a Jesuit priest. One might reasonably wonder how he combined the two roles, especially since his critical approach could so easily be seen as undermining the faith of ordinary Catholics. Actually, Thurston (1952, 120) himself addressed this very issue in his final essay on the stigmata: "The role of Devil's advocate is a thankless one and does not make for popularity. Indeed ... I have [often] felt at times, in spite of good intentions, that I was playing a mean and unworthy part. Why, I have asked myself, should a skeptical line of argument be put forward which may possibly trouble the simple faith of many good people much nearer and dearer to God than I can ever hope to be?" But Thurston the rationalist had his answer ready, and he continued:

And yet in these days of widespread education, universal questioning and free discussion, a premature and ill-grounded credulity cannot in the long run be of advantage to the Church ... We have to meet adversaries who of late years have paid a vast amount of attention to the study of psycho-pathology and even a slender acquaintance with the literature of hysteria and other nervous disorders suffices to show how extensive is the vista of possibilities which have opened up, and also how great are the perplexities with which the whole subject is beset.

I have immense admiration for the attitude that Thurston expresses here, and for his willingness to maintain that attitude in essay after essay. His suggestion that the literature of "psychopathology," "hysteria," and "other nervous disorders" might provide insight into many areas of Catholic practice quite obviously accords well with the spirit of this book. But there is one instance (and only one) where I think that Thurston the priest got the better of Thurston the rationalist, and it has to do with the Sacred Heart of Jesus.

On the face of it, devotion to the Sacred Heart is precisely the sort of devotion that should have attracted Thurston's attention. After all, it is a devotion organized around what is, at the very least, a rather unusual physical object, the actual heart of Jesus Christ. It was also a devotion that was supposedly initiated during an apparition, and so was precisely the same sort of tradition that Thurston had subjected to critical scrutiny in the case of the Rosary and the Brown Scapular. Finally, at the turn of this century, devotion to the Sacred Heart was one of the most popular of all Catholic devotions. Nevertheless, Thurston virtually ignored it.

Thurston (1903) did discuss the Nine First Fridays, a form of devotion to the Sacred Heart that is based upon the pious belief that anyone who receives Holy Communion on each of Nine First Fridays in honour of the Sacred Heart will not die without the grace of final repentance. But he limited himself to what for him was a relatively minor matter: did Margaret Mary Alacoque, the nun whose visions established the popularity of devotion to the Sacred Heart, really believe in the efficacy of the Nine First Fridays? (He concluded that she did, and left things at that.) This minor essay aside, I know of no other essay by Thurston in which he discusses devotion to the Sacred Heart. Why did he avoid subjecting this particular devotion to the same thorough scrutiny to which he subjected so many others?

Possibly he was just being considerate of his organizational colleagues. While it was one thing to demystify the Rosary, a devotion most associated with the Dominicans, or the Brown Scapular, a devotion most associated with the Carmelites, it would have been quite another thing to demystify the Sacred Heart, a devotion that for centuries had been most associated with the Jesuits, Thurston's own order.

But there was also, I think, a second reason why Thurston avoided this subject. In the late nineteenth century, after centuries of ambivalence, the Church, particularly the papacy itself, had finally endorsed devotion to the Sacred Heart in a clear and unambiguous manner. This in turn had made the devotion the object of erudite theological discussions to a degree that was never true, say, of devotion to the Rosary or the Brown Scapular. Faced with a popular devotion endorsed strongly by his own religious order, by the papacy itself, and by a range of highly respected theologians, Thurston, prudently, decided against confrontation.

For us this was unfortunate. The analysis presented in this chapter would undoubtedly have benefited greatly had Thurston subjected devotion to the Sacred Heart to the same critical scrutiny to which he subjected so many other Catholic devotions. Still, precisely because the Sacred Heart of Jesus became the object of so much theological discussion, there are many learned commentaries available on this devotion, and these can be mined with great profit if we are careful to separate the parts that analyse the devotion from those that try to promote it.

HISTORY

Central to the emergence of a truly popular devotion to the Sacred Heart was a series of apparitions experienced by St Margaret Mary Alacoque (1647–90) at Paray-le-Monial, France, in 1673–75. In these apparitions Christ himself appeared to Alacoque, showed her his "Sacred Heart," and told her to promote devotion to it. Catholic theologians, however, go to great lengths to establish that devotion to the Sacred Heart existed long before the apparitions at Paray-le-Monial.

Almost all theological discussions of the Sacred Heart, for instance, make some attempt to locate the origins of this devotion in the Patristic period (see, for instance, Bainvel 1924, 127–9; Hugo Rahner 1958). But an examination of those passages written by Patristic authors which supposedly reveal early forms of the devotion to the Sacred Heart invariably turn out to be passages in which the author is discussing the wounds of Christ, and in particular the side wound. Christ's heart, if it is mentioned at all, is mentioned only in passing.

On the other hand, it is true that since the end of the twelfth century any number of well-known mystics and clerics have made explicit reference to the Heart of Jesus in their writings, and professed a personal devotion to it. Nevertheless, all commentators agree that during the medieval period devotion to the Sacred Heart remained a purely private devotion (see for instance Bainvel 1924, 130–222; Stierli 1957a).

It was only in the latter part of the sixteenth century, and the early part of the seventeenth century that a sustained effort was made by some Catholic religious leaders to convert this private devotion into a popular cult. Included among these would-be popularizers were people like Louis of Blois ("Blosius"; d. 1566), St Peter Canisius (1521–97), and St Francis de Sales (1567–1622). But the most important was St John Eudes (1601–90), a French cleric who established an order of secular priests in 1643. It was Eudes who caused the first feast in honour of the Sacred Heart to be celebrated at a seminary at Rennes, France, in 1670, and who in 1672 published an Office, that is, a set of systematized prayers, hymns, lessons, and parts of a Mass, in honour of the Sacred Heart. Centuries later, in 1903, Pope Leo XIII identified Eudes as the originator of the cult of the Sacred Heart.

Yet though Eudes and others did much to lay the foundation for a formal cult organized around the Sacred Heart, they did not succeed in fostering any noticeable devotion to the Sacred Heart among the laity. That was not to happen until after Margaret Mary Alacoque experienced her apparitions.

Alacoque had entered the cloister of the Visitandine nuns (an order co-founded by St Jane de Chantal and St Francis de Sales, who was himself an early devotee of the Sacred Heart) at Paray-le-Monial in 1671. She experienced her first major apparition in 1673. In that apparition Christ appeared to her and exposed his Sacred Heart, an object she described as follows: "The heart of Jesus was represented to me as on a throne formed of fire and flames, surrounded by rays more brilliant than the sun and transparent as crystal. The wound He received on the cross was clearly seen there. Around this Sacred Heart was a crown of thorns, and above it a cross which was planted in It."[1] In later apparitions Christ instructed Alacoque to promote public devotion to his Sacred Heart, and this she did, mainly by enlisting the support and aid of her Jesuit advisor, Claude de la Columbière.

When accounts of Alacoque's experiences spread, it seems clear that devotion to Sacred Heart did – finally – become the basis for a public cult in some places. The first public celebration in honour of the Sacred Heart, unconnected with a religious community, seems to have taken place at Marseilles in 1720 (Bainvel 1924, 301). In that year Marseilles had been struck with the plague, and another Visitandine nun, Anne-Madeleine Rémuzat, reported having experienced an apparition in which Christ told her that the disease could be counteracted by devotion to his Sacred Heart. As a result a large number of the city's inhabitants started wearing small scapulars to which were affixed an image of the Sacred Heart and the phrase "Arrête! le Coeur de Jesus est là!" in order to "safeguard" themselves against the plague.[2] These scapulars were consequently called *sauvegardes*. The ending of the pestilence was widely attributed to this practice, with the result that Marseille was publicly consecrated to the Sacred Heart. The plague struck again in 1722, and this time the city council responded by celebrating the feast of the Sacred Heart with a Mass and a solemn procession. Other French cities struck by plague around this time – including Aix, Arles, Avignon, and Toulon – also sought relief from the Sacred Heart. The eighteenth century also saw the establishment of the first confraternities dedicated to the Sacred Heart (Beringer 1925b, 126).

On the other hand, the initial popularity of this new cult should not be exaggerated. As late as the 1780s for instance, the curé of La Chapelle-en-Valgaudemar, Hautes-Alpes, could complain to the bishop of Gap that his parishioners showed no interest at all in the creation of a confraternity dedicated to the Sacred Heart (Tackett 1986, 232n). A confraternity was finally established in this curé's parish, but only after an epidemic had struck the region. In any case, at least in France, many of the Sacred Heart confraternities that were established during the eighteenth century were suppressed during the Revolutionary period (Hamon 1953, column 1038).

It also seems clear that the devotion never established itself at all in certain parts of the Catholic world. When William Christian (1972, 80–5) began his investigation of local religion in the Nansa Valley region of northern Spain in the late 1960s, for instance, he found that devotion to the Sacred Heart was among the most popular of all Catholic devotions. One indication of this was that images of the Sacred Heart were found in a greater number of churches than the images associated with any other devotion. Yet Christian's inspection of church records revealed that devotion to the Sacred Heart had been introduced into the area only in 1910.

Furthermore, the modest increase in the popularity of this devotion in the eighteenth century should not be taken to mean that devotion to the Sacred Heart had received the full backing of the Church. On the contrary, the Church's attitude was ambivalent. Though Rome did not outlaw the devotion, it did refuse a request in 1697 to establish formally an official feast in honour of the Sacred Heart. The same request was made in 1726, and refused (again) in 1729. Moreover, in 1704, a book on the Sacred Heart written by Jean Croiset, who had been an associate of Claude de la Columbière, Alacoque's confessor, was put on the Church's *Index of Forbidden Books*. Rome did finally grant permission for a special feast in honour of the Sacred Heart in 1765, but only to dioceses that specifically requested the right to celebrate the feast. It was not made a feast of the Universal Church until 1856.

Only in the nineteenth century, in particular during the last half of the century, did devotion to the Sacred Heart of Jesus become one of the most popular of all Catholic devotions.

PUZZLES

The great efforts by Catholic commentators to establish that a number of prominent people were devoted to the Sacred Heart before the apparitions experienced by Margaret Mary Alacoque gives rise to an interesting question: if this is true, why did devotion to the Sacred Heart only become a popular devotion after the Paray-le-Monial apparitions? A devotional answer might be that it was at Paray-le-Monial that Christ himself appeared and gave his approval to the devotion. But over a dozen people before Alacoque had also experienced apparitions in which Christ had revealed his Sacred Heart.[3] Early would-be popularizers of the devotion, like St Francis de Sales and St Jean Eudes, could easily point to these earlier apparitions as evidence that the devotion was divinely approved. Why then did the devotion still not become popular?

The most likely possibility would seem to be that devotion to the Sacred Heart only become a popular devotion after the apparitions at Paray-le-Monial because those apparitions added something to this devotion that had not previously been present. Actually, even a casual inspection of Alacoque's message will indicate what that something was: an emphasis upon reparation.

In the first of Alacoque's apparitions, which occurred in 1673, Christ appeared to her, revealed his Sacred Heart, and told her that he had chosen her as the instrument that he would use to spread devotion to his Sacred Heart. In what was either a later phase of this first apparition or a second, separate apparition (see the discussion in Bainvel 1924, 18–19), Alacoque saw only the Sacred Heart (and not Christ) and came to understand the necessity of honouring Christ through the image of his physical heart. If Alacoque's apparitions had ended here, her experience would not have been much different from that of the many other mystics in preceding centuries who had had apparitions in which Christ revealed his Sacred Heart, and nothing new would have been added to the traditions surrounding the Sacred Heart.

But in her next apparition, which seems to have occurred sometime in 1674, something new *was* added. Christ talked of the great love he had for human beings but complained that in return for this love he had received "ingratitude and forgetfulness" and "coldness and rebuffs." He then specifically asked Alacoque to make *reparation* for the ingratitude directed against his heart: "Do you, at least, give me this pleasure by supplying for their ingratitude as far as you are capable of doing." He also told Alacoque what form this reparation should take: first, she was to receive Holy Communion on the first Friday of every month, and second, she was to rise every Thursday night at eleven, prostrate herself face down on the ground for an hour, and pray. She was told by Christ that this second act of reparation was in commemoration of his suffering in the Garden of Olives and would help to "soften in some sort the bitter sorrow that I felt at being abandoned by my Apostles."

In Alacoque's next apparition, which devotional accounts usually call her "Great Apparition," and which occurred in 1675, Christ again showed her his Sacred Heart. He then asked for a public feast in honour of his Sacred Heart, telling her very clearly that the celebration of this feast should be seen as reparations for the attacks on his heart. Thus, Alacoque reports Christ as saying: "I ask you to have the first Friday after the octave of *Corpus Christi* kept as a special feast of honor of my Heart, by receiving communion on that day *and making it a reparation of honor for all the insults offered to my Heart* [emphasis added] during the time that it has been exposed on the altars [a reference, presumably, to Christ's exposure on the altar in the form of the Blessed Sacrament]." From this point forward, the idea of reparation – which had not been emphasized previously in connection with the Sacred Heart – became a central element in the devotion to the Sacred Heart. Indeed theologians who have discussed this devotion usually call particular attention to the centrality of the reparation element (see, for instance, Karl Rahner 1957, 147–50).

That the idea of reparation was something added by the Paray-le-Monial apparitions to the traditions surrounding the Sacred Heart is by no means a novel suggestion (it seems implicit, for instance, in Hamon 1953, column 1034; and Callahan 1985, 14–20). But no one has yet drawn the obvious conclusion: if devotion to the Sacred Heart only became a truly popular devotion only after the widespread dissemination of information about Alocoque's apparitions, and if the main difference between these apparitions and pre-existing traditions was Alacoque's emphasis on reparation, it seems likely that this emphasis upon reparation is central to the popularity of this devotion.

But reparation for what? Devotional accounts sugest simply "reparation for indignities against Jesus." Kleinian theory, by contrast, leads us to expect that the first and most important reparations are those made in response to phantasy attacks on the mother. I have already argued that the desire to make reparation for these attacks lies behind the stigmatization process and explains the popularity of the Forty Hours devotion and the Brown Scapular. The conscious emphasis on reparation in connection with devotion to the Sacred Heart suggests that something similar is operating here as well, and the best way to find out if that is true is to examine the other associations evoked by the Sacred Heart.

PSYCHOLOGICAL ASSOCIATIONS

Because the Sacred Heart is a physical heart, it is a body part, and in particular, a body part belonging to an adult male, Jesus Christ.[4] But surely one of the most interesting things about the Sacred Heart, at least as it is usually depicted in devotional art, is that it is a body part that is simultaneously internal and external. It is an internal body part because hearts are in the normal course of things internal organs. But this particular heart is also an external body part because it is invariably displayed outside the body of Christ. When the community at Paray-le-Monial first began to make images of the Sacred Heart, it simply represented the heart by itself, without the body of Christ. This portrayal, while quite common over the centuries, has generally been discouraged by the Church, which has always preferred that the Sacred Heart be represented as resting exteriorly on the chest of Christ (Dineen 1906; Morris 1967). But in either case, the Sacred Heart is an external image.

There is one other psychological association that the image of the Sacred Heart evokes in the Catholic mind, and it emerges clearly when we consider the iconography of the Sacred Heart over the centuries.

Since Alacoque's apparitions in the seventeenth century, the most common representation of the Sacred Heart portrays it as (1) a real heart (which means that it is slightly asymmetrical and has an aortic opening at the top), (2) that has a spear wound in either the left or right side, (3) that is encircled by a crown of thorns (today this usually means that the thorns are wrapped around the heart, but in the seventeenth and eighteenth centuries the crown of thorns often encircled but did not touch the heart), and (4) that is surmounted (at the aortic opening) by a "clutch" of flames out of which emerges a cross. In fact, this is the description of the Sacred Heart given in the *New Catholic Encyclopedia* (Morris 1967).

Alacoque did not invent any of these iconographic elements. On the contrary, an inspection of earlier representations of the Sacred Heart (presented in Grimoüard de Saint-Laurent 1880), that is, representations made *before* the apparitions to Alacoque, make it clear that virtually every one of these iconographic elements had long been in use. The portrayal of Christ's Heart as a real heart became popular in the late sixteenth and early seventeenth centuries, something that Kehoe (1979) has attributed to the increasing familiarity of Europeans with Aztec art, in which "realistic" hearts were quite common; a heart surmounted by a cross had long been a symbol associated with St Catherine of Siena (1347–80), who herself had experienced an apparition in which Jesus had revealed his Sacred Heart.

On the other hand, it is also true that the iconography of the Sacred Heart has never been completely standardized. Both before and after Alacoque, for instance, some Sacred Hearts have been idealized (rather than real) hearts; not all Sacred Hearts have had a cross on top; and the circlet of thorns has sometimes been missing entirely.

If we survey the entire range of representations of the Sacred Heart, from the Middle Ages, through the period of Alacoque's apparitions, down to the twentieth century, we find that only two iconograph elements appear in virtually all Sacred Heart representations: the Sacred Heart is invariably (1) lacerated and (2) punctured. The laceration takes the form of a slit in the heart (sometimes on the right, sometimes on the left), from which blood usually drips, and which is supposed to be the spear wound received by Christ on the cross. Likewise, the Heart is almost always punctured, though not always in the same way. In modern representations, this puncturing is done by the circlet of thorns wrapped tightly around the heart. In older representations, by contrast, especially those in the pre-Alacoque period, this puncturing was often effected either by three arrows or by three large nails that penetrated the heart (see, for example, images 4 and 5 in plate v and image 6 in plate vi in Grimoüard de Saint-Laurent 1880).

All in all then, the primary associations evoked by the Sacred Heart seem to be that it is a body part belonging to an adult male, that is simultaneously both inside and outside that male's body, and that it is lacerated and punctured. In Klein's clinical investigation of reparation and fantasy among young children, she discovered something involving similar imagery.

THE ABSORBED PENIS

It was Klein's contention that children come to an awareness of the shape of both male and female genitalia at a very early age. But, she argued, the child did not become conscious of the sexual relationship between its parents until it had experienced the depressive position for quite some time, which means that the child is well past the point where it comes to think of its mother and father as "whole" individuals. Once developed, the child's phantasy image of the parents "locked in intercourse" dominates much of its phantasy life. Projecting his or her own sexual desire onto this dual-person "parental monster," for instance, a child often imagines that intercourse between the parents is nearly continuous.

According to Klein, one of the most important developments at this point is the child's emerging belief that phantasy attacks on the mother will damage the father. This belief derives from the child's belief that the father's penis is absorbed by the mother during intercourse and thus is located inside the mother. The image of the father's penis inside the mother, Klein felt, gives rise to the "woman-with-a-penis" images often encountered in dreams and other fantasy material (see Klein 1928, 315; 1952, 76–80).

Freud himself had come across the image of the "woman-with-a-penis" in the dreams he analysed, as had Abraham (1922). Psychoanalytically inclined anthropologists like Róheim (1945) had discovered the same image in their analyses of myths. But for Freud and his more orthodox followers like Abraham and Róheim these were images of the phallic mother; that is, they reflected the early infantile belief that everyone – including males and females, fathers and mothers – had a penis. For Freud then, the penis associated with the "woman-with-a-penis" was the mother's own penis, while Klein saw it as the father's penis which had been absorbed by the mother.[5] Generally, it seems that Klein's view of these "woman with a penis" images is now more accepted than Freud's.

As usual, the logic of Kleinian theory suggests that these phantasy attacks on the father's "absorbed" penis should produce guilt and a consequent desire to make reparation. It is this desire for reparation that is being gratified in the devotion to the Sacred Heart.

In short, my hypothesis is that in making reparation for the indignities directed at the Sacred Heart of Jesus (a normally internal body part belonging to an adult male that is seen externally) devotees are gratifying the infantile desire to make reparation for those phantasy attacks on the mother that damage the father's penis (a male body part this is normally external but which becomes an internal body part when absorbed by the mother during intercourse). This hypothesis interrelates most of the defining features of the devotion: the focus upon the body part of an adult male, the simultaneous association of this body part with the concepts "external" and "internal," and the strong emphasis on reparation. But there is still the association with laceration and puncturing, which I have already identified (in chapter 5) as oral modes of attack. Can the hypothesis account for these emphases as well?

Klein argued that when the child was forced to give up the mother's breast, it would tend – at least in phantasy – to see its father's penis as a substitute for the oral gratification previously provided by the breast (see Klein, 1931, 241–2; 1945, 409–1; 1952, 78–9).[6] The child in other words phantasizes about sucking on the father's penis as he or she had once sucked on the mother's breast.

But given this strong "oral" component to the child's image of its father's penis, Klein argued that attacks on the father's penis – the "absorbed" penis inside the mother – would become attacks using oral-sadistic means. This in turn produced phantasies in which the child imagined eating, biting, lacerating, or cutting the father's "absorbed" penis (see Klein 1928; 1931, 241–2; 1945, 402–11). Under the interpretation presented here, the emphasis upon laceration and puncturing in visual representations of the Sacred Heart has been shaped by the infantile memory of these oral-sadistic attacks on the father's "absorbed penis."

HEART SYMBOLISM

The suggestion that the heart is a phallic symbol is central to the hypothesis being offered here. How plausible is that? As far as I can tell, a heart never appeared as a central element in any of the dreams that Freud himself analysed. On the other hand, I do know of four discussions of heart symbolism in the later psychoanalytic literature. Three of them (Hall 1946, 219; Fenichel 1945, 219-20; Schneck 1958) do in fact argue that the heart images that appear in the dreams and other fantasy material being analysed are representations of the penis. The fourth investigator (Schneider 1954; 1955), who is concerned with heart symbols (e.g., an hour glass, a vase, etc.) rather than with actual images of the heart, argues that the heart symbols that appear in dreams are usually the condensation of two concepts, penis and babies. Seeing the heart as a phallic symbol, then, is hardly novel.

Still, none of this bears directly on the particular heart being considered here, namely, the Sacred Heart of Jesus. Is there any evidence that this heart can reasonably be considered a phallic symbol, and more specifically, a symbolic representation of the father's penis that is absorbed by the mother during intercourse? The best way to look for evidence that bears on this question is, I suggest, to inspect accounts of apparitions in which the Sacred Heart appears.

A fairly large number of Catholics over the centuries have seen apparitions of this sort, and detailed accounts of these apparitions have been widely published. If we rule out supernatural causation, then these apparitions are almost certainly hallucinations. If we further assume that these hallucinations, like hallucinations generally, are shaped at least in part by the unconscious impulses and desires of the persons involved, then accounts of these apparitions should provide some evidence of the link between the Sacred Heart of Jesus and the father's absorbed penis *if* that link does in fact exist.

The most well-known apparitions in which the Sacred Heart appears are those experienced by Margaret Mary Alacoque herself, and in the first of

Alacoque's apparitions we do find an incident that evokes imagery which can reasonably be seen as reflecting the infantile memory of the father's absorbed penis. After telling us that Christ had instructed her to promote devotion to his Sacred Heart, Alacoque continues:

> Then he asked for my heart, which I implored him to take, and having done so, he placed it within his adorable Heart, showing it to me as a little atom being consumed in a glowing furnace; and then withdrawing it thence like a burning flame in the shape of a heart, he replaced it whence he had taken it, saying: "Behold, my beloved, a precious pledge of my love, which is inserting into your side a tiny spark of its most fiery flames, to serve as your heart and to consume you until your last moment." (Stierli 1957b, 115–16)

In plainer words: Christ removed Alacoque's heart from her body, merged it with his own, and then inserted back into her body a new heart, which contained a "spark" of his own, and he did all this as a "pledge of his love." Theological commentators (like Merton 1950, 15) insist that this "exchange of hearts" should be viewed in purely metaphorical terms, that is, as a metaphor for mystical union with Christ. But the line that immediately follows the quotation above suggests that Alacoque herself probably thought of it in a more literal way: "And as a sign that the great favour I [Jesus] have just done you is *not* [emphasis added] imaginary, but the foundation of all those I still have to bestow upon you, although I have closed the wound in your side, the pain of it shall ever remain with you." Alacoque did experience the pain mentioned in the last sentence, and this is the basis for the claim sometimes made that she experienced the "invisible" stigmata.

Under the interpretation being offered here, this exchange of hearts represents the infantile memory of the father's absorbed penis; that is, Alacoque "absorbed" Christ's physical heart during mystical intercourse with him just as the mother absorbs the father's penis during sexual intercourse.

If this exchange of hearts appeared only in Alacoque's apparitions of the Sacred Heart, the argument presented here would not be all that convincing. After all, if the Sacred Heart really is a representation of the father's absorbed penis, then similar absorbed heart imagery would probably appear in the many Sacred Heart apparitions experienced by other seers. But then, it does.

Remember that a fairly large number of mystics and clerics from the medieval period on had a strong personal devotion to the Sacred Heart long before it became a devotion widely popular with the laity. A great many of these mystics, like Alacoque, experienced apparitions in which Christ revealed his Sacred Heart, and during these apparitions an exchange of hearts was quite common.

The most well-known such incident is probably the one involving St Catherine of Siena (1347–80):

For it seemed to her [Catherine] that He appeared in His own person, and opening her side, took out her heart, and carried it away.

Two days later, being in the chapel ... She remained when her companions had gone away, and continued her prayers; until at last, as she arose and prepared to return home, a great light surrounded her, and in the midst of the light our Lord again appeared, bearing in his Hand a Heart of vermilion hue, and casting forth bright rays of fire. Then he approached her, and *once more opening her side, He placed there this Heart* [emphasis added], and said, "Daughter, the other day I took thy heart; today I give thee Mine, which shall henceforward serve thee in its place." (Drane 1880, 109)

Bainvel's (1924) historical account of the devotion to the Sacred Heart mentions eight other persons who "exchanged" hearts with Jesus during an apparition. They are St Lutgarde of Aywières (1182–1246), St Mechtilde (d. 1298); Marina d'Escobar (1554–1633; Suzanne de la Pomélie (1571–1616); mother de Jasse of Ussel (1614–56); Sister Antoinette Miette of Roanne (1592–1627); Giovanna Benigna Gojoz (1615–42); and mother Anne-Marguerite Clement (d. 1661). Cabassut's (1953) article on "heart exchange" in the *Dictionnaire de Spiritualité* suggests that we should add Dorothea of Montau (1347–94), Osanna Andreasi of Mantua (1449–1505), St Catherine dei Ricci (1522–90), and Michael de los Santos (1591–1625) to this list. In all these cases, Christ appeared to the seer, removed her or his heart, and then inserted back into the seer's body a new (or at least a refurbished) heart.

Notice that in all fourteen instances of heart exchange just mentioned, with only once exception (Michael de los Santos), the seer who receives Christ's heart is a woman. The fact that in almost all instances of heart exchange a woman "absorbs" the heart of Jesus seems consistent with the suggestion that this hallucinatory element is shaped by the infantile memory of the mother who absorbs the father's penis during intercourse.

A COMPARISON: THE IMMACULATE HEART OF MARY

Were it possible to inform Catholic thinkers of the mid-seventeenth century that a devotion centred on a physical heart would become one of the most popular of all Catholic devotions, I doubt that they would be very surprised. What might surprise them, however, is that the physical heart in question would belong to Jesus, rather than the Virgin Mary. St Jean Eudes, for instance, now identified by the Church as originating the cult of the Sacred Heart of Jesus, was actually more devoted to the Immaculate Heart of Mary and did more to promote the latter devotion than he did to promote the former. Eudes caused a feast dedicated to the Heart of Mary to be celebrated at the Rennes seminary in 1648, twenty two years before he caused a feast dedicated to the Heart of Jesus to be celebrated at the same seminary. He also published a treatise on Mary's heart, entitled *The Admirable Heart of the Most Sacred Mother of God*, in 1681. Though he is supposed to have written a similar work on the Heart of Jesus, there are no extant copies of that work, and it seems likely that it was never published (Phelan 1946, xxv). The book now available as *The Sacred Heart of Jesus* by Jean Eudes (1946) is really just volume 12 of his work on Mary's heart.

Yet devotion to Heart of Mary has never enjoyed the wide popularity enjoyed by devotion to the Heart of Jesus. Even the great upsurge in Marian devotion in the nineteenth century, an upsurge fuelled by the well-publicized apparitions of the Virgin at Paris (1830–31), LaSalette (1846), Lourdes (1858), Pontmain (1981), and Knock, Ireland (1879), did not give devotion to Mary's heart the popularity enjoyed by devotion to Jesus' heart. The feast of the Immaculate Heart of Mary was not even made a feast of the Universal Church until 1944.

Some further indication of the relative appeal of the two devotions can be seen in the coverage given to each in the *Catholic Encyclopedia*: eight columns of text are devoted to the Heart of Jesus (Bainvel 1913a) but only three to the Heart of Mary (Bainvel 1913b). Virtually this same ratio is preservd in the *New Catholic Encyclopedia*, which devotes five and a half columns to the Sacred Heart (Moell 1967; Larkin 1967; Morris 1967) and less than two to the Immaculate Heart of Mary (Murphy 1967).

At first sight, the fact that devotion to the Immaculate Heart of Mary has fared less well than devotion to the Sacred Heart of Jesus would seem quite damaging to my argument. After all, most of the same psychological associations evoked by the Sacred Heart would also seem to be evoked by the Immaculate Heart. In both cases a physical heart lies at the core of the devotion, and in both cases the heart is displayed exteriorly, which means that in both cases the heart involved is a body part that is internal and external simultaneously.

In the case of the Sacred Heart of Jesus, I have argued that its assocation with an adult male makes it easier for it to represent the father's absorbed penis. On the other hand, because the Heart of Mary is a woman's heart, it is an organ that would normally be contained within a woman's body. As such it too, it seems to me, could also function as a symbol for the penis that is "within" the mother's body.

Similarly, many of the elements that define the iconography of the Sacred Heart also define the iconography of the Heart of Mary. In both cases the heart is usually a real heart, and in both cases a cluster of flames regularly emerges from the aortic opening.

True, the emphasis upon laceration and puncturing, so evident in depictions of the Sacred Heart, is less evident in depictions of the Immaculate Heart of Mary. Most nineteenth- and twentieth-century depictions of Mary's Immaculate Heart show it tightly encircled by a garland of flowers, rather than the more painful circlet of thorns that encircles the Sacred Heart. But there is a second iconographic tradition that depicts Mary's heart as pierced with a sword. This almost certainly derives from the tradition of portraying Mary as the *Mater Dolorosa* whose chest is pierced with one or more swords (see for example the illustrations in Jameson 1903, 120), which in turn derives from Simeon's prophecy at Christ's Purification that Mary's soul would be pierced with a sword (Luke 2:35). Furthermore, this tradition of Mary's heart pierced with a sword tradition was established before the Paray-le-Monial apparitions (see the illustrations of "early" Immaculate Hearts in Grimoüard de Saint-Laurent 1880, plates IV, V, and VI). This means that before those apparitions there was at least one iconographic tradition associated with Mary's heart that did convey the same emphasis on laceration and puncturing found in association with the iconography of the Sacred Heart.

In summary then, a reasonable case could be made to the effect that by the middle of the seventeenth century *all* the elements – with one notable exception – which combine (under my hypothesis) to make devotion to the Sacred Heart so appealing were also associated with devotion to the Heart of Mary. That one missing element of course is an emphasis on reparation, which was the same element missing from devotion to the Sacred Heart before the Paray-le-Monial apparitions. Just as Eudes, for example, did not stress reparation in discussing the Heart of Jesus, neither did he stress it in discussing the Heart of Mary.

Since I have argued that the addition of the reparation element was critical for the devotion to the Sacred Heart, what all this suggests is that the reparation element had been added to the traditions surrounding the Heart of Mary, this devotion would have become at least as popular as devotion to the Sacred Heart. But things did not happen that way.

During her apparitions, Margaret Mary Alacoque associated the Sacred Heart of Jesus with a strong emphasis upon reparation, but no one performed a similar function for the Heart of Mary. As a result, devotion to Mary's physical heart never achieved the popularity of devotion to Jesus's physical heart. The moderate increase in the popularity of devotion to Mary's Heart over the centuries is probably attributable to the fact that most commentaries on the Immaculate Heart of Mary link it to the Sacred Heart of Jesus.

THE SACRED HEART IN THE NINETEENTH CENTURY

I have already mentioned the great upsurge in the popularity of the devotion to the Sacred Heart in the late nineteenth century. One indication of this upsurge is the increasing number of confraternities, and especially in the increasing number of *arch*confraternities, dedicated to the Sacred Heart. An archconfraternity is a confraternity empowered to aggregate unto itself other confraternities in other locations and to impart to those other confraternities the indulgences and privileges it itself has been granted. The first arch-confraternity dedicated to the Sacred Heart was established at Rome in 1803. There were fifteen hundred confraternities associated with this archconfra-ternity in 1818; by 1900 there were more then ten thousand (Beringer 1925b, 127). Morever, the last half of the nineteenth century saw the establishment of five additional Sacred Heart archconfraternities, each of which was the organizational focus for a great many other confraternities scattered through-out the world.

The last half of the nineteenth century, in particular, saw a great number of developments that indicate the great increase in the popularity of this devo-tion. Thus, in 1856 Pius IX made the feast of the Sacred Heart a feast of the Universal Church; in 1864 Margaret Mary Alacoque was beatified; in early 1875 Pius IX asked the Congregation of Rites to develop a standardized for-mula to be used in consecrating groups and individuals to the Sacred Heart; he then urged all Catholics to use this formula to consecrate themselves to the Sacred Heart on 16 June 1875, the second centenary of Alacoque's Great Apparition; and finally, in 1899 Leo XIII consecrated "the entire human race" to the Sacred Heart of Jesus. Increasingly as well, the leadership (ecclesiastical or governmental or both) in a great many Catholic nations made formal vows consecrating their nation to the Sacred Heart. Thus, Ireland was consecrated to the Sacred Heart in 1873; San Salvador in 1874; Venezuela in 1900; Col-ombia in 1902; Spain in 1919; Nicaragua in 1920; Poland in 1920; Costa Rica in 1921; Brazil in 1922; and Bolivia in 1925 (Verheylezoon 1955, 143).

It is hardly coincidental, I think, that this striking upsurge in the popularity of devotion to the Sacred Heart, a devotion whose appeal (under my hypothesis) derives from an unconscious desire to make reparation for phan-tasy attacks on the father, should coincide exactly with the two most serious attacks on the authority of the pope in modern history, attacks that took place in Italy and Germany respectively.

Italy

The *Risorgimento*, the drive for the unification of Italy, had begun in the 1830s under the leadership of men like Giuseppe Mazzini (1805–72) and Giuseppe Garibaldi (1807–82). In 1848 riots in Rome, which was then part of the Papal States, forced Pius IX to promise a more democratic form of government. The violence intensified and the pope fled the city in disguise. The revolutionaries then established a Roman republic, which quickly abolished the temporal authority of the pope. A few months later French troops intervened, the pope returned to Rome, and papal authority was re-established.

In the late 1850s the Kingdom of Sardinia (which included Piedmont) under the leadership of King Victor Emmanuel and Camillo di Cavour (1810–61), began to annex other Italian states. By 1860, the Kingdom of Sardina had annexed all of Italy, except Venice, but including – over the strenuous objections of the pope – all the Papal States except Rome and its immediate environs. In (1861) the new Italian government, meeting in Florence, declared Rome the capital of Italy, even though Rome was still under the temporal authority of the pope.

Garibaldi raised an army and marched on Rome in 1862 but was defeated by troops of the Italian government. A second attempt by Garibaldi to march on Rome in 1867 was thwarted by French troops sent by Napoleon III. French troops remained in Rome to protect the pope until they were withdrawn in 1870 as a result of the Franco-Prussian War. In late September 1870, the Italian army entered the city. The next month, after a plebiscite showed that the Romans were overwhelmingly in favour of annexation, Rome was annexed to Italy, thus bringing to an effective end the temporal authority of the pope.

The Italian government tried to be conciliatory by passing the Law of Guarantees, which guaranteed the saftey of the pope, his authority in all spiritual matters, and his right to communicate freely with foreign governments and with the Catholic hierarchy. The pope was also granted a measure of territorial independence in connection with the Vatican. But Pius IX, who refused to acknowledge the validity of this law, called upon all Catholics not to recognize the legitimacy of the Italian government. This papal position was not to be relaxed until after 1900.

One response by Catholics loyal to the pope to this Italian assault upon the pope's temporal authority was a general willingness to affirm and strengthen the pope's spiritual authority. Thus in 1864 Pius IX had announced his intention to call a council of the Church. That council, the first Vatican Council, was convened in December 1869 and suspended on 1 September 1870, just a few weeks before the Italian army entered Rome. It was at this council that the bishops of the Church endorsed the doctrine of Papal Primacy (the doctrine that the pope has ultimate jurisdictional authority over all other bishops and over the laity) and promulgated formally, for the first time in the history of the Church, the doctrine of Papal Infallibility (which holds that the pope is infallible when speaking *ex cathedra* on matters of faith and morals). I now want to suggest that the increased popularity of devotion to the Sacred Heart among the laity and the increased willingness on the part of Church authorities to endorse this devotion, were jointly yet another response, however unconscious, to these same Italian assaults upon the temporal authority of the pope.

Remember what the appeal of this devotion is, if I am correct: the devotion is appealing because it allows for the gratification of the infantile desire to make reparation for phantasy attacks against the father's absorbed penis. By extension, the devotion provides a means of making reparation for attacks against the father generally. I take it as self-evident that in the mind of loyal

Catholics the pope is an authoritative father-figure. In the minds of those individuals firmly committed to papal authority, laity and clerics alike, the dissatisfaction and anxiety produced by attacks on papal authority would reactivate and intensify their infantile desire to make reparation for the phantasy attacks on the father's absorbed penis. This in turn would predispose them to a devotion, like that organized around the Sacred Heart, that allows for the symbolic gratification of just this infantile desire.

This, I suggest, was one of the reasons why devotion to the Sacred Heart became more appealing to lay Catholics during the late nineteenth century and why the clerical administrators of the Church themselves became more favourable to this devotion. I might note also that the assembled bishops at the Vatican Council, who committed themselves to Papal Primacy and Papal Infallibility, also presented a petition to the pope asking that he upgrade the feast of the Sacred Heart to the highest possible liturgical rank (Bainvel 1924, 308).

Germany

But it was not just in Italy that the authority of the pope was under attack during the late nineteenth century. By the 1870s another attack, this time on the ecclesiastical authority of the pope, was under way in the German-speaking regions of Europe. This second attack on papal authority was part of what historians usually call the *Kulturkampf*,[7] a term that refers to a political movement in Germany and in other German-speaking regions that led to the passage of a variety of laws limiting the influence of the Catholic Church. The *Kulturkampf* was in some sense the result of a number of trends that coalesced in the late 1860s and early 1870s, including here the efforts to establish a unified Germany, the extension of the democratic franchise, and the proclamation of Papal Infallibility at the Vatican Council (see in particular Anderson 1986). But the first piece of *Kulturkampf* legislation was passed only in 1871. This was the Pulpit Law, designed to prevent Catholic priests from engaging in political activity while preaching in a church.

In that same year, Bismarck asked the pope to censure the Catholic Centre Party for its parliamentary opposition to some of Bismarck's policies; the pope refused. In 1872, Prussia passed a law that in effect excluded Catholic clergy from the supervision of schools. In 1872, the Reichstag passed a number of laws that led to the expulsion of the Jesuits from Germany. In 1873 similar laws were extended to other religious groups, including the Redemptorists, Lazarists, Fathers of the Holy Ghost, and the Ladies of the Sacred Heart.

In the period 1872-4, Bismarck's Minister of Education and Public Worship, Adalbert Falk, drafted and had passed a number of laws that put the clergy in Germany firmly under the control of the state. Thus, all appointments to ecclesiastical offices were to be approved by the civil authorities, and all decisions by ecclesiastical courts could be appealed to the civil authorities. For priests to administer the sacraments without having been authorized by the civil authorities was made a criminal offence. Finally, in May 1873 the penalties were increased for priests and bishops who did not comply with the earlier laws. These "May Laws," as they came to be called, were strengthened in 1874. In February 1875, Pius ix declared the May Laws to be invalid.

In 1875, Prussia passed a law that allowed for the suspension of state grants to the Church, confiscated all Church property, and turned this property over to lay administrators selected from each parish. Criticism of the state from the pulpit was made a criminal offence. Over the next few years, hundreds of priests were arrested, thousands deprived of their right to teach religion in the schools, and 292 monastic institutions closed. Only with the accession of Leo xiii in 1878 did relations between Prussia and the Vatican begin to improve.

Though the *Kulturkampf* was most marked in Prussia between 1865 and 1880, similar struggles took place in other German-speaking regions, including Baden, Hessen-Darmstadt, Bavaria, Austria, and many German-speaking parts of Switzerland (Freudenthal 1967, 268–9).

In 1871, following the outbreak of the *Kulturkampf*, two separate petitions were presented to the pope, one from the Empress of Austra and one from "German Catholics," both asking him to upgrade the feast of the Sacred Heart (Bainvel 1924, 308). Here again then, we have some evidence that loyal Catholics responded to attacks on papal authority by an increased emphasis upon devotion to the Sacred Heart. It was also at the height of the *Kulturkampf*, in 1875, that Pius ix asked all Catholics to consecrate themselves to the Sacred Heart.

The relationship between devotion to the Sacred Heart and the onset of the strong and successful attacks on papal authority that occurred in both Italy and Germany during the late nineteenth century has not been missed entirely by Catholic thinkers. For instance, one of the "Sacred Heart" archconfraternities established in this period was established in 1877 and located at the then new *Sacré Coeur* (Sacred Heart) church in Montmartre. The full title of this archconfraternity was "The Archconfraternity of the Sacred Heart, for the liberty of the Pope and the Preservation of Society." One of its goals was to propagate the cult of the Sacred Heart in families and in society, as a way of making reparation (*expiation*) for the outrages committed against religion, against the rights of the Church and the Holy See, and against the holy person of the Vicar of Christ" (Beringer 1925b, 131), and this is presumably a reference to the attacks on papal authority in Italy and Germany. Even so, in most theological and devotional discussions the coincidence in time between the upsurge in the popularity of the Sacred Heart and these attacks on papal authority has been missed entirely.

In principle, attacks on papal authority are not the only attacks that should lead Catholics to emphasize devotion to the Sacred Heart. On the contrary, any attack on authority should reactive infantile memories of the phantasy attacks on the father's penis, which in turn should predispose Catholics towards this devotion. This theoretical consequence allows us to understand at least two other patterns associated with the history of Catholic devotion to the Sacred Heart. The first is the association between the Sacred Heart and the French monarchist cause.

Originally, the kings of France did not show any especial attachment to the Sacred Heart. On the contrary, in 1688 Margaret Mary Alacoque reported a vision in which Christ had instructed her to request the reigning King, Louis XIV, to consecrate himself and all of France to the Sacred Heart. It is unclear if this message was ever transmitted to the king (Bainvel 1924, 26), but in any event no such consecration was made.

Only with the Revolution did things change. There is a tradition that Louis XVI consecrated himself, his family, and his Kingdom, to the Sacred Heart in 1790, just after the Revolution had begun. Since this tradition appeared only in 1815, its authenticity is open to question. For our purposes though, it does not really matter whether the tradition is true or not; what matters is that so many people in the early nineteenth century found it reasonable to believe that a king whose authority and person was under attack would endorse devotion to the Sacred Heart.

The most important link between the French monarchy and the Sacred Heart occurred in the early 1870s, when devotion to the Sacred Heart became intertwined with the attempts to reestablish the monarchy and restore the Bourbon pretender, the Comte de Chambord, to the throne (see Kselman 1983, 125–7). Monarchists used the occasion of pilgrimages to Paray-le-Monial to make important speeches on behalf of the restoration, and a popular "Sacred Heart" hymn of the period, "Sauvez Rome et la France, au Nom du Sacré Coeur" came to be interpreted to mean that France would prosper with the restoration of the Bourbon monarchy. In 1873, when the Archbishop of Paris petitioned the government for funds to build a new basilica at Paris dedicated to the Sacred Heart, the cause of the new basilica was strongly supported by the monarchist party, and the eventual passage of the resolution endorsing construction of the basilica was taken as a sign of monarchist strength.

Why should this one devotion have become so intertwined with the monarchist cause? Partly because the Comte de Chambord was known to have a strong personal devotion to the Sacred Heart, and partly because monarchist groups were obviously attempting to elicit public support by associating themselves with a form of folk religion that had long been popular in France. But the argument in this chapter provides a third explanation that complements these first two: devotion to the Sacred Heart will always have an appeal to Catholics upset by attacks on authority, since this devotion gratifies the infantile desire to make reparation for attacks on the father, the prototypical authority figure.

There is one final example of the link between the onset of attacks on authority and a relatively sudden endorsement of the Sacred Heart. It should be mentioned if only because it concerns the Jesuits, who have long been seen as the greatest champions of the Sacred Heart.

A casual inspection of the historical record might suggest that Jesuitical attachment to the Sacred Heart derives from the fact that Jesuits like Claude de la Columbière and Jean Croiset worked hard to popularize Alacoque's apparitions. But despite the actions of individual Jesuits like de la Columbière and Croiset, in the early part of the eighteenth century the Jesuit hierarchy was generally cool to the new devotion. Though Jesuit officials did not condemn it, they did discourage it (Bainvel 1924, 295). The change in Jesuit policy came only in the late 1760s and early 1770s, when Lorenzo Ricci (1703–75) was General of the Order. It was only during Ricci's tenure that the Jesuits began to practise devotion to the Sacred Heart as a group. The timing here is (once again) significant since it means that the Jesuits only began to endorse devotion to the Sacred Heart during the period of their suppression.

The King of France dissolved the Society of Jesus in his country in 1764, and required the Jesuits remaining in France to renounce their vows. Similar suppressions of the Jesuit order took place in Spain, Naples, and Parma, where thousands of Jesuits were arrested and deported. Finally, under pressure from a variety of European governments, Pope Clement xiv in 1773 issued a Brief of Suppression that suppressed the Society of Jesus throughout all of Europe. Though the Brief (which among other things forbade Jesuits from living in community with one another) was carried out to different degrees in different parts of Europe, the net effect was to strip the Jesuits of a substantial amount of their power and authority.

It was during this period, when the authority of the order was under such severe attack, that the Jesuits first turned to the Sacred Heart, just as Catholics loyal to the pope did two centuries later when his authority came under attack.

MASTER AND KING IN THE HOME

My interpretation of the Sacred Heart, like my interpretation of the Stigmata, assumes that Jesus Christ functions as a father-figure in folk Catholicism, even though Catholic theology recognizes him only as the Son of God. In chapter 5 I justified this assumption by arguing that theology aside, Catholic ritual and tradition are overwhelmingly Christocentric and that the net effect of this is that Jesus Christ is the most "authoritative" of all the male beings in the Catholic pantheon. This means that Jesus Christ is available as a conscious symbol for the unconscious image of the authoritative father. In the case of the Sacred Heart, there is some additional evidence that can be brought to bear on this issue, and it concerns a ritual called the "Enthronement of the Sacred Heart."

This ritual emerged in the late nineteenth century as part of the upsurge in the popularity of the Sacred Heart devotion that occurred at that time. Basically, the ritual entails placing an image of the Sacred Heart in a prominent room of a family's home, and with all members of the family present, as well as a priest, consecrating the family to the Sacred Heart. At the same time family members pledge to uphold the Commandments, the teachings of the Church, the directions of the pope, and so on. Although in principle any group can use this procedure to consecrate itself to the Sacred Heart, in fact the Enthronement ceremony has always been a family-oriented ceremony. This strong association between the Sacred Heart and the family seems generally consistent with the Kleinian argument developed here, since in that argument it is the child's perception of the (sexual) relationship between the parents that gives rise to the infantile desires being gratified by the Sacred Heart devotion.

But what is most important for us is the imagery surrounding the Sacred Heart in the Enthronement ceremony. Consider Bainvel's (1924, 328-9) description of this ceremony:

The Act to which we refer is that of the Enthronement of the Sacred Heart in the home, where it is henceforth to preside not merely as a guest and a witness, but as *Master and King* ... enthronement implies that hereafter this image (picture or statue) will have its place in the home and will be honoured by the inmates ... For the enthronement consists, as the word ("enthronement") shows, in bringing the Sacred Heart into the house, to be henceforth *Master and King*. (emphasis added)

But who in the normal course of daily events is the person who would most reasonably be regarded, at least in the infantile mind, as the "Master and King" of the household? Surely it is the father. That the Sacred Heart of Jesus is enthroned in the household as "Master and King" is therefore in itself clear evidence of the strong association between Jesus and father in the Catholic mind. But the final line in the actual formula prescribed for use during the Enthronement ceremony (Beringer 1925a, 176-7) removes all doubt: "Long live the Heart of Jesus, our King and our *Father*" (emphasis added).

In other words, it appears that the words of the Enthronement ceremony come very close to expressing in a clear and conscious way what I have argued is the underlying appeal of the devotion to the Sacred Heart: that in making reparation to the physical heart of Jesus, a heart that has been lacerated and punctured, devotees are really gratifying the infantile desire to make reparation for the oral-sadistic attacks launched in phantasy against the father's penis.

CHAPTER NINE

The Splintering of Religious Devotion in Catholicism

Theologians and historians have often written of the doctrinal differences between Catholicism and Protestantism – differences having to do, say, with attitudes towards the Eucharist, the role of faith in achieving salvation, the relationship between the institutional church and its members, and so on. Less well-studied are the systematic differences between the practice of Catholicism generally and the practice of Protestantism generally. One such difference, and the one of concern of this chapter, has do with the greater proliferation of separate and distinct religious devotions in Catholicism. Quite apart from those devotions that are part of the official liturgy (like the Mass, the Eucharist, and the Sacraments), Catholics engage in a wide variety that of extra-liturgical devotions of precisely the sort discussed in this book. Though Protestants also engage in extra-liturgical devotions (a home or office Bible study group would be a good example), the range and variety of such devotions hardly match what is found in Catholicism.

In part this particular difference in religious practice derives from a doctrinal difference concerning the Virgin Mary and the saints. Catholicism holds that Mary and the saints can intercede with God on behalf of the faithful; this view has always been rejected by all Protestant groups. Seeing Mary and the saints as potential intercessors with God obviously creates a psychological atmosphere that facilitates the emergence of cults and devotions organized around these beings.

But the greater proliferation of cults and devotions in Catholicism does not derive entirely (or even mainly) from the fact that the Catholic pantheon is peopled with a greater variety of supernatural beings who can benefit humanity. It derives also from the fact that Catholics seem more willing to splinter the devotion to particular supernatural beings into a wide range of separate and distinct devotions, each of which is logically independent of the others, and (apparently) gratifying in itself.

This splintering of religious devotion is most evident in the case of devotion to the Virgin Mary. Although it is convenient to talk about *a* cult of Mary among Catholics, what is most striking about Catholic Mariolatry is the enormous range of separate and distinct devotions that each have Mary at their focus. There are for example separate prayers or rituals associated with Mary under the titles of the Immaculate Conception, the Name of Mary, the Immaculate Heart of Mary, Our Lady of the Blessed Sacrament, Our Lady of Lourdes, Our Lady of Fatima, Our Lady of Guadalupe, Our Lady of Miracles, Queen of the Rosary, Mother of Sorrows, Our Lady of the Angels, Our Lady of Perpetual Help, Our Lady Help of Christians, Our Lady of Mt Carmel, Our Lady of Reparation, Our Lady of Mercy, Our Lady of Compassion, Our Lady Help of the Sick, and Our Lady of Hope. Nor is this list complete. On the contrary, I have taken it mainly from Beringer (1925a; 1925b), which lists only those Marian titles associated with prayers or confraternities that convey papal indulgences. It thus does not include the large number of traditional Marian titles that associate Mary with some particular quality or attribute, or tie Mary to some particular village or region but without being associated with an indulgence. To all this we must add all the widely popular devotions, already considered in earlier chapters, that have a Marian focus, like the Rosary, the Angelus, the Brown Scapular and, the Miraculous Medal.

The simplest way to explain this splintering of Catholic devotion to Mary would be to see it as an expression of the great importance that Catholics have traditionally assigned to Mary – but that line of reasoning leads to a prediction easily disproved. If it were the relative importance of a supernatural being which gave rise to a splintering of the devotion to that being, we would expect to find a greater splintering of Christocentric devotion among Protestants. After all, to say that Protestants emphasize Mary and the saints less is to say that they emphasize Christ more. But the fact is that even in regard to *Christocentric* devotions, splintering is more evident in Catholicism.

Within the Catholic tradition, for example, there are separate devotions associated with the Sacred Heart of Jesus, the Stations of the Cross, the Eucharistic Heart of Jesus, the Holy Name of Jesus, the Holy Face of Jesus, the Precious Blood of Jesus, the Holy Agony of Jesus, Jesus as the Infant of Prague, Jesus under the appearance of the Blessed Sacrament, and so on. Each of these Christocentric devotions has its own separate set of prayers, each is promulgated by one or more different archconfraternities, and many of them have their own unique rituals. Some of these already splintered devotions have been splintered even further. Devotion to the Sacred Heart of Jesus has given rise to the Nine First Fridays devotion, to the Enthronement of the Sacred Heart in the Home ceremony, and to the wearing of various Sacred Heart scapulars (see chapter 8). Similarly, devotion to the Blessed Sacrament has been splintered into devotions concerned with daily visits to the Blessed Sacrament, nightly adoration of the Blessed Sacrament, the Forty Hours Adoration of the Blessed Sacrament, the veneration of the Blessed Sacrament by children five to fifteen years old, and so on.[1] To all this we must add the Christocentric devotions, like the Mass and Holy Communion, that are part of the official liturgy.

In short, whether we look at the Virgin Mary or Christ, we find that the splintering of religious devotion is more evident in Catholicism, not Protestantism. Why should that be?

THE PSYCHOLOGY OF SPLINTERING

Although social scientists have commented on some of the broad differences between Catholicism and Protestantism,[2] none, as far as I know, have been concerned with the greater Catholic predilection to splinter the devotion to particular supernatural beings like Mary or Christ. On the other hand, though psychoanalytic investigators have rarely addressed the differences between Catholicism and Protestantism they have discussed something that bears at least a passing resemblance to the splintering of religious devotion found in Roman Catholicism.

Thus, in his analysis of the Schreber case, Freud (1911) found that Schreber split the figure of his physician, Dr Flechsig, into two aspects – "God" and "the Flechsig soul" – and felt persecuted by each. Later still, Schreber felt persecuted as well by the soul of the chief attendant at the institution where he was being treated, something Freud saw as yet another split-off image of Flechsig. Finally, each of these two souls – the "Flechsig soul" and the "attendant's soul" – was splintered into a number of "soul divisions," each of which then proceeded to persecute the unfortunate Schreber. The Flechsig soul alone had as many as sixty "soul divisions," and the attendant's soul seems to have had about the same. For Freud, this sort of splintering, which he called "decomposition," was typical of paranoia.

Can Freud's explanation of Schreber's paranoia help to explain the splintering of Christ and of the Virgin Mary found in Catholicism? I doubt it. For Freud, this sort of excessive splintering was the result of pathological conditions. On *a priori* grounds it seems to me that in trying to explain a phenomenon that is widespread (like the splintering found in Catholicism), we should try to relate that phenomenon to some process that occurs routinely during the normal (read: typical) course of psychological development, not to abnormal processes associated with relatively atypical outcomes (like paranoia).

Melanie Klein, whose work has already proved so useful in this book, also discusses a type of splintering, and in this case the splintering *is* an integral part of normal development. Klein argued, remember, that during the first few months of an infant's life, the image of the mother breast is split into two images: the Good Breast, which supplies milk, and the Bad Breast, which withholds milk. This splitting process is reinforced not only by innate tendencies (which Klein calls the "Life Instinct" and the "Death Instinct"), but also by the infant's experience of warm gratifying experiences (when being nursed) and by frustrating, unpleasant experiences (produced when the infant wants to be nursed but is not). These two images, Klein argued, are introjected; that is, the infant comes to see them as objects in its own mind, and they become the core around which the ego develops. The Good Breast becomes the prototype for all satisfying experiences and objects, and the Bad Breast for all unpleasant and persecutory experiences.

But the process does not stop there. As a defence against the persecutory anxiety produced by the infant's image of the Bad Breast, the Bad Breast is splintered into a number of parts. These parts are then projected onto things in the infant's environment. The Bad Breast might be splintered into say, a "greedy Breast" and a "biting Breast," and each of these images then projected onto objects in the infant's environment, which subsequently become "greedy" or "biting." If the child projected these images onto parts of its mother's body, her eye for example, the result might be a "greedy eye" or a "biting eye" or both. In most cases, these external objects will then be re-introjected, that is, brought back into the child's mind.

The process of splitting a single image (in this case the Bad Breast) into several parts, projecting those parts onto objects in the environment, and then re-introjecting these external objects, is what Klein calls "projective identification". Klein's isolation of this process is generally regarded as one of her most important psychoanalytic discoveries,[3] if only because the objects brought into the infantile mind as a result of projective identification constitute a template that largely determines the shape of the adult personality.

For Klein, the splintering of the Bad Breast is a defence mechanism, since it is a way of keeping the Bad Breast separate from the Good Breast, and so preventing the Bad Breast from despoiling the Good Breast. In principle the same effect could be achieved by splintering the Good Breast as well, and Klein does in fact argue that some splintering of the Good Breast takes place: "It is however not only the bad parts of the self which are expelled and projected, but also good parts of the self. i.e., the loving parts of the self ... The projection of good feelings and good parts of the self into the mother is essential for the infant's ability to develop good object-relations and to integrate his ego" (Klein 1946, 8–9). But too much splintering and projection of the Good Breast would lead to the feeling that the good parts of the personality were lost forever, and this in turn would weaken the developing ego. This for Klein explains why in the normal case the Bad Breast is splintered more excessively than the Good Breast.[4]

Our goal was to isolate a period during the normal development of a child that is characterized by a sort of splintering that seems at least vaguely similar to the splintering in folk Catholicism. If Klein is correct, then the first few months of life, during what she calls the paranoid-schizoid position, is just such a period. The splintering of, say, the Virgin Mary into a number of separate and distinct Madonnas and the splintering of the mother's breast into a number of different images may differ with regard to content, but the two phenomena are clearly similar in structure. Furthermore, remember that the excessive splintering during the paranoid-schizoid position is not characteristic of later stages in psychological development. On the contrary, such splintering declines in favour of increasing integration (at least in the normal case), so that movement into the depressive position is in fact defined by the perception that the Good and Bad Breasts are just two aspects of the same person.

Am I really suggesting that events in the first six months of life can affect the structure of religious belief among adults? Yes. As contrary to common sense as this may seem to some, clinical investigators working in the Kleinian tradition have come to precisely this sort of conclusion over and over again. In discussing the paranoid-schizoid position, Hanna Segal (1973, 35) puts the matter succinctly: "No experience in human development is ever cast aside or obliterated; we must remember that in the most normal individual there will be some situations which will stir up the earliest anxieties and bring into operation the earliest mechanism of defence ... [The] achievements of the ego in the paranoid-schizoid position are indeed very important for later development, for which they lay the foundations." If we want to discover the origins of the splintering of religious devotion found in Catholicism, then, a good place to start is the excessive splintering character of the paranoid-schizoid position, an experience common to us all.

Simply advancing an argument, of course, does not make it correct. That can only be done by using the argument to generate specific hypotheses that are then shown to have explanatory power. In this particular case, the specific hypothesis that would seem to be most easily derivable from Klein's argument is this: the more the memories of the paranoid-schizoid position (and thus the memories of the splintering characteristic of this period) are activated by events in later life, the more the individual involved should be likely to splinter his or her religious devotion to a particular supernatural being, like the Virgin Mary or Christ.

Ultimately, I believe that this hypothesis will allow us to explain the splintering of religious devotion evident in Catholicism. But before this explanation can be constructed, it is necessary to consider one particular variant of Catholicism, a variant in which the splintering of religious devotion is especially intense and which has always exerted a strong influence on Catholicism in general. This variant is Italian Catholicism.

ITALIAN CATHOLICISM
AND SPLINTERING

Studies of the folk religion found in Italian and Italian-American communities[5] invariably agree that Italian folk religion is an admixture of two quite different sets of elements.[6] On the one hand, there are those obviously "Catholic" elements that are to some degree approved by Church authorities, at least at the local level, and in which the local clergy participates, at least to some extent. Into this category fall all the beliefs and practices associated with the many supernatural beings who populate the Italian pantheon, including the God of Christianity (under the guises of Father, Son, and Holy Ghost), the Souls in Purgatory and – most important of all – the Virgin Mary and a multitude of saints. On the other hand, Italian folk religion also includes a range of beliefs and practices that commentators variously label "pagan," "non-Christian," or "occult." The most important beliefs and practices in this second category are those associated with human beings who are seen to have preternatural abilities, notably witches, who use their magical powers for malevolent ends; healers (often priests) who can cure disease and deformity; and those with the Evil Eye, whose gaze is sufficient to cause misfortune, whether intentional or not.

This is not to deny that some of the occult elements in this second category sometimes invoke Catholic imagery. Quite the contrary. One of the most common charms used to ward off the Evil Eye in South Italian communities is a folded copy of the "One True Letter of Jesus Christ," and candles or other objects blessed in church on the feast of St Blaise are often used as a remedy for sore throats. The point is rather that these occult elements have not received the approval of Church authorities, and the local clergy have not officially promulgated such beliefs and practices.

By far, most studies of Italian folk religion have tended to focus upon the occult elements in Italian folk religion. The Evil Eye complex alone has attracted a great deal of scholarly attention. In connection with the explicitly Catholic components of Italian folk religion, investigators have examined mainly the nature and functions of the *festa* and upon the "logic" and "specialization" that characterize the cult of the saints.

Less well-studied, but directly relevant to our concerns here, however, is the predilection of Italian Catholics to splinter their religious devotion, in particular, their devotion to the Virgin Mary. For instance, if we limit ourselves to the separate madonnas mentioned in Besutti's (1972, 52–77) short list of Marian shrines in Italy, we find that Mary is venerated variously as the Madonna di Crea; the Madonna di Tirano; the Madonna della Ghianda; the Madonna dell'Olmo; the Madonna di Lonigo; the Madonna del Borgo; the Madonna dei Miracoli; the Madonna della Stella; the Madonna delle Grazie; S. Maria della Consolazione; the Madonna di S. Maria in Trastevere; the Madonna della Quercia; the Madonna delle Vittorie; the Madonna della Catena; the Madonna delle Lacrime; the Madonna del Carmine; the Madonna del Paradiso – and this is only a start. By consulting more extensive works on Italian sanctuaries (like Vinciotti 1962), we could easily expand this list of Italian Madonnas to several hundred distinct titles. Moreover, the simple fact that two Madonnas in different parts of the country share the same title is not evidence of a historical link between the two. It seems likely, for instance, that at least some of the many madonnas throughout Italy who are called "Madonna dei Miracoli" developed independently of one another, and the same thing is probably true of the many madonnas called "Madonna delle Grazie" and "Madonna dell'Olmo" ("Madonna of the Elm").

In trying to make sense of this panorama of madonnas, it is easy to draw a conclusion that severely distorts the nature of the Mary cult in Italy. For instance, it is abundantly clear that in Italy itself the veneration of some particular madonna varies from region to region. Furthermore, studies of Italian-American communities in the United States show that groups of Italian immigrants often formed themselves into regional societies that were organized around some madonna who was especially popular in the region from which they had come.

From all this it would be easy to conclude that Marian devotion in Italy consists mainly in venerating Mary under some particular title that happens to be popular in one's village. Such a conclusion would be misleading, since it overlooks the fact that in most regions of Italy, several different madonnas are venerated simultaneously and considered to be at least somewhat distinct.

In the village near Rome studied by Silverman (1975, 150–3), important community-wide ceremonies were organized around at least two different madonnas, the Madonna Addolorata and the Madonna dei Portenti. In the Sicilian village of Milocca, the two most important festas were organized around the Madonna Immacolata and the Madonna Addolorata, but there was some devotion also to the Madonna del Carmine, the Madonna Assunta, the Madonna di Trapani, and the Madonna del Monte Racalmuto (Chapman 1971, 172–3). In the Lucanian village studied by Banfield (1958, 131), five separate madonnas were the focus of cultic activity: the Madonna di Pompei, the Madonna del Carmine, the Madonna della Pace, the Madonna Assunta, and the Madonna Addolorata.

Furthermore, this tendency to splinter the image of Mary seems to have been a part of Italian Catholicism for quite some time. In his study of popular religion in Florence during the fifteenth century, for instance, Trexler (1980, 62–73), observes that, although the most important Florentine madonna was the Madonna di Impruneta, several other madonnas were venerated in Florence at the time. More important, Trexler argues that each of madonnas was invested with psychic power, sensate qualities, and "individuality and animism."

The way in which Italian Catholics regard the various madonnas is perhaps best expressed in an incident reported in Banfield (1958, 131n). When an ex-seminarian tried to explain to a woman of the village that there was really only one madonna, the woman replied: "You studied with the priests for eight years and you haven't even learned the differences between the madonnas?"

It is difficult to imagine a remark that more clearly indicates the psychological reality of the splintering process.

In short, Italian Catholics don't really venerate simply "Mary" under some particular title. They venerate simultaneously a *range* of "Marys," each designated by a separate title, each venerated at a different time of the year (since all madonnas have different feast days), and each addressed in at least slightly different prayers. Though there is no denying that all these Marys are perceived to be linked in some way, they are to a large extent considered to be separate and distinct.

The fact that the splintering of religious devotions in Italian Catholicism seems more extensive than in Catholicism generally and more focused on Mary exclusively (as opposed to both Mary and Christ) means only that Italian Catholicism bears much the same structural relationship to Catholicism generally as Catholicism bears to Protestantism.

ENVY, ITALY, AND EXCESSIVE SPLINTERING

In his review of anthropological studies of Mediterranean societies, including Italy, Gilmore (1982, 189) notes that a recurring theme is that Mediterranean communities are characterized by an "intense competition among social equals as a way of life." He is referring to the widespread feeling that because of the competition for valuable resources in such societies, individuals feel at odds with virtually everyone outside their immediate family, and often even with many of their immediate family members. Gilmore also notes that this sense of competition is usually coupled with an "image of limited good."

The limited-good concept was first introduced by George Foster (1965) on the basis of his study of a peasant community in Mexico. According to Foster, an ideology of limited good prevails in a society when all the valuable things in that society – including wealth, love, power, and so on – are believed to exist in limited quantities, with the consequences that a person can only enrich himself at the expense of someone else. Foster's work produced a lively debate in anthropology during the late 1960s and early 1970s, and in light of that debate parts of Foster's original argument have to be modified. For instance, Foster tended to believe that the scarcity that gave rise to the image of limited good derived ultimately from a material scarcity caused by a harsh physical environment. Critics have argued that this view ignores the role played by the exploitation of one class by another in creating scarcity. Foster also believed that the image of limited good worked against a high need for achievement, and thus against economic development. But even Foster's students have now shown that under certain conditions the image of limited good and a high need for achievement can coexist (see for instance Wagner 1979). Foster saw the image of limited good as a characteristic of peasant economies. But others have found similar ideologies among the urban poor. In his study of a neigh-bourhood in Naples with chronic underemployment, Belmonte (1979, 94–7) argues that local residents adopted the image of limited good simply because it was a fairly realistic assessment of their economic situation.

Still, whether produced by harsh material conditions of life, exploitation, or both, the image of the limited good does seem prevalent in a great many Mediterranean regions, as does the "intense sense of competition with social equals" also mentioned by Gilmore. Though these two psychological condi-tions may not have the effects upon economic development posited by Foster, they may have other effects. In fact, it seems obvious that these two condi-tions would be likely to produce widespread feelings of envy. After all, in such societies, another person who has gained a valuable resource can only have done so by reducing the probability that *you* will some day gain that same resource. Foster (1972) in fact did argue that envy was especially intense in societies characterized by the image of limited good.

For the most part ethnographic studies of Mediterranean communities do *not* report that informants express excessive envy in any explicit way. Instead, they report that informants regularly attribute excessive envy to others, usually in connection with the Evil Eye.

Belief in the Evil Eye is found in most Mediterranean cultures, and, as in other parts of the world where a belief in the Evil Eye is found, the emotion most often associated with this belief is envy.[8] This association is established by the widespread belief that the person with the Evil Eye lets his or her gaze fall upon you (thereby causing you misfortune) because they are envious of something that you possess. The usual interpretation is that the envy asso-ciated with the Envy Eye is a projection of the envy found within the indi-vidual who believes in the Evil Eye, an envy that that individual is unwilling to express directly.

At this point it may seem that we have drifted away from a consideration of the excessive splintering of religious devotion found in Italian Catholicism. In fact, we are now in a position to explain that phenomenon, because Kleinian theory provides a theoretical rationale for linking such splintering to the envy that is chronically experienced in Italian communities.

In Klein's reconstruction of the infantile development, the first experience of envy occurs during the paranoid-schizoid position. During this period the infant comes to believe the Good Breast has an unlimited supply of milk, and thus, by extension, is able to provide unlimited gratification. When the Good Breast is not dispensing milk to the infant, the infant will conclude that the Good Breast is keeping its milk for itself – and this makes the infant envious.

As Klein's clinical investigations progressed, she came more and more to consider this first experience of envy to be of paramount importance in the development of the child, and thus envy became one of the most important concepts in Kleinian theory.[9] Most of Klein's own discussion of envy is concerned with what happens when the infant experiences excessive envy, something that Klein believed impeded normal development. But she also argued (see Klein 1957, 190) that the experience of envy in later life routinely activates the memory of our infantile experience of envy, even if that early envy was not particular intense. This last insight gives us a theoretical basis for explaining the splintering of religious devotion to supernatural beings.

Very simply, if the conditions of life that have prevailed historically in Italian communities have ensured that the experience of envy among adults is relatively intense and chronic, the result should be to activate systematically the memory of the very first experience of envy, the envy of the Good Breast, that we all experienced during the paranoid-schizoid position. But the paranoid-schizoid position is also the period which the infantile mind is most characterized by a tendency to splinter the most important object in its environment, the mother's breast, into a wide range of separate and distinct images. The experience of chronic and intense envy in later life should therefore reactivate as well the infantile memory of this splintering.

In summary, then, the conditions of life in Italian communities have historically led to chronic and relatively intense envy, which activates the infantile memory of the splintering of the mother's breast during the first few months of life, and this memory makes the individual more willing to splinter his or her devotion to important supernatural beings like the Virgin Mary and Christ.[10]

ITALY AND THE
UNIVERSAL CHURCH

Even granting that the argument just presented might explain the excessive splintering evident in Italian Catholicism, we still need to explain the emphasis on splintering in Catholicism generally. I could of course simply postulate that envy has traditionally been more intense in Catholic societies than in Protestant societies. But this, I think, would be insupportable. While there is much evidence that the image of limited good (which is the root cause of the sort of envy we have been discussing) does prevail in many Mediterranean Catholic communities, it would be difficult to argue that it has been more prevalent in, say, Catholic societies like Bavaria and Austria, than in the Protestant societies of northern Europe. Instead, it will be more useful to proceed by looking at an issue that has been touched upon only lightly in earlier chapters.

The popularity of every devotion considered in this book has been explained by suggesting that the devotion gratifies one or more infantile desires. But though the infantile desires being gratified in these devotions are universal, these devotions, once introduced, did not always become widely popular in all parts of Catholic Europe right away. On the contrary, in several cases the devotion at first established itself only in some particular area, something I have usually attributed to social conditions that had intensified the particular infantile desire(s) being gratified in the devotion. Only when a devotion came to be endorsed and promulgated by the administrators of the Universal Church at Rome was its wide popularity throughout all the Catholic world assured.

What this suggests is that the hypotheses introduced in the earlier chapters must be modified a little. Though each of the devotions analysed earlier may indeed be appealing because it gratifies some infantile desire, this appeal is never strong enough in itself to ensure the popularity of the devotion in question. Rather if these devotions are widely popular throughout the Catholic world it is because they gratify some universally experienced infantile desire *and* because they have been promulgated by the administrators of the Universal Church. In short, I am suggesting that if these devotions had not been endorsed by the Church, they would not have acquired the transnational appeal that they have, and the differences between folk Catholicism and folk Protestantism would not be as large as they are.

What we need to explain, in other words, is why the administrators of the Universal Catholic Church, unlike their organizational counterparts in Protestantism, have been so willing to endorse the splintering of religious devotion to beings like the Virgin Mary and Christ. Without denying that every policy of the Church is the result of many different processes, I would nevertheless like to advance the following hypothesis: the administrators of the Catholic Church have been so willing to endorse the splintering of religious devotion to beings like the Virgin Mary and Christ because all the institutions responsible for administering transnational devotions have been dominated by men raised in a society in which such splintering was both excessive and legitimate. Simply put, the administration of the Church has been dominated by Italians.

ITALIAN DOMINATION IN THE CHURCH

Three institutions, in particular, have had responsibility for regulating religious devotions in the Universal Church, that is, for regulating religious devotions that transcend national boundaries. These are (1) the office of the papacy itself, (2) the Roman Curia (which is the name given to the total of all the bureaucrats who aid the pope in administering the Church), and (3) the College of Cardinals, the "princes of the Church" who are supposed to advise the pope, who often head departments in the Curia, and who elect a new pope when an old one dies – and each has been dominated by Italians for centuries. The Polish John Paul II, elected in 1978, was the first non-Italian pope since 1523. Table II shows the national origins of the College of Cardinals

TABLE 11

Nationality of the Members of College of Cardinals, twentieth Century

Year	Total Membership of College	Number (Percentage) of Italians
1916	59	29 (49)
1923	63	31 (49)
1939	59	32 (54)
1961	85	34 (40)
1968	109	35 (32)
1981	127[a]	33 (26)
	115[b]	29 (25)

Source: Adrianyi *et al*. (1981, 17); Foy (1981, 182–95)

[a] includes all Cardinals.
[b] excludes Cardinals over eighty and thus ineligible (by reason of rules introduced in 1970) to participate in papal elections or be members of Curial departments.

at various points in this century. It is clear that until the reforms introduced by John XXIII in the early 1960s, Italians constituted nearly half the membership of the College of Cardinals; they were always four or five times the size of the next largest national group. A precise breakdown of the national origins of the Curia over the centuries is more difficult to come by, but historians investigating the Curia have had no doubts about its domination by Italians (see, in particular, Hay 1977, 41–8).

Though there is no great novelty in the suggestion that the administration of the Universal Catholic Church has been dominated by Italians, only a very few commentators have given any thought to what influence Italian Catholicism, the Catholicism of the men administering the Church, might have had upon the shape and texture of Catholicism generally. The neglect of this issue is in my view one of the most important lacunae in the study of folk Catholicism.

Perhaps the most well-known of the commentators who did address this issue was John Henry Newman (1801–90). At several points in his writing, Newman makes it clear that his celebrated conversion from Anglicanism to Roman Catholicism was made easier by the recognition that much of what the general public considered Catholicism to be really only Italian Catholicism. In his works written before his conversion, Newman consistently denounced popular Catholic devotions like those centred on the Virgin Mary and the saints as among the most blatant of the Catholic Church's deviations from early Christian practice (see Newman 1836, III–30; 1841, 305–9). But even then he argued that these devotions were not an essential part of the basic traditions of the Roman Church. Rather they were suspect practices that had emerged spontaneously in certain parts of the Catholic world and had subsequently been magnified by Church leaders. Newman at first did not explain why the leaders of the Roman Church would magnify such practices, but eventually he came to a conclusion similar to the one reached here: they did it because they were Italian.

In his *Apologia Pro Vita Sua* (1864, 176–8), Newman's great autobiographical account of his gradual conversion, he tells us that Catholic "Mariolatry," the emphasis that Catholics place upon Mary and Marian devotions, had always been one of his greatest stumbling blocks. Reading a translation of some writings by St Alphonsus Liguori (1696–1787), a Neapolitan whom Newman knew to be one of the most excessively Mariological authors in the Roman Catholic tradition, he was puzzled by the absence of any passages in which Liguori's excessive Mariolatry seemed evident. On consulting the Catholic publisher of the book, he was pleased to learn that these passages had been deliberately omitted. To Newman, this demonstrated that much of the excessive Mariolatry "as are found in the words of Italian Authors were not acceptable to every part of the Catholic world."

Elsewhere Newman tells us that at the time of his conversion he received all sorts of helpful advice from Catholic leaders anxious to nurture his attachment to the Church. In thinking back on that advice twenty years later Newman (1865, 21) recalls: "only one warning remains on my mind, and it came from Dr. Griffiths ... [who] warned me against books of devotion of the Italian school ... I took him to [be] caution[ing] me against a character and tone of religion, excellent in its place, [but] not suited for England." A recognition of the Italianate influence on Roman Catholicism is also apparent in Newman's many rebuttals to those Protestant critics who charged that Roman Catholics had elevated the Virgin Mary to the status of a minor deity. Newman consistently argued that most of the Marian devotions that seemed excessive to non-Catholics were of Italian or Spanish origin, and could be safely ignored by English Catholics. In speaking again of St Alphonsus Liguori (who was clearly Newman's favourite whipping boy in this regard), Newman (1864, 98–9) argues:

As to his practical directions, St. Alphonso wrote them for Neapolitans, whom he knew, and we do not know ... Whatever these writers [like St. Alphonso] may have said or not said, whatever they may have said harshly, and whatever capable for fair explanation, still they are foreigners; we are not answerable for their particular devotions ... I suppose that we owe it to the national good sense, that English Catholics have been protected from the extravagances which are elsewhere [in the Catholic world] to be found.

This theme was repeated over and over again (see Newman 1864, 89–119).

If there is a flaw in Newman's analysis, it is only that he did not go far enough. By the nineteenth century, the influence of Liguori and other Marian devotees was not limited to Italy and Spain. Newman himself (1865, 21) hints that "works of the Italian school" were becoming popular in England, and in fact during this same period (the mid to late nineteenth century) such works were becoming popular throughout the Catholic world. This could not have been the case except for the fact that the devotions proposed by Italian authors like Liguori were now being promulgated throughout the Universal Church.

Still, Newman did address the relationship between Italian Catholicism and Catholicism generally, and for that he must be given credit, if only because this relationship has been otherwise ignored. Even Herbert Thurston, another Englishman who often turned his critical Anglo-Saxon eye to the study of popular Catholic devotions, failed to address this issue.

I am only adding to Newman's insight by suggesting that excessive Mariolatry is not the only consequence of the Italianization of the Catholic Church. Such Italianization, I am suggesting, has as well ensured that the men administering the Church have been highly receptive to the splintering of devotion to supernatural beings like Mary and Christ.

AN INDEPENDENT TEST

Despite legends that devotions like the Rosary and the Brown Scapular developed during the Middle Ages, the fact is that all the devotions considered in this book (except for the Angelus) first emerged as popular devotions in the second half of the fifteenth century or later. This is not to deny that some devotions with a transnational appeal did exist before say, 1450. They did. Included among these would be devotion to the Holy Name (and the associated use of *jetons*; see chapter 1), the *Agnus Dei*, the Angelus, and a few others. But the number of such transnational devotions was not great; certainly it does not compare with the dozens upon dozens of extra-liturgical devotions with a transnational appeal that emerged after 1450.

Under the hypothesis developed here, the simplest way to explain the post-1450 proliferation of transnational devotions would be to assume that during this period the administration of the Church came under Italian control – and to a large extent that is exactly what happened.

Italians have of course influenced the papacy since the earliest days of the Church. But we must remember that the Bishop of Rome was not always accorded the authority over the Church that he now enjoys, especially with regard to the practice of religion outside of Italy. In the centuries before 1054, for instance, the authority structure of the Eastern Church was centred more on Constantinople than Rome, and the split that occurred in that year only formalized an existing separation.

Just as important, other national groups have often had an influence over the papacy that rivalled the Italian influence. The most obvious indicator is the number of times the Pope was not an Italian during the Middle Ages.

Thus of forty-nine popes who reigned between 1054 (the year of the schism between the Western and Eastern Churches) and 1378 (the beginning of the Great Schism), eighteen popes, or more than one-third of the total, were non-Italian. In particular, the seven popes who reigned between 1305 and 1378 were all French, and the papacy was centred at Avignon, not Rome.

The Great Schism itself was evidence of the relatively strong influence of non-Italian national traditions upon the papacy. In 1378, having just elected Urban VI (a Neapolitan) as pope, the (mainly French) College of Cardinals decided to nullify its decision and elected a new pope. This new pope was a Frenchman who took the name Clement VIII and who took up residence at Avignon. At Rome, Urban VI was succeeded by Boniface IX and Innocent VII, while at Avignon Clement VIII was succeeded by Benedict XIII. In 1409 the Council of Pisa, attended by supporters of both existing popes, tried to resolve the split by deposing both existing popes and electing a new one, who took the name Alexander VI. Alexander died shortly thereafter and was succeeded by John XXIII. Since neither the pope at Rome nor the pope at Avignon would step down, the only effect of Pisa was that there were now three papacies.

In retrospect Catholic historians usually identify the three Avignonese popes and the two Pisan popes as "antipopes" (see for example McGuire 1967, 576). Nevertheless, in the eyes of much of the Catholic world during the early part of the Schism, the Avignon papacy, not the Roman papacy, was the legitimate one. Support for the Avignon papacy was especially strong in France, Naples, and Scotland (Holmes and Bickers 1983, 109). Most historians also seem to agree that in the period after 1410 the Pisan pope John XXIII had more support across Europe than either of his rivals.[11]

The end of the Great Schism was made possible only as a result of compromises made by all the national traditions within the Church and by a willingness of each faction to give the others a role in administering the Church. In 1414, John XXIII, under pressure from King Sigismund of Germany, convened the Council of Constance. One of the first decisions of the Council was to organize all the delegates into national groups. Initially, this resulted in English, French, Italian, and German groups; a Spanish group was added later. Each national group met separately, and each collectively cast a single vote in the deliberations of the council as a whole. The net effect was to weaken the influence of the very large Italian delegation in comparison with the smaller delegations from other areas.

After the Council had deposed all three existing popes, it was agreed that a new pope would be elected by a two-thirds majority of an assembly composed of (1) the twenty-three members of the College of Cardinals who were at Constance *and* (2) six delegates from each of the five national divisions. This fairly international conclave elected Cardinal Colonna, a Roman, who took the name Martin V. He was quickly recognized as the one legitimate pope in almost all parts of Europe, and the Great Schism was over.

To maintain the spirit of compromise and internal co-operation that had

TABLE 12

Italianization of College of Cardinals following Council of Constance (1414–18)

Date of Papal Conclave	Total Number of Cardinals Voting	Number (Percentage) of Italians
1431	12	6 (50)
1447	18	11 (61)
1455	15	8 (53)
1458	18	9 (50)
1464	19	11 (58)
1471	19	14 (74)
1484	26	22 (85)
1492	23	21 (91)
1503	36	22 (61)
1513	25	19 (76)
1522	39	36 (92)
1523	36	32 (89)
1534	34	23 (67)
1550	49	31 (63)
1555	39	32 (82)
1555	45	35 (78)
1559	42	33 (78)
1566	49	46 (94)
1572	52	46 (88)
1585	41	36 (88)
1590	53	47 (89)

Sources: Hay (1977, 38) for conclaves held in period 1431–64; Hallman (1985, 4) for all later conclaves.

ended the Schism, the Council of Constance had explicitly called for an internationalization of the College of Cardinals (and thus by implication an internationalization of the papacy, given that the Cardinals elected the pope). The delegates at Constance also suggested that the different national traditions should be represented proportionally within the Curia. Nevertheless, the hundred years following Constance saw one national tradition – the Italian – come to dominate the administration of the Universal Church.

Of the fourteen popes who reigned between 1417 and 1523, only three (Callistus III, Alexander VI, and Adrian VI) were non-Italians. Of the forty-five popes who reigned between 1523 and 1978, *all* were Italian. Italians also came to dominate the College of Cardinals. This is evident in Table 12, which shows the proportion of Cardinals who were Italian in each of the twenty-one papal conclaves following the Council of Constance:

During the fifteenth century, the Roman Curia also fell to the Italians. True, in the years immediately following Constance, the merger of the Curias from Avignon and Rome did produce some internationalization. But scholars who have studied the development of the Curia during the fifteenth century (Hay 1977, 41–8; Thomson 1980, 95–113) estimate that by the middle of that century Italians predominated in the Curia, and that the few non-Italians who remained were in positions of little importance. The domination of the Curia by Italians is reflected in the fact that towards the end of the fifteenth century Italian replaced French and Latin as the language used by Curial members to communicate among themselves (Hay 1977, 42).

One of the capstones to the Italianization process occurred at the Council of Trent (1543–63), that very influential council whose pronouncements defined the shape of the Counter-Reformation. Only a century and a half earlier, the delegates to the Council of Constance had been organized into national groups, each of which had only one vote. But at Trent the delegates voted as individuals, and the Italians were the largest single national group among the delegates (see Jedin 1960, 154–8; 1965, 36–40). Although the Italians at Trent were by no means united on every issue, their numerical superiority ensured at the very least that reforms at variance with the ethos of Italian Catholicism would almost certainly not be passed by the Council.

Some time ago, Hay (1977, 46) noted that the effects of the Italianization of the Curia upon the practice of Catholicism in Italy had not been well studied by historians. His remark remains valid, but it is far too limited: scholars have not been much interested in the effects of the Italianization of the Curia (and other administrative agencies of the Church) upon the practice of Catholicism *generally*, either inside or outside Italy. What I am arguing here is that one effect was that the administrators of the Universal Church became more and more receptive to the splintering of devotion to important supernatural beings like Christ and Mary.

I grant that most of the Italians who came to control the papacy, the College of Cardinals, and the Curia were not from the poorest strata of society. I am therefore not arguing that they would have directly experienced the scarcity and the corresponding envy that gives rise to the splintering characteristic of Italian Catholicism. But such men, being Italians, would have been raised in a society in which the splintering of religious devotion was preferred by the vast majority of ordinary lay Catholics. These men would therefore have been relatively sympathetic to the splintering of religious devotion, and to the emergence of new devotions – in Italy or anywhere else – that resulted from such splintering.

WHY MARY?

So far, the main concern in this chapter has been with explaining why

Catholics in general, and Italian Catholics in particular, are more likely to splinter their devotion to supernatural beings. But devotion to some supernatural beings is more likely to be splintered than the devotion to other beings, and so far this issue has not been addressed. It seems clear, for instance, that devotion to the Virgin Mary has been more excessively splintered than devotion to Christ or anyone else. Evidence of this can be found in Beringer's (1925b) list of Catholic devotions associated with indulgences.

If we count as a separate and distinct instance of splintering any devotion that (1) honours a supernatural being under a distinct title or in connection with a distinct object and (2) that is promulgated by one or more archconfraternities, we find that Beringer lists only nine such devotions associated with Christ but eighteen associated with the Virgin Mary. Furthermore no other supernatural being (for example, the Holy Spirit or any of the saints) is associated with more than two such devotions. Why has devotion to the Virgin Mary been splintered the most?

Under the argument developed in this chapter, the greater splintering of religious devotion in Catholicism derives – ultimately – from the infantile memory of the splintering that occurred during the paranoid-schizoid position. But the object that was most excessively splintered during this period was the mother's breast. It seems likely then that when the memories of this period are activated in later life, it will be easier to splinter maternal images than others sorts of images. Given this, the fact that devotion to the Virgin Mary has been splintered so excessively can be attributed to the fact that Mary has always been regarded as a prototypical mother figure in the Catholic tradition.

SUMMARY OF THE ARGUMENT SO FAR

Because this chapter has ranged widely over a number of subjects, a short summary of the overall argument will be useful:

1 A most important (but little studied) difference between Catholicism and Protestantism is the Catholic tendency to splinter devotion to particular supernatural beings, mainly Christ and Mary, into a range of separate devotions, each logically independent of the other and each satisfying in itself.

2 There seems a structural similarity between this splintering of religious devotion in Catholicism and the splintering that takes place during what Klein calls the paranoid-schizoid position.

3 The splintering of religious devotion seems especially evident in Italian Catholicism. This was explained, within the logic of Kleinian theory, by suggesting that the conditions of life in Italian communities have histori-

cally worked to activate infantile memories of the intense envy associated with the paranoid-schizoid position, which in turn activated memories of the excessive splintering that is characteristic of this period.

4 The willingness of the Catholic Church to promulgate practices that reflect the splintering of religious devotion to Mary or Christ derives from the fact that the administration of the Church has long been dominated by men raised in a society, Italy, in which such splintering was both excessive and legitimate.

5 This argument allows us to understand the increase in transnational devotions that began in the late fifteenth and early sixteenth centuries (since this was a period in which Italian domination of the Church's administrative structures increased substantially) and why devotion to Mary has been more excessively splintered than devotion to any other supernatural being.

This argument, first of all, provides an explanation for what we set out to explain, namely, the greater emphasis upon the splintering of religious devotion in Catholicism as compared to Protestantism. But it also leads to a perspective on Church history that is somewhat a variance with the views held by a great many Church historians, and I would like to bring this chapter to a close by considering that perspective.

THE CENTURY PRECEDING THE COUNTER-REFORMATION

While Church historians have not been much interested in uncovering the appeal of specific Catholic devotions, they have been more than willing to offer global explanations for the appeal of all the extra-liturgical devotions that have emerged within the Catholic tradition over the past few centuries. Simply put, most commentators have seen these devotions as a response of some sort to the Counter-Reformation. Some, for example, suggest that when the Council of Trent (1543–63) purged the Church of the excesses that had been criticized so effectively by Protestant reformers, the result was a new, sparser liturgy that held little appeal for ordinary Catholics. In this view the new extra-liturgical devotions that emerged after Trent are seen as an attempt to fill the emotional void created by the unappealing Tridentine reforms. Muller (1981, 541) summarizes his version of this argument by suggesting that "given the great discrepancy between the official church service and a religiosity that people were able to comprehend, it is not surprising that they intensely cultivated extra-liturgical forms."

Other commentators have argued that these new devotions, rather than being a reaction against the Counter-Reformation, were instead an integral part of it. Jedin (1980, 564), for example, believes that the popular devotions that emerged after Trent "stressed new anti-Reformation ideas and aimed to revive a Catholic consciousness of faith and arouse enthusiasm for it." But perhaps the most well-known argument of this sort, and certainly the most controversial, was put forward by Jean Delumeau (1971).

Delumeau believes that before the Reformation, Christianity had had little if any influence outside the cities of Europe. The history of the Counter-Reformation, he suggests, is really a history of Catholic missionaries who, their commitment to Catholicism kindled to a blaze by the Tridentine reforms, went out into the countryside to convert the pseudo-pagans. In their zeal, however, these missionaries were forced to "folklorize" their Christianity, that is, to adapt their Catholicism to the type of thought prevailing among the illiterate masses of Europe. Since such "folkloric" thought emphasized the concrete and the magical, those elements were allowed to creep into popular Catholic devotions. Thus, so Delumeau's argument goes, because odd numbers usually have special properties in magical thought, the Church came to emphasize the pre-eminence of such numbers in its own theology, and the result was an emphasis upon "three theological virtues, three members of the Trinity, seven gifts of the Spirit, seven capital sins, and so on" (Delumeau 1971, 167). In Delumeau's reconstruction, this folklorization of Christianity produces the superficial similarities between folk Catholicism and pagan practice that are so often the basis for the facile claim that many Catholic practices are "survivals" of earlier pagan practices.

Delumeau's specific suggestion that Christianity had made no headway in the European countryside before Trent is still controversial (see for instance Fenlon 1982; O'Malley 1982; O'Neil 1986, 222-3), and so it would be wise to reserve judgment on that particular issue until more evidence becomes available.

On the other hand, in focusing upon the process whereby the "thought" of the average person in the rural areas of Catholic Europe gave rise to new forms of Catholic devotion, Delumeau is advocating an approach to popular religion that bears a strong resemblance to the approach taken in this book. After all, the master hypothesis that had guided the analysis in earlier chapters is that the key to understanding the appeal of popular Catholic devotions is to see them as gratifications of an unconscious desire. In trying to discover the nature of the desire being gratified, we have inevitably been led – like Delumeau – to concentrate upon those aspects of Catholic devotions that are most visible and most concrete in the minds of ordinary Catholics, rather than on theology or abstract doctrine.

Nevertheless, despite the appeal of the general approach taken by Delumeau, two objections can be made against his specific argument, and in fact against any argument that the Counter-Reformation was responsible for the emergence of the new extra-liturgical devotions with a transnational appeal. First, the timing is all wrong: at least some of these new devotions emerged *before* Trent. The Stations of the Cross, remember, was widely popular in Germany and the Low Countries by 1500. Furthermore, the Tridentine Reforms spread slowly. Thus it is difficult to see the Brown Scapular and the Forty Hours, both of which were widespread by the end of the sixteenth and the beginning of the seventeenth centuries, as a reaction to those reforms. But it is the case of the Rosary that most clearly indicates the historical distortion introduced by the scholarly insistence that Trent was critical in the emergence of these transnational devotions.

First, a number of scholars indeed believe that the Rosary is one of most important of the new transnational devotions to have become popular after Trent. For instance, towards the end of her otherwise excellent account of Roman Catholicism in nineteenth century America, Taves (1986, 89–111) proposes her own version of the new-devotions-as-a-response-to-Trent argument. According to Taves, the post-Tridentine church promoted new transnational (what she calls "general") devotions "in order to bind the laity more closely to the institutional church, both to ensure the church's survival in this world and to ensure the orthodoxy of the laity and thus their survival in the world to come." Taves (1986, 90) very explicitly lists the Rosary among the devotions she is discussing here. Similarly, in discussing altars dedicated to the Rosary in various churches in the dioceses of Vence and Grasse (in eastern Provence) during the eighteenth century, Froeschlé-Chopard (1982, 160–4) also calls the Rosary one of the most important of the new devotions promulgated by the Council of Trent. Yet, the discussions by Taves and Froeschlé-Chopard notwithstanding, there is abundant evidence, already reviewed in chapters 1 and 7, that the Rosary emerged as a popular devotion in the German-speaking states in the late 1400s and was widely popular throughout Europe by the early 1500s. It can thus hardly be called a "post-Tridentine" phenomenon.

None of this is to deny that the Counter-Reformation might have increased the popularity of existing transnational devotions (like the Rosary) or given rise to new ones. My point is only that the emergence of transnational devotions in the Catholic world seems to have begun in the late 1400s and to have been well underway in the early 1500s, before the Counter-Reformation.

But another objection can be raised as well against any argument that sees the new devotions as a response to the Counter-Reformation: such arguments do not usually explain why these devotions emerged in Catholicism but not Protestantism. Delumeau, for instance, would have us believe that in their zeal to Christianize Europe, Catholic missionaries in Europe were led to condone devotions that were at variance with the strict spirit of the Tridentine reforms. But he also argues that Protestant leaders of the same period were also engaged in an attempt to Christianize the countryside. If the proliferation of Catholic devotions during this period was simply a pragmatic adaptation to the "concrete and magical thought" prevailing in Europe (and that is what Delumeau is arguing), we would expect to find a proliferation of similar devotions in Protestant regions – yet we do not. Similarly, if the new devotions were a response to the sparseness of the Tridentine liturgy, why didn't such devotions appear among Protestants? After all, it would be difficult to argue that the Tridentine liturgy was any sparser than the liturgies used by the various Protestant confessions.

By contrast, the argument in this chapter is that the administrators of the Universal Church were so willing to promulgate devotions that reflected the splintering of religious devotion because these men were from a society – Italy – where the conditions of life ensured that such splintering would be widespread. This hypothesis explain both why the proliferation of the new extra-liturgical devotions began in the late 1400s (it was during this period that the Italianization of the papacy, the College of Cardinals, and the Curia increased dramatically) and why Protestant denominations (not dominated by men from countries where the conditions of life fostered a splintering of religious devotion) did not develop similar devotions.

This is not to say that the character of popular Catholicism over the past few centuries would have been totally different if the administration of the Church had been dominated by national traditions other than the Italian. On the contrary, the very same conditions that result in chronic envy in Italy have also prevailed in other parts of the Mediterranean world. Spain is the obvious example here, and studies of local religion in Spain (Christian 1972; 1981a; 1981b) show that it is also characterized by the excessive splintering of devotion to Mary and Christ. This suggests that if the Spanish had dominated the administration of the Universal Church, Catholicism would still probably have come to be characterized by as wide variety of extra-liturgical devotions.

But the conditions that produce chronic envy seem less in evidence in northern Europe. This means that a Catholic Church dominated, say, by the English or the Germans would very likely have produced a Catholicism in which such devotions were not as common. The fact that the administration of virtually all Protestant groups *has* been dominated by northern Europeans means that they have been dominated by men from societies where the conditions of life have not produced a strong predilection for the splintering of religious devotion. It is this, along with doctrinal differences regarding the intercessory role of Mary and the saints, which has inhibited the growth and maintenance of extra-liturgical devotions in the Protestant tradition.

Conclusion

When the editors of the original *Catholic Encyclopedia* needed someone to write on popular devotions, they not-unexpectedly turned to Herbert Thurston. Athough the brief article that Thurston submitted (see Thurston 1913f) was informative, Thurston was unable to recommend to his readers a general reference work that dealt with popular Catholic devotions. "There seems," he said in the bibliographical note at the end of the article, "to be no authoritative general work on [these] devotions." The best he could do was to refer readers to some of his own earlier articles in *The Month* and to a few works – like earlier editions of Beringer (1925a; 1925b) – that discussed the indulgences associated with different devotions. Not much has changed.

What Thurston called "popular devotions" were in all cases Catholic devotions with a transnational appeal. In the introduction to this book, I pointed out that these devotions have been ignored by psychoanalysts; in fact, they have also been ignored by almost all scholars interested in the study of religion. True, some scholars have occasionally described the practice of some particular devotion, like the Forty Hours or the Rosary, in some particular historical and social setting, and many of these studies have been cited in this book. But there have been no attempts to develop a systematic overview of these transnational devotions and no attempts to determine their general psychological appeal in any systematic way. Over the course of his own career, even Thurston seems to have lost interest in the subject.

Crehan (1953, 46), Thurston's biographer, notes that there is a fairly obvious difference between Thurston's early articles, written before the First World War, and those written later. Whereas his early articles emphasized the popular devotions that had always been widely practised throughout the Catholic world, his later articles were more and more concerned with mysticism and spiritualism, and with related phenomena (like levitation, inedia, telekinesis, and so on). These later articles are the ones for which Thurston is today best known. His *Physical Phenomena of Mysticism* (1952), a posthumous collection of his essays on mystical phenomena, is still widely cited in books on the occult, and his *Surprising Mystics* (1955), a collection of his essays on individual mystics, seems to be available in most university libraries. Yet no one has yet thought to publish his early essays on popular Catholic devotions in book form, and books like his *Stations of the Cross* (1906) are relatively difficult to find except in a few theological libraries.

Even so, nothing much has come along to replace Thurston's early works, and so they continue to be cited. Most of the (usually short) articles on various Catholic devotions in *The New Catholic Encyclopedia* (1967), for instance, still refer readers to Thurston, as do the essays on similar subjects in recent issues of the *Dictionnaire de Spiritualité*. Even modern authors who challenge Thurston on minor matters are still willing to accept his judgment on the larger issues. Ousterhout (1981, 32m), for example, rejects Thurston's suggestion that the "replica Jerusalem" at Bologna was erected in the fifth century (Ousterhout prefers a twelfth century date), but he still accepts the main outlines of Thurston's general argument relating the Stations of the Cross (the European devotion) to the Way of the Cross (the pilgrimage site) in Jerusalem. The continuing use of Thurston's work as a basic source in the study of popular Catholic devotions is evidence of how little research has been done on this subject over the last half century.

Given that there has been an explosion of scholarly interest in "local religion" over the past few years, one might expect that interest in popular Catholic devotions would increase. But it has not. Most studies of local religion are concerned with the interrelationship between the religion practised in a region and the unique features of the social and cultural milieu of the region. Such a concern, by its very nature, leads researchers away from a detailed consideration of those religious devotions that *transcend* cultural boundaries. Some mention of these transnational devotions is often made in discussions of local religion, of course, but such remarks are usually unspecific and vague. Delumeau (1971, 148–51) argues that one of the best measures of "religious vitality" in the French diocese of La Rochelle during the seventeenth century can be had by plotting the geographical distribution of the Rosary confraternities that sprang up on the diocese. Such an approach makes absolutely no sense except on the presupposition that the Rosary was an important religious devotion in the area. Yet Delumeau does not discuss the practice of the Rosary devotion in any detail, or speculate on why it, rather than some other devotion, should have become so popular in this region. Someone reading Delumeau's book in the distant future would in fact have no basis whatsoever for knowing what the Rosary was.

The study of popular Catholic devotions seems to have fallen through the cracks of the intellectual edifice that modern scholars have erected in order to study religion. Those interested in local religion pay little attention to such devotions because such devotions, being transnational, seem unrelated to the unique features of the local situation. Commentators who address differences between Catholicism and Protestantism ignore such devotions because they seem incidental to those "important" doctrinal and liturgical concerns – like those associated with the Eucharist, with "immanence," or the structure of the Church – that have always dominated the discussion of these broad differences.

Yet the undeniable fact remains: these devotions have been practised by large numbers of Catholics for hundreds of years. In some places and in some periods of history it seems likely that such devotions were more important to ordinary Catholics than were the practices associated with the official liturgy. This suggests that these devotions have a broad psychological appeal. To uncover the nature of that appeal has been the goal of this book. I have tried to use a fairly consistent and parsimonious set of psychological principles. The explanations that have resulted, it seems to me, do account for most of the idiosyncracies of a broad range of those most popular Catholic devotions.

The specific explanations aside, I hope that one effect of this book will be to suggest to scholars interested in the study of popular religion that psychoanalysis is perhaps more relevant to their concerns that they previously thought. As I stated in the introduction, I am making no grand claims about the need to make psychoanalysis the dominant theoretical perspective in the study of religion. Religious beliefs, like all beliefs, are shaped by a variety of forces, some social and cultural, some political, some that originate in the local environment, some that originate outside. Many, perhaps most, of these forces, have little or nothing to do with the things discussed by Sigmund Freud or Melanie Klein. My point is only that some of them do. Some aspects of religious belief, in other words, *are* shaped by the psychological processes discussed by psychoanalysts. In particular, I have argued that the fairly extreme and relatively unusual nature of so many popular Catholic devotions makes it likely that psychoanalysts can be particularly useful in uncovering the psychological processes that have given shape to these devotions and that have made them so popular over the centuries.

And what of the future? Does anything in the arguments advanced here allow us to make predictions about the likely course that "popular Catholicism" will take? The key variable would seem to be the attitude of the Church hierarchy. I have already argued that though traditional Catholic devotions have some universal appeal, this is never sufficiently strong to ensure the popularity of these devotions unless they are actively promulgated by the Church, and the post-Vatican II Church does not seem much inclined to do that. Furthermore, the Italianization of the Church hierarchy, itself so important in fostering Church approval of these devotions, seems on the wane (though perhaps not as much on the wane as most people think). In any case it also appears that the social and economic conditions that have historically given rise to a psychological predilection among Italians for the splintering of religious devotions (see chapter 9) are also on the decline. This means that even if Italians continue to exert a disproportionate influence on the texture of Catholicism generally, the nature of that influence will not necessarily be what it was before.

On the other hand, one thing you develop when studying the history of popular devotions in the Roman Catholic Church is a sense of time and historical perspective. The Second Vatican Council, which seems to have wrought so many changes in the practice of Catholicism, is less than two generations in the past. In the long history of the Church, two generations is not much. Many of the complaints now being voiced by a number of Catholics about the sparseness of the post-Vatican ii liturgy are similar to the complaints voiced four centuries ago about the sparseness of the Tridentine liturgy. Yet the austere tone of the Tridentine degrees did not prevent the emergence of popular devotions like the Brown Scapular and the Sacred Heart; there is no particular reason why the austere pronouncements of Vatican ii will necessarily impede a revival of interest in the old devotions or the emergence of new ones.

The Angelus Prayer

The Angel of the Lord declared unto Mary. And she conceived of the Holy Ghost.
  Hail Mary, full of grace ...
Behold the handmaid of the Lord. Be it done unto me according to Thy Word. Hail
  Mary, full of grace ...
And the word was made flesh. And dwelt among us. Hail Mary, full of grace ...
Pray for us, O holy Mother of God, that we may be worthy of the promises of Christ.
(Let us pray). Pour forth, we beseech Thee, O Lord, They grace into our hearts; that,
  as we have known the Incarnation of Christ Thy Son by the message of the Angel,
  so by his Passion and Cross we may be brought to the Glory of the Resurrection.
  Through Christ our Lord. Amen.

Sources: Elwell *et al.* (1956, 56); Beringer (1925a, 221–2)

The Liquefaction of the Blood Relics

Although there is no definitive answer to the question of why the blood relics of Naples liquefy, it can be established that these liquefactions are roughly correlated with a number of variables. These rough correlations, I think, can at least provide us with some clues as to the identity of the different processes that produce the real or apparent liquefaction of these relics.

TRICKERY

It would be naive to overlook the possibility that the liquefaction of these relics is the result of deliberate deception. The suggestion, often made, that trickery is unlikely since the clerics in charge of these relics have been men honestly committed to serving God is unconvincing. Throughout the history of the Church there have always been men and women who were quite sincere in their desire to serve God and yet who for that very reason felt no compunction about, say, exaggerating the reports of a miracle in order to bring people closer to God.

The best reason for rejecting the trickery hypothesis, at least as an explanation for the vast majority of liquefactions, was given by Thurston (1909a, 803–4): over the centuries too many people have been involved in administering these liquefactions. Even apart from the clerics who have administered the St Januarius cult at the Tesoro for the past six hundred years, for instance, in the last century or so the actual ceremonies have been administered by local civic officials as well. Add to this the clerics who have administered the ceremonies surrounding the blood relics at other locations, and the number is easily in the thousands. If there was a trick to the liquefaction of a blood relic, it seems likely that one of these people would have revealed it.

Moreover, there are instances in which a single church maintains several liquefying blood relics, some of which stop liquefying while others of which continue to liquefy. A good example involves two of the blood relics associated with John the Baptist. Both relics were liquefying in the sixteenth century, and both ended up at San Gregorio Armeno. The first came to San Gregorio Armeno from San Arcangelo at Baiano in

1577, and the second came to San Gregoria Armeno from Santa Maria di Donnaromita in 1828. Initially both relics continued to liquefy on feasts associated with John the Baptist. By the early twentieth century, however, only the relic originally from San Arcangelo was liquefying regularly. This is not what you would expect if the custodians at San Gregorio Armeno were using trickery to produce liquefaction.

Nevertheless, though trickery seems unlikely as an explanation for *most* instances of liquefaction, it seems highly unlikely that a single relic could continue to liquefy and solidify over and over again for a period of centuries without at least occasionally being "renewed" in some way, and so I assume that particular individuals at particular points in time have done just that.

TEMPERATURE

In everyday experience, the passing of a substance from a solid to a liquid state is most often due to an increase in temperature. Presumably for that reason the single hypothesis about these relics that has been investigated most often is that they liquefy as a result of being heated up, either by the ambient temperature or by the candles so often placed behind the relic to enable the faithful to see if it has liquefied. It now seems clear that there is no obvious correlation between the temperature of the relic (established by means of a thermometer placed near or on the relic) and the time it takes the relic to liquefy after being exposed on the altar. This sort of study has been done several times (at least in connection with the Januarius relic at the Tesoro), and the relevant data have often been published by those arguing for a supernatural origin of this phenomenon (see, for instance, Kehoe 1871, 49–55; Grant 1929, 49–52). Thurston (1930, 122) concedes that heat alone could not account for the liquefaction.

On the other hand, the evidence does suggest that relatively high *seasonal* temperatures are at least a predisposing factor in these liquefactions. Remember that in May and September the St Januarius relic at the Tesoro almost always liquefies, whereas it does not at the ceremony in December, a much cooler month (see Tables 4 and 5). It also seems too coincidental that so many of these relics liquefy on feast days that "just happen" to fall in or near the month of August, which is the hottest month of the year in Naples. Thus, there have been three blood relics that liquefied on the feast of St Pantaleone, which is 27 July; two relics that liquefied on the feast of St Lawrence, 10 August, and one relic that liquefied on the feast of St Patricia, 25 August (see Table 6).

The case of the three relics associated with St John the Baptist is particularly interesting. This saint's feast day is in fact 24 June, but his various blood relics liquefied most often on 29 August. I have already attributed this in part to the fact that a liquefaction on the feast of the Baptist's Decollation (decapitation) enhances the associated castration imagery, but this hardly rules out the possibility that the higher temperatures in August as compared to June might also be a precipitating factor. Similar evidence of a clear "preference" for blood relics to liquefy in the hotter months is evident in the case of the relics associated with St Stephen. This saint's feast day is 26 December, and his relics sometimes liquefied on that day. Far more often, however, the relics associated with St Stephen liquefied on 3 August, the feast of the Invention of St Stephen, which commemorated the discovery of his relics in AD 415. (The Catholic Church ceased celebrating the Invention of Stephen in 1955.)

The most notable exception to the liquefies-in-August pattern is of course the Tesoro relic associated with St Januarius. But here it is worth quoting from the earliest documentary account of the St Januarius miracle: "On the 17th of August this year [1389] there took place a great procession on the occasion of the miracle which our Saviour Jesus Christ showed with the blood of St Januarius. This blood which is kept in a phial, became liquid just as it had that day flowed from the body of the blessed martyr" (quoted and translated by Thurston 1909, 804). The reference to a *single* vial in itself raises some interesting questions, since there are now two vials in the reliquary, one of which is empty. If the vial in this early account is a reference to the smaller vial that is now empty, it would suggest that the relic has been "renewed" at least once by the addition of the vial that is now full. On the other hand, if the reference is to the vial that is now full, what accounts for the presence of the empty vial?

But perhaps the most important element in this earliest account of the miracle is the statement that the liquefaction took place on 17 August. In the modern era, the nearest liquefaction (in time) of this relic takes place on 20 September, the saint's feast day. One defender of the Januarius cult (Petito 1983, 164) suggests the 1389 miracle occurred in August of that year because at that point certain ecclesiastical quarrels connected with the Western Schism (and thus the conflict between the Roman and Avignon papacies) had reached a peak in Naples and the miracle was God's way of "calling for order" among the warring parties. This, however, seems to be a later rationalization; certainly there is nothing in original account of the miracle which links it to the Great Schism.

Part of the discrepancy between these two dates 17 August and 20 September can be accounted for by the calendar reforms introduced by Gregory XIII in 1583. But these reforms had the effect of adding ten days to the calendar, not thirty-four. In fact, if we add ten days to 17 August, we get 27 August, which "just happens" to be close to the two days (25 August and 29 August) on which the relics of St Patricia and St John the Baptist started to liquefy in later centuries. In other words, there appears to be some evidence that the first of the St Januarius blood relics was also a blood relic that liquefied in August.

COASTAL LOCATION

Most of the liquefying blood relics listed in Table 6 are located in cities or towns (Naples, Pozzuoli, Amalfi, Ravello) on or very near the coast. This is not to say that liquefying blood relics never exist at inland locations. The liquefaction of a blood relic, for instance, is recorded as having occurred at Avellino, which is approximately thirty-five kilometres (twenty-two miles) inland. But on average there are fewer liquefying relics at inland locations, and the relics at inland locations that do liquefy are less likely to continue liquefying for long periods of time. This suggests that liquefaction might somehow be facilitated by a coastal climate.

WEIGHT GAIN

The fact that liquefactions in the Naples area seem most likely to occur 17 August, which is both the hottest month of the year in Naples and a month during which the relative humidity averages 62 per cent (according to records kept since the beginning of this century), plus the association of these liquefactions with coastal locations, would seem to suggest that at least some of the "liquid" involved in the liquefaction process is drawn from the air. If something like this were happening, of course, the relic would increase in weight and at least on some occasions this has indeed happened.

One study conducted in the early part of this century (and reported in Grant 1929, 53; Mioni 1908, 253-4) compared the weight of the reliquary when the vials was half full with its weight when it was "almost full." The result: the reliquary had gained twenty-seven grams. Grant (1929, 53) notes in connection with this study that "the weight [that is, the twenty-seven grams] thus realized corresponds to a similar volume of blood." No doubt, but it would also come close to being the equivalent of a similar volume of any liquid.

For the relic to draw liquid from the air, it is necessary to postulate that it is not perfectly sealed. In fact, inspections of the reliquary (reported in Thurston 1930, 123) have suggested that the plug at the top of the vial is probably traversed by a great many minute cracks and that there is no particular reason to believe that the outer case of the reliquary is airtight.

THE CEREMONY

Thurston believed that something about the simple act of removing these relics from their vaults and putting them on display facilitated liquefaction. He suggested exposure to light as a possibility; another would be that the liquefaction is aided by the very act of handling the relic, as occurs for instance when it is turned upside down in order to establish that liquefaction has occurred.

Whatever the proximate cause, the best evidence that something connected with the actual ceremony facilitates liquefaction occurred in the late sixteenth century, when the Gregorian calendar reforms were introduced. Since all feast days were in effect displaced ten days, this reform approximates a naturally occurring experiment. In other words, after the reform, did the relics continue to liquefy at those times which in some objective sense were the same times of the years that they had always liquefied, or did they liquefy ten days later, on the occasion of the feast days with which they had historically been associated? Generally, records from the late sixteenth century suggest that these relics liquefied on the feast days of the saints with which they were associated (Thurston 1909a, 804). The simplest way to explain this would be to hypothesize that, indeed, there was something about the actual ceremony on these feast days that exerted a powerful influence on liquefaction.

MISPERCEPTION

The case that presents the strongest argument *against* the hypothesis that handling facilitates liquefaction involves the blood relic of St Pantaleone at Ravello. This relic is contained in a reliquary that sits in a square aperture cut through a wall separating the back of the church at Ravello from a side chapel, called the Chapel of the Blessed Sacrament. Grant's (1929, 21) description makes it clear that access to the reliquary is impossible: "The top, bottom and sides of this aperture are covered with bronze, and upon its bottom, as upon a floor, stands the reliquary. This ... is barred by an iron-gilt railing in front and by a double iron-gilt railing in rear. There is also a sheet of thick glass let permanently into the woodwork in front and another in rear." This relic is usually viewed from a small platform that is directly behind the aperture. Liquefaction of the relic occurs on 26 July, which is the day before the feast of the saint.

The reliquary containing St Pantaleone's blood at Ravello differs in several ways from that containing the blood of St Januarius at Naples. First, the substance in the reliquary is contained directly between two pieces of round, convex glass, rather than in a vial. Second, in Grant's (1929, 29–30) description, there are clearly observable layers in the material contained in this relic, which he identifies (moving from the bottom up) as "soil, dust, blood," a "milky substance," "blood," and a "fatty substance." Finally, the glass on one side of the relic is cracked near one side and there are bits of a red substance on top of these cracks, that is, on the outside of the pane. This crack is supposed to have been made in 1759, at a time when the relic *was* handled during the liquefaction ceremonies. A priest, anxious to establish that liquefaction had occurred, brought a candle too close to the relic and the heat from this candle cracked the glass. The blood in the relic immediately began to seep through (so the story goes), and the frightened priest promised to erect a small silver statue of Pantaleone if the flow stopped. It did. The red blotches on the outside of the crack, then, are supposed to be dried blood.

The fact that the Pantaleone relic seems to liquefy even though it cannot be touched, turned, or agitated is inevitably adduced by defenders of the cult as evidence that liquefaction is not produced by natural processes (see for instance Alfano and Amitrano 1951, 174). On the other hand, the fact that it cannot be touched also means that liquefaction must be "verified" by visual inspection of the blood's appearance alone. This is in contrast to, say, the case of the Januarius relic at the Tesoro or the Patricia relic at San Gregorio Armeno, in both of which cases the "liquid" quality of the blood is demonstrated by turning the reliquary and observing a "flow." In Grant's (1929) account of the Pantaleone relic, liquefaction was established solely on the basis of changes in the translucency and colour of the layer of blood that lay across the middle of the reliquary. From the diagrams drawn by Grant (1929, 29–30) it is evident that this layer (of blood) was exceedingly narrow: that is, it is far narrower than the other layers containing the "fatty substance" and the "mixture of blood, soil and dust." Here is Grant's (1929, 33) description of the relevant changes in this narrow layer of blood during a liquefaction: "We fell upon our knees [to pray] and then rising to our feet, we instantly recognized that the liquefaction had already begun. The left half of the ribbon of blood was no longer the perfectly opaque strip of dark reddish brown matter it was a few months previously; it had suddenly become a perfectly lucent, transparent, a bright brilliant red, the redness of a ruby." Taken at face value, such an account seems impressive. But other remarks in Grant's account of his experiences indicate that he was not always quite certain of just what he was seeing.

For instance, in commenting upon the appearance of the "congealed drops of blood" on the outside of the reliquary, he tells us he is certain they were wet, "but the conditions of the artificial light were confusing, and I am not prepared to pronounce definitely as to their color." Problems of lighting aside, remember that Grant (and everyone else) was viewing this relic through two panes of glass (the glass in the reliquary itself and the "thick" pane of glass covering the aperture where the reliquary rests), as well as two layers of metal grating.

On another occasion, Grant was looking at some reddish blotches that appear inside the relic near the top. To Grant they seemed to have changed from their usual brown to red. But just to be certain, he asked the sacristan who was standing nearby to look at them and give his own judgment as to their colour. According to Grant (1929, 35) the following interchange then took place: "'Rosso, Signore, proprio rosso' [red, truly red] was [the sacristan's] reply. 'Truly, really red?' I again asked him. 'Most truly so,' was his answer. There could, in all truth, be no doubt about it; they [the splotches] had changed in color from their original brown." At the very least, this interchange suggests that Grant was letting another observer influence his own opinion as to whether liquefaction had actually occurred. More generally then, it seems plausible to suggest that at least some instances of the liquefaction of the Pantaleone relics (and probably others as well) are believed to occur because everyone else says liquefaction has occurred.

Another point about the Pantaleone relic: in the opinion of the priest in charge of the church at Ravello during Grant's visit, the crack in the relic was large enough that it would be impossible – under normal circumstances – for a container so cracked to "contain blood without leaking" (Grant 1929, 36). That the container did contain blood during the liquefaction of the relic was therefore for this priest yet another of the several miracles surrounding this relic. From our perspective, however, the fact that the relic is cracked and that blood does not leak out during liquefaction is itself evidence that no liquefaction, at least no substantial liquefaction, had taken place.

In this section I have relied entirely upon Grant's account of the Pantaleone relic because I assume that what Grant saw at Ravello in the 1920s was what others around the same period saw. The relic that *I* saw during a visit to Ravello in 1987, however, seemed somewhat different from the relic described by Grant. Nevertheless, my own experience with that relic (described in appendix c) makes the "misperception" hypothesis even more likely.

Nor is the Pantaleone relic the only one where there is room for perceptual error. I have already mentioned (see chapter 4) that the Januarius relic has often been classed as "full," which means that the substance inside the vial covers the entire inside surface of the vial, making it impossible to tell if the substance is liquid or solid. Given that such ambiguity can occur, there must have been several occasions over the centuries that were just as ambiguous but in which the desire of the participants to see liquefaction led them to see just that.

CONCLUSION

The one thing that most prevents us from knowing with certainty what produces the liquefaction of, say, the St Januarius relic at Naples, is the very fact that it is indeed a relic, and as such is the object of religious veneration. It would be a simple matter to establish if "coastal location" were an essential variable in facilitating liquefaction by removing the relic to, say, Avellino or some other inland city near Naples, and seeing if it still liquefied at the appropriate time. The role of handling in liquefaction could be easily settled by exposing the relic publicly at times of the year other than May, September, and December. And so on. Yet precisely because of the cultic importance of this relic and the others like it, they cannot be treated in such a manner. As Durkheim long ago reminded us, religion is ultimately organized around sacred things, which by definition are things that cannot be used freely, in the manner of the "profane" objects that we encounter in everyday life.

I see no great loss to science in any of this. Though experimental procedures for ferreting out the secret of these liquefactions might satisfy the intellectual curiosity of a few non-believers, I cannot image that it would advance our understanding of physics or chemistry. Nor would it shed any light on the sociology or psychology of religion. In this last regard, the only thing that really matters is that the adherents of these cults *believe* that liquefaction occurs. Given this, the theoretically important task is to discover the appeal of that belief – and that of course is what chapter 4 is all about.

Three Blood Relics Still Liquefying

Apart from the Januarius relic at the Tesoro, I know of only three blood relics that continue to liquefy. Although a few English-language accounts of these relics are available, none published since Grant's (1929) account have been written by anyone who has actually seen them. For this reason it seems worthwhile to record here my own encounter with these relics during a visit to Naples in August 1987.

THE RELIC OF ST PATRICIA

There seems to be a widely prevalent view that Naples is somehow more unsafe than other cities. The result is that while thousands of tourists pass through Naples on the way to Pompeii and Herculaneum, only a relatively small number stop to see the city itself. This is unfortunate. Nothing in my own experience suggests that Naples is any more or less unsafe than other cities of comparable size in Europe or North America, and those who bypass Naples are missing one of the great combinations of geography and civilization to be found anywhere in Europe.

Naples is a city steeped in the Catholic traditions distinctive of southern Italy and a home to countless churches. One of these churches, located in the old section of Naples about midway between the Duomo and the church of Santa Chiara, is the convent church of San Gregorio Armeno. Unlike many of the other churches in Naples, which were heavily damaged during the Second World War and whose interiors are now relatively sparse, the interior of San Gregorio Armeno – though decaying a little – is a baroque explosion of gilt-covered ceilings and walls. Although the church does not seem to contain individual pieces of art which earn much praise from guidebook authors (thus ensuring that it attracts hardly any of those few tourists who do visit Naples) the effect of the paintings and statues set amongst the gilt-encrusted interior is quite impressive.

But appearances aside, this particular church is important because it contains both the body of St Patricia (*Santa Patrizia*) and a relic of this saint's blood. (For the traditions surrounding this blood relic, see chapter 4.) This particular blood relic liquefies on the saint's feast day, 26 August. What is more interesting, perhaps, is that it also liquefies every Tuesday, since Tuesdays in Naples are specially dedicated to St Patricia, and on the St Patricia's feast day, 26 August. My first visit to San Gregorio Armeno took place at nine o'clock on a Tuesday morning, and the reliquary containing the blood relic was set on a small stand to the viewer's left of the altar. Masses were held continuously throughout the morning, and each Mass was attended by about twenty people, including older men and women as well as several families with young children.

At the conclusion of each Mass, a sister from the convent attached to the church brought the reliquary to the officiating priest, who in turn moved to the gap in the communion rail, where he held the reliquary so that its glass front could be kissed by the faithful. Most of those who had attended the Mass did kiss the relic.

No pictures of the reliquary were available, and my request to sketch it was refused. The best I can do is to describe it as consisting of two panes of glass enclosed by a thick silver frame whose shape vaguely resembles a squat heart measuring roughly eight inches by eight inches. The frame seems about four inches thick. Inside the reliquary, and clearly visible through the glass panes, are two vials, both spherical and both of which are supposed to contain some of St Patricia's blood. In overall appearance it is quite unlike the reliquary pictured in Alfano and Amitrano (1951, 190), and so I assume that it is relatively new.

At the conclusion of the first Mass, I asked the sacristan if I could get a closer look at the reliquary. She was more than willing to oblige. I was brought into the sanctuary to the small stand on which the reliquary sat, and one of the sisters held it up for me to inspect. I asked if the relic was truly liquid, and in response the sister slowly tilted the reliquary. The interior surface of the smaller vial to my right was too darkened for me to see what was inside. In the larger vial on the left, however, whose diameter I estimated to be about three inches, there was a darkish-red substance that filled the bottom inch or so. Without question this substance *was* liquid: when the reliquary was tilted, the substance flowed and seemed to have the viscosity, say, of warm maple syrup. I might note that all this is consistent with the eye-witness report by Alfano and Amitrano (1951, 190–1), who also note that only the substance in the larger of the two vials liquefies.

On days other than Tuesday, the reliquary is not kept in the church, and I was not able to secure permission to see it. Therefore, neither I nor the rest of the public has any certain knowledge about whether the substance in the vial flows on these occasions.

The Tuesday following my first visit to San Gregorio Armeno was in fact the feast of St Patricia. This was a special occasion that had been well advertised by posters throughout the neighbourhood, and which involved the continuous celebration of the various Masses from 7:00 AM to 2:00 PM. One of these Masses was concelebrated by several priests, including the Archbishop of Naples. There was an additional Mass at 6:00 PM, which is the one I attended.

The church of San Gregorio Armeno is not large, and it was full, though not crowded, by the time the evening Mass started. By my estimate, there were 250 to 300 people sitting in the pews or standing in the aisles (most of those standing, I should note, stood in front of the side chapel to the right of the altar that contains the body of St Patricia). During this Mass the blood relic was not exposed to public view. Generally, it seemed to me that a conscious attempt was being made to de-emphasize the relic itself. For instance, the priest who celebrated the Mass and gave the sermon was a well-known orator who had been brought in especially for this occasion. Though his sermon was about St Patricia, his theme was that St Patricia is important because she was a "Bride of Christ" in the same way that the Church is the "Bride of Christ." The relic was hardly mentioned. By contrast, the priest who had preached the previous Tuesday had made many references to this relic and to "blood prodigies" generally. Similarly, when the Mass on the feast day was over, the presiding priest conducted a Benediction. Thus what was "exposed" to the public was not the blood relic but rather a monstrance containing the Blessed Sacrament. (The monstrance, incidentally, was a beautiful example of the "sunburst" type discussed in chapter 6). After the Benediction (involving exposure of the monstrance, prayers to the Blessed Sacrament, and the blessing of the congregation with the monstrance), the officiating priests left the altar and the church with the monstrance in hand. Only after they had left the church did another priest appear in front of a side altar with the blood relic and hold it to be kissed. It appears then that when church authorities above the local level take part in the St Patricia cult, the blood relic itself is de-emphasized.

Incidentally, I moved close enough to the relic on the feast day to see that as the priest moved the reliquary around, the substance inside the larger vial did flow, just as it had done the preceding week.

There are some physical resemblances between the Januarius reliquary in the Tesoro and the Patricia reliquary at San Gregorio Armeno that, as far as I know, have never been commented upon. Although the shape of each reliquary is certainly different, both reliquaries contain two vials, in both cases the smaller vial is to the viewer's right and the larger is to viewer's left, and in both cases the phenomenon of liquefaction takes place in the larger vial on the left. There is no point in reading too much into this, but it is at least some evidence of imitation. In other words, it raises the possibility that at some point in the past the cult centring on the blood relic of St Patricia was modelled in some precise way upon the cult centring on the blood relic of St Januarius at the Tesoro.

Finally, reports dating from the sixteenth century onwards make it clear that at that time the convent of San Gregorio Armeno had several other blood relics in its possession for long periods of time. One of the most famous was a blood relic (already mentioned in appendix B) associated with John the Baptist, which liquefied regularly. For instance, a decree passed in 1586 by Council of the Knights of Malta, at the request of the abbess of the convent, invited the Knights who happened to be in Naples on 29 August, the feast of the Decollation of St John the Baptist, to visit the church and witness this relic "which [was] seen by all [on that occasion] ... to glow and boil in its phial like a living ruby" (Thurston 1909a, 805). Alfano and Amitrano (1951, 52–74) say this relic was still liquefying on 29 August early in this century.

I inquired about a John the Baptist relic at San Gregorio Armeno, but none of the sacristans had ever heard of it. Even so, there seems to be a special relationship between this church and John the Baptist. For example, the posters advertising the various events to be celebrated at San Gregorio Armeno in honour of the feast of Santa Patrizia on 25 August also advertised a special Mass in honour of the death of St John the Baptist on 29 August. Though I cannot claim to have made a systematic survey of the churches of Naples (several of which were closed for restoration), I did visit many churches during this period, and San Gregorio Armeno was the only one I came across that was advertising a special celebration for 29 August. It thus strikes me as quite likely that the John the Baptist relic might still have been liquefying at San Gregorio Armeno until relatively recently, even though the memory of this has been lost to those now administering the cult.

That the current administrators of a cult might not be aware of cultic traditions going back only a few decades is not as unlikely as some might think. For example, during this same visit to the Naples area I also went to the inland town of Avellino, because reports dating from the eighteenth century and proceeding into the early twentieth century indicate that during this period the cathedral there possessed a blood relic of St Lawrence that liquefied regularly. The cathedral at Avellino does have a relic of St Lawrence, and it resides in a small cage set into the lower half of a gilded silver half-figure stature of the saint. All this seems very similar to a 1709 report (see Thurston 1927b, 128) that describes the phial containing the liquefying blood relic of St Lawrence as "set like a jewel in the breast of a silver-gilt bust of the saint." Yet when I asked the sacristan what type of relic was contained in the St Lawrence reliquary, he said that though they were certain it was from the body of the saint, they did not know what part of the body was involved. Nor is the St Lawrence relic discussed in the official history of the cathedral published in 1966. In fact, the only reference to the St Lawrence reliquary in that book occurs in a passage listing the twelve different "reliquary-busts," each associated with a different saint (including St Lawrence), that are carried in procession on 10 June (Sarro 1966, 24).

Because the official Church has always been ambivalent about many popular devotions, it is not unlikely that over the centuries, or even decades, the popular beliefs associated with these devotions might be lost, even in the places where they were once important.

THE ST PANTALEONE RELIC AT RAVELLO

Ravello is a small town of great antiquity in the hills just above Amalfi, which is located on the lower edge of the Sorrentine Peninsula just below Naples itself. Ravello can be reached from Amalfi by public bus, though the tour buses that flock to the Amalfi coast routinely include Ravello on their itinerary. The view of the Mediterranean coast from Ravello is one of the most breathtaking and spectacular in all of Italy. To my mind it requires that the dictum "See Naples, then die" be revised to "See Naples and Ravello and then die, unless, of course, you can go back."

The relic of St Pantaleone is contained in the Ravello Cathedral, in a side chapel on the congregration's left. Though Grant (1929, 21) calls this the Chapel of the Blessed Sacrament, it is now called the Chapel of St Pantaleone. The appearance of the chapel is for all practical purposes the same as in Grant's description. The only element not mentioned by Grant (and which may have been added since his time) is some metal grillwork that bars direct entrance to the chapel. The sacristan, however, was quite willing to open the door embedded in this grillwork.

The reliquary containing the relic is set into a niche cut into the wall directly above the tabernacle on the altar. Because of the height of this niche, plus the fact that it is covered with an ornamental grill, the relic is not visible from within the chapel. There is, however, a door on either side of the altar, each leading to a set of five steps that curve up to a platform. Standing on this platform, you can view the reliquary from the back of the niche. I should mention that the existence of this viewing platform behind the rear wall of the chapel is not obvious. There are no signs indicating its presence, and someone who had not read Grant's book before coming to Ravello would be likely to miss it entirely.

Between the viewer (standing on the viewing platform) and the reliquary in the niche are (1) a pane of glass, (2) an ornate metal grating, and (3) a simpler metal grating. The gaps in both sets of grating, however, are large enough that the reliquary can easily be seen, though sometimes getting a clear view of the reliquary requires moving your head around a bit. The sacristan switched on an electric light located in front of the niche (on the altar side). The light makes it even easier to get a clear view of the reliquary, and more important, it also provides a light source that shines directly through the blood contained in the reliquary.

The shape of the reliquary is as Grant described it. The blood is enclosed directly between two glass discs (imagine two glass saucers stuck together on concave sides) about five inches in diameter. The glass discs are held together by a circular metal frame and are set upon a pyramidal base. On top of the frame is a small cylindrical platform on which stands a miniature stature of St Pantaleone. By my estimate, the height of the reliquary, from the tip of the small statue to the bottom of the base, is about twenty inches. The crack in the glass disc visible from the platform side is curved (moving from the lower left to the upper right) and (unlike the crack on the other side, which I did not see) does not extend into the blood. The shape of this crack is exactly as given in Grant's (1929, 29) drawing, which suggests that he and I saw the same reliquary. This is worth mentioning because when we come to a description of the blood contained in the reliquary, Grant and I appear not to have seen the same thing.

Grant reported that the glassed-in portion of the reliquary was half full, and I saw it half full too. What I did not see, however, were the layers described by Grant, consisting, in order, of "soil, dust, blood," "a milky substance," "blood," and "a fatty substance." Alfano and Amitrano (1951, 173) also describe layers of this sort in the relic (though they may simply be repeating Grant's account, which they cite later in another regard). On the other hand, the relic I saw seemed to be half full of blood, period; that is, I saw it half full of a substance that was for the most part entirely dark and reddish-black.

Just above the surface of the blood, apparently clinging to the inside surface of the glass, were what looked like drops of liquid amber. These presumably correspond to what Grant called a "line of dried up bubbles" (though there was one fairly large amber spot that does not appear on Grant's drawing). Although these "bubbles" did undeniably seem like drops of a liquid, I eventually concluded that they might possibly be air bubbles trapped in the structure of the glass itself.

The information obtained by Grant at Ravello suggested that the relic started to liquefy a few days before the Vigil of St Pantaleone's feast (26 July) and that liquefaction was usually complete when the vigil arrived. This is still the case, at least in the sense that complete liquefaction is expected to occur on 26 July. Grant did not say when the liquefaction ended, but both the sacristan and literature supplied at the cathedral say that the liquefaction lasts until 14 September, the Feast of the True Cross.

So now to the important question: *was* the blood liquid? My visit, after all, did fall at the end of August and was thus within the traditional period of liquefaction, 26 July to 14 September. The short answer is yes, it did appear to be liquid. Although most of the blood was dark, there was a narrow layer at the top (about half an inch thick) that, with the light from the electric lamp shining through it, was a bright ruby-red and did look exactly like fresh blood.

Here, however, I must mention that whether I saw this layer of fresh blood depended upon my line of sight. Because of the two grates between the viewer and the reliquary, it is not possible to view the reliquary from all angles. If you have a clear view from one angle, you might easily have to move your head quite a bit in order to obtain a clear view from another angle. From some angles, I caught the light from the lamp just right and the layer did appear ruby red; from other angles the entire amount of the blood seemed equally dark and reddish-black throughout.

The entire effect just described is consistent with the hypothesis that what resides in the reliquary is a continuously liquid, or possibly crystalline, substance that does or does not appear liquid depending upon the viewer's angle of vision with respect to the light coming from the lamp. In other words, at any given time, whether the observer sees liquefaction or non-liquefaction is to a large extent under the observer's control. If observers therefore see liquefaction only during one period of the year (26 July to 14 September), it is probably because this is the period during which they want to see liquefaction.

One final note: there is a permanent memorial to Grant in the St Pantaleone chapel. The memorial consists of a stylized picture of the reliquary done in coloured marble and set in the floor of the chapel directly in front of the altar. The dedication beneath the picture reads "A Divozione di Jean Grant Capitano Inglese 1925." Grant's (1929) book may now be hard to get, but his efforts to spread devotion to the saint's relic have not been forgotten by the people of Ravello.

THE STONE AT POZZUOLI

Pozzuoli is a town on the coast just north of Naples and is the site of a church built in the sixteenth century and now called San Gennaro di Solfatura. Pozzuoli has always been identified as the place where St Januarius was beheaded in AD 305, and this church is supposed to be near the site of that beheading. More important, the church contains what is supposed to be the stone block on which that beheading took place.

The stone is kept in a side chapel just to the right as you enter San Gennaro di Solfatura. Two niches are cut into the rear wall of the side chapel, one on either side of the altar. The niche on the right contains a half-bust of St Januarius executed in marble; the niche to the left contains the stone.

The stone's dimensions (a glass pane about 4 inches in front of the stone prevents exact measurements) are about 40 inches high and 30 inches wide. What is now the lower section of the stone contains a cavity that measures approximately 15 by 11 inches, by about 8 inches deep. Here and there on the bottom of this cavity (or, rather, what would be the bottom if the stone were laid flat) are some fairly large discolourations. The discolouration are reddish-brown and are supposed to have been produced from the saint's blood when his head tumbled into the cavity immediately after he was decapitated. This dried blood is supposed to liquify and turn a brighter shade of red during those same periods in May and September when the relic in the Naples Tesoro liquifies. I can find no record of it's liquefying during the 16 December feast on which the Tesoro relic sometimes liquefies.

The earliest reference to the liquefaction associated with the Pozzuoli stone dates from the end of the seventeenth century (Alfano and Amitrano 1951, 151). Thus it is not as old a phenomenon as the liquefactions associated with the Tesoro relic or the relics found at Ravello and at San Gregorio Armeno.

In 1926 a piece of cotton that had supposedly been drawn across the surface of the cavity bottom during a liquefaction was subjected to a chemical analysis that indicated that the cotton showed traces of human blood. But even defenders of the Januarius cult (see for instance Petito 1983, 325) concede that this was a questionable test, given the length of time that had elapsed between drawing the cotton across the stone and the chemical analysis, and given the number of different people who had handled the cotton during that interval. For the most part then, the claim that liquefaction occurs in connection with the Pozzuoli stone rests entirely upon the fact that the discolourations *appear* to liquify and turn a bright red.

Before explaining what I think produces the appearance of liquefaction at Pozzuoli, it will be useful to review a report made by investigators in 1902 and quoted at length in Grant (1929, 71–4). These investigators observed the stone during a liquefaction and made careful measurements in order to compare the temperature of the stone at various times with the surrounding temperature. At various times during one day they also compared the discolouration of a glass plate containing squares representing different shades of red. They found that the discolourations did change colour and that these change did *not* correlate with temperature in any way. Putting aside their remarks about temperature, let me quote some passages from their report that I think are significant:

I first saw to it that no candles should be lit before the niche in which the Stone is walled in, as *the daylight sufficed for my observation* ... [Later] we saw liquid drops *glinting* upon the stone at half-past ten [their observations had started at 9:30] ... and [these] gradually became bigger ... They extended over so much of the surface that by eleven o'clock the entire Stone, as seen behind the glass, *looked wet* all over, as though it had had water poured all over it. (emphases added)

Although the authors of the report concluded that all this was "no delusion," my own experience at Pozzuoli leads me to conclude that that is exactly what it was.

When staring at the stone straight on, I found that the discolourations in the cavity were indeed a dull reddish-brown. In itself this is not problematic since I viewed the stone in late August, when liquefaction is not expected. Nevertheless, when I moved my head slightly to the left, the same surface did quite clearly "glisten" and "seem wet." After experimenting a little with my line of sight, and carefully inspecting the cavity itself, I concluded that the glistening was an optical illusion produced by the play of the ambient light in the chapel (and the 1902 instigators, like almost everyone else, made use of that same ambient lighting, most of which is provided by sunlight entering through windows and skylights) and by peculiarities of the surface on which the discolourations appear. This surface, it turns out, is not at all smooth. Rather it is marked by a number of closely spaced ridges of the sort seen on roughly quarried stone. It seemed to me that the glistening which appeared on the stone was mainly on the tops of these ridges. Looking carefully at the surface from various angles, I eventually came to the conclusion that this was because the upper surfaces of these ridges had been worn especially smooth.

The fact that the surface of the stone seemed to glisten (at least when I positioned myself properly) not only made it seem wet but also gave the impression that the discolourations were somewhat lighter than they had seemed originally. I believe that those optical effects produce the appearance of liquefaction on this stone. That these effects seem so dependent upon the sunlight that infuses the chapel also seems consistent with the fact that the stone is not reported to liquefy on the occasion of the December feast, when the Neapolitan sky is usually more overcast than in May or September. Furthermore, the fact that investigators staring straight on at the stone saw changes in colouration over the course of a morning could be due to nothing more than changes in the intensity and angle of the sunlight entering the chapel.

Here again, then, as with the Ravello relic, the appearance of liquefaction seems very much under the control of the observer. I therefore conclude (again) that if an observer wants to see liquefaction at certain periods and not others, presumably for the reasons outlined in chapter 4, that is exactly what will happen.

Notes

1 This chapter is an expanded and revised version of an article that originally appeared in the *Journal for the Scientific Study of Religion*; see Carroll 1987c.

2 By "most poular" Taves means those twenty-three prayer books that were issued and re-issued most often during this period. She found that twenty-two of these twenty-three books mentioned the Rosary. By contrast, the devotions mentioned next most often were the benediction of the Blessed Sacrament, which was mentioned in fifteen of these twenty-three books, and devotion to the Sacred Heart of Jesus, mentioned in thirteen books.

3 For an account of these Rosary sessions in Catholic schools, written with gentle humour, see Cascone 1982, 106–15. A similarly humorous account, dealing with the recital of the Rosary during Mass, is given in Meara *et al.* (1986, 100–1).

4 The second most common Rosary, for instance, is the Bridgettine Rosary. This is similar to the Dominican Rosary, except that it has six decades (rather than five) as well as a group of three Hail Mary beads. The sixty-three Hail Marys associated with this Rosary correspond to the sixty-three years that the Virgin Mary is supposed to have lived on earth. While the historical St Bridget did popularize the idea that the Virgin Mary died at age sixty-three, the Bridgettine Rosary came into use only long after St Bridget's death in 1373 (see Thurston 1902c). Other rosaries which involve groupings of Our Fathers and Hail Marys that differ from the groupings associated with the Dominican Rosary are the Rosary of Our Lady of Consolation, the Rosary of the Immaculate Conception, the Rosary of the Immaculate Heart of Mary, and the Seraphic Rosary. Each of these variants is described in Attwater (1956, 255–6); see also Shaw (1954, 69–79).

5 Most readers familiar with the Rosary will know that a small tassel is usually attached to the circle of beads I have described. This tassel consists of a crucifix (on which is usually prayed the Apostles' Creed), an Our Father bead,

three Hail Mary beads grouped together, and another Our Father Bead. A religious medal of some sort is often found at the spot where this tassel joins the main strand of Rosary beads. But neither the tassel nor the associated prayers forms part of the Rosary as officially defined by the Church (Attwater 1956, 250–1; Hinnebusch 1967, 667). Moreover, it is clear from the archaeological evidence (Thurston 1901d, 396) that the tassel was not found on the Rosary when the Rosary first became popular in the late fifteenth and early sixteenth centuries. It seems likely that the three-beaded tassel, which had always been part of the Bridgettine Rosary, was added to the Dominican Rosary when Church authorities in the early eighteenth century began trying to discourage the use of the former and encourage the use of the latter (see "Gaining of Cumulative Indulgences 1909; Thurston 1901d, 201–3). Finally, many Catholics also add a short prayer after each "Glory be to the Father," namely, "O my Jesus, forgive us our sins, save us from the fires of hell, lead all souls to Heaven, especially those who have most need of your mercy." This is a fairly recent innovation, introduced only since the Second World War, in response to a request supposedly made by Our Lady of Fatima in 1917.

6 Perhaps the best evidence *against* the historicity of the tradition linking St Dominic to the Rosary comes from the history of art. Kaftal's (1952; 1965; 1978; 1985) discussion of the iconography of St Dominic in Italian art, for instance, makes it clear that in the fourteenth and fifteenth centuries there were at least three distinct iconographic traditions surrounding St Dominic which involved either "an apparition of the Virgin Mary" or "the transmission of a physical object during the course of an apparition" or both. Thus, it was common to depict (1) St Dominic praying for the bedridden Reginald of Orleans while Reginald has a vision of Mary in which she gives him the new habit of the Dominican order, (2) St Dominic having a vision of Saints Peter and Paul in which they gave him a staff, and (3) a vision in which the Virgin Mary presents both St Dominic and St Francis to her son Jesus Christ. There appear, however, to have been *no* depictions of St Dominic in this period (the fourteenth and fifteenth centuries) receiving a Rosary from the Virgin Mary. It seems inconceivable that such a tradition would have been ignored by artists of the period had it in fact existed.

7 In presenting this brief history of the Rosary, I have drawn upon a number of sources, including Attwater (1956); Hinnebusch (1967); Shaw (1954); Thurston (1900d; 1900e; 1900f; 1913g); William (1953).

8 This was not the Hail Mary known to modern Catholics, since the entire second half of the modern prayer (which begins "Holy Mary, Mother of God, Pray") was missing. See the discussion in Willam (1953, 82–90).

9 A "confraternity" is officially defined by the Church to be an organization that promotes some form of religious devotion among the public.

10 For a more detailed account of the founding of the Rosary Confraternity at Cologne, see Duval (1964).

11 Several commentators have suggested that a concern with Marian devotion

and a concern with witchcraft derived from the same sources. See for instance Rothkrug (1987, 249).

12 An ex voto is a token left at a shrine when the supernatural being associated with the shrine, say, Mary or some saint, has granted a request. In the usual case, the ex voto is linked in some clear visual way to the type of request made. Most of the painted ex votos being discussed here depict the accident, sickness, or calamity from which the supplicant sought deliverance (for themselves or others). Thus, these painted ex votos might show a woman dying in bed, a man being attacked by bandits, a farmer being run over by his cart, and so on. For some examples of painted ex votos from the sixteenth century that explicitly depict supplicants praying a Rosary in order to obtain the favour they want, see D'Antonio (1979). Incidentally, that the Rosaries depicted in these paintings were *Marian* Rosaries, rather than, say, paternoster beads, seems obvious from the fact that the supplicants are invariably portrayed as directing their prayers to an image of Mary floating in the sky above them. Although the systematic study of ex votos has been well under way for some decades now (see, for instance, Besutti 1972, 127–40), their importance as sources of information on the spread of popular devotions seems to have been generally overlooked.

13 This lack of interest in Freud's argument linking infantile anal-eroticisim to the anal personality has been discussed by Brown (1959), whose own work is an exception to this pattern. For some speculation on why this part of Freud's argument has generated so little research, see Kline (1981, 108–9).

14 The Blue Army of Our Lady of Fatima, for instance, which is an organization devoted to spreading the message associated with the apparitions at Fatima, believes that praying the Rosary and wearing the Brown Scapular of Our Lady of Mount Carmel are the two most potent weapons in the fight to convert Russia from Communism; see Blue Army (1982). For more on the relation between the Rosary, and Marian devotion generally, and Catholic opposition to Communism, see Kselman and Avella (1986); Christian (1984).

15 Others, however, have been less cautious than Dundes. Rosenman (1986), for example, points to reports which suggest that child abuse has historically been far higher in Germany than in surrounding areas, and develops from this an argument that would explain the intense anal-eroticism that Dundes posits for German culture.

16 Catholicism is of course not the only religion to have flourished in German-speaking areas. The logic of the argument presented here quite clearly leads us to expect that, say, the German Protestant tradition should also be characterized by strong anal-erotic concerns. In fact, a number of investigators have argued that this is the case. For a discussion of anal themes in Luther's work in particular, see Brown (1959); Dundes (1984, 59–62); Erikson (1962, 122 and 245–50); Domhoff (1970). More generally, Scribner (1981, 81–6) provides some examples of the use of anal imagery in the popular woodcuts disseminated by Protestant propagandists during the early phases of the Reformation.

17 Although the Church has now declared that St Christopher was a purely legendary character, St Christopher medals are still being sold in stores specializing in Catholic religious goods.

18 The following account of the history of Catholic religious medals is based upon Thurston (1913c) and Mulhern (1967).

CHAPTER TWO

1 For the full text of the modern Angelus devotion, see appendix A.

2 For the history of the Hail Mary, see Thurston (1901f); Willam (1953, 82–90).

3 My account of the history of the Angelus is based mainly upon Thurston (1901f; 1901g; 1902a; 1902b; 1904a; 1913a); Henry (1924); and De Marco (1967).

4 For a discussion of the development of the midday Angelus, see Thurston (1902b); Henry (1924, columns 2074–7).

5 The final prayer of the Angelus (see appendix A) does make a passing reference to the Passion and Resurrection of Christ, as well as the Incarnation. But as I have mentioned, this prayer was a later addition. It was also not considered an essential part of the Angelus. This prayer could be omitted, for instance, and devotees could still obtain all the indulgences associated with the Angelus (O'Loan 1894).

6 For some clinical material showing traces of this infantile desire in both males and females to impregnate the mother, see Klein (1923, 98–100; 1945, 401–5).

7 For an account of the successive indulgences attached to the Angelus, see Lea (1896); "Recitation of Angelus" (1909); "The Angelus" (1913); Beringer (1925a, 221–4).

CHAPTER THREE

1 For a discussion of these and other apparitions of the Virgin Mary, as well as some discussion of the influence of Vatican II in the de-emphasis of the Mary cult, see Carroll (1986a).

2 All four Gospel accounts do mention that the Roman soldiers supervising the crucifixion threw lots for Christ's clothes while he was still alive on the cross; see Matthew 27: 27–29; Mark 15: 24; Luke 23: 34, John 19: 23–25. Though this suggests that at least some of Christ's garments were removed when he arrived at Golgotha, nothing in the Gospel accounts suggests that this was a particularly painful experience.

3 The basic reference work on the Stations of the Cross is still Thurston's (1906) *The Stations of the Cross*, and I have relied heavily on this work in discussing the history of this devotion. More recent works, which are more accessible but which add little to Thurston's discussion, include Alston (1913), Brown (1967), and Peters (1985). Thurston's 1906 book, I might add, is an expansion of three earlier articles (Thurston 1900a; 1900b; 1900c) that appeared in *The Month*.

These three articles were the first in a series of articles entitled "Our Popular Devotions" that Thurston wrote for that journal. The fact that he thought to begin such a series with an investigation into the Stations of the Cross presumably implies that considered it to be a particularly important Catholic devotion.

4 "Dives" was the rich man in the parable about the rich man who goes to Hell and the poor man, Lazarus, who goes to Heaven; see Luke 16: 19–31. The word "dives" simply means "rich man" in Latin, but was used as a proper name during the Middle Ages. In pointing to the site where the house of Dives stood, pilgrims were obviously expressing the belief that he was a historical character.

5 In this regard, the Stations of the Cross might be contrasted with the experience of the Stigmata. As we shall see in chapter 5, stigmatics do identify with the Christ and do strive to experience the suffering of the crucified Christ.

6 Throughout this book, I will conform to common psychoanalytic usage by using "fantasy" when referring to conscious images and "phantasy" when referring to unconscious images.

7 In Catholic eschatology, the souls of the dead go to one of three places: Heaven, Hell, or Purgatory. Purgatory is the place where sinners must experience unremitted punishment for the sins that they have committed in life. Only when this punishment is discharged are they allowed to enter Heaven.

8 For more on the Catholic doctrines relating to indulgences, see Beringer (1925a; 1925b); Kent (1913); Markham (1967).

9 For a fuller discussion of the factors that facilitate regression to the anal-sadistic stage, see Freud (1913; 1916–17, 339–91; 1919, 174–5).

CHAPTER FOUR

1 What the young man remembered was *"Exoriare ex nostris ossibus ultor*; the correct quote was *"Exoriare aliquis nostris ex ossibus ultor*, a literal translation of which would be "Let someone arise from my bones as an avenger"; see Freud (1901, 9).

2 This seems to be a garbled version of a very common story involving a *French* general (rather than the Italian general Garibaldi). In the original story, the blood relic failed to liquefy in 1799, and the French commander present at the time threatened to have the cleric in charge shot if the relic did not liquefy within the next ten minutes – which it promptly did. Thurston's (1926, 59–60) view was that the story was entirely apocryphal.

3 My account of the circumstances surrounding the liquefactions of the blood-relic of St Januarius is based mainly upon Thurston (1909a; 1909b; 1913c; 1921; 1926; 1927a; 1927b; 1927c; 1930); Alfano and Amitrano (1951); Petito (1983); and Grant (1929). But see also Kehoe (1871); Mioni (1908, 252–9); Rogo (1983, 186–202); and Cruz (1984, 182–9). I have relied on these same sources for the

information relating to the other blood miracles discussed in this chapter.

4 The May ceremonies commemorate the translation of St Januarius' relics to Naples in the late fourth century.

5 The December festival commemorates the deliverance of Naples from the ravages of a volcanic eruption of Mt Vesuvius on 16 December 1631.

6 Throughout this chapter I will for convenience use the word "blood" to denote the substance which is considered blood by the members of the cult being discussed and which liquefies during the ceremonies of the cult. Nevertheless, whether these relics really are remnants of human blood is something that has never been established by direct examination.

7 Geary (1985) points out that the ritualized abuse of saintly relics was a common practice in some parts of Europe during the Middle Ages, although he also suggests that such behaviour declined dramatically during the thirteenth century in response to strong opposition from Church authorities. Mioni (1908, 301–4) reached similar conclusions. Yet even in the late nineteenth century, at least in southern Italy, the use of abuse as a means of coercing a patron saint was common. Describing the relationship between a Sicilian peasant and his saint, for instance, Salomone-Marino (1897, 174) noted, "The peasant, though, turns against his Saint, threatens him, insults him, beats him, inflicts upon him the severest punishments – until his prayer is granted and his boon given," and then goes on to give several specific examples. Although most of the "humiliations" described by Salomone-Marino involve images of a saint, rather than relics, the activities of the *Zie di San Gennaro* seem to me to be part of this same Southern Italian "humiliation of saints" tradition.

8 On the other hand, it is probably not possible for anybody to read through the literature dealing with the liquefaction of blood relics and not be slightly curious as to what might be producing the effect. For those who are curious, appendix B and appendix C present some information that seems relevant to the search for the physical processes that produce the liquefaction of these relics.

9 Strictly speaking, the English term "castration" refers to the removal of the testicles, but Freud consistently used the term more in the sense of "penis-detachment."

10 Using these criteria produces a list of relics that is more or less the same as what Alfano and Amitrano (1951) call their "First Group" of blood relics.

11 For my own account of these two relics, associated with St Pantaleone and St Patricia respectively, see appendix C. I might note that while the St Patricia relic is now supposed to liquefy every Tuesday, reports from the seventeenth century indicate that at that time it liquefied every Friday afternoon, in honour of Christ's death on the cross.

12 The traditions about St Patricia given here are based upon the information distributed to visitors at the church of San Gregorio Armeno in Naples. In the version of the St Patricia legend presented in Delaney (1980, 447) Patricia is

described as a noblewoman from Constantinople who died c.665 (which would have made it impossible for her to have been the Emperor Constantine's niece). In most other regards, however, the two accounts are in agreement. I might add that the blood relic of St Aloysius Gonzaga at Gesù Vecchio was also supposed to be blood that flowed during the extraction of a tooth (Thurston 1927b; 132).

13 For discussions of the iconography associated with St Stephen, see Kaftal (1952, 949–64; 1965, 1057–72; 1978, 945–53; 1985, 600–22); and Réau (1958, 444–56). These works also reproduce examples of paintings and frescoes depicting the martyrdom of Stephen, Stephen with a stone on top of his head, and Stephen bleeding from the top of his head.

14 I say that castration imagery is "most pronounced" in the case of the Januarius relic at the Duomo because of the cultic insistence that the decapitated head of the said must be exhibited next to the blood relic itself; see earlier discussion. On the other hand, I should note that some of the other features of the Januarius cult at the Tesoro, features that are often emphasized in popular accounts, are *not* found in these other blood liquefaction cults. For instance, these other cults, as far as I can tell, are not associated with any group that resembles the *Zie di San Gennaro*. Likewise, the suggestion that the failure of the blood relic to liquefy is a portent of calamity – something invariably mentioned in popular accounts of the *tesoro* cult – is also missing from these other cults. Even in the case of the *tesoro* cult itself, I think, this element has been exaggerated. This relic, remember, quite often fails to liquefy in December, at a ceremony which even more than the ceremonies in May or September is associated with the memory of a disaster (the eruption of Vesuvius in 1632), and yet such failures do not seem to provoke any great degree of anxiety. In any event, my inference is that those elements which might appear in the Januarius cult at the Tesoro, but not in these other cults, probably have little to do with explaining the general appeal of blood liquefaction cults.

15 Most of the discussion which follows, relating to the effects of the father-ineffective family on the oedipal process for males, is reprinted with slight modification from Carroll (1986a, 53–5 and 62–3) with the permission of Princeton University Press.

16 These passages are from *Belief, Magic and Anomie* by Anne Parsons. Copyright © 1969 by The Free Press, a division of Macmillan, Inc. Reprinted by permission of the publisher.

17 For some discussion of this feminization of Catholicism, see Pope (1988).

CHAPTER FIVE

1 An earlier and somewhat shorter version of this chapter was previously published in the *Journal of Psychoanalytic Anthropology*; see Carroll (1987a).

2 Thurston (1952, 32–43), for instance, reviews much of the historical data on

possible stigmatics before St Francis.

3　For an account of some Protestant stigmatics, see Crehan (in Thurston 1955, 203).

4　Inedia among Catholic mystics is also discussed in Bell (1985), Pater (1946), and Bynum (1987).

5　Inedia is not the only characteristic associated with the stigmata for which we have evidence of faking. For instance, around the time that Louise Lateau had developed her "crown of thorns," the local curé walked into her room to find a leech attached to her forehead. Asked to explain herself, Lateau denied any knowledge of the leech or how it had ended up on her head. The curé recognized that the marks left by a leech were similar to the puncture marks from Lateau's "crown of thorns," but concluded that the Devil had placed the leech on her head to discredit her. The leech was put into a container and stored in a cupboard in Lateau's house. Shortly thereafter the container vanished, something else blamed on the Devil (see Didry and Wallemacq 1931, 107–8). Similarly, some of the people who had kissed Padre Pio's hands reported that they smelled iodine. Since iodine stains could simulate the appearance of blood stains, Pio's supporters are quick to point out that Pio himself stated that he did *not* put iodine on his wounds, and thus that the "iodine smell" must have been a manifestation of the "perfumed odor" that so often emanated from Padre Pio (see Carty 1953, 85). While it would be easy to smirk at the credulity of the devout in face such clear evidence of faking, I think that would be missing the important point. The fact that people believe in the supernatural origin of the stigmata, despite such clear evidence of faking, proves that the desire to believe in the stigmata is especially strong. It is this strong desire to believe that needs to be explain.

6　For Freud's views on hysteria, see Breuer and Freud (1895) and Freud (1908a; 1908d).

7　For a review of these more recent approaches to hysteria, see Gutheil (1985), Marmor (1953), and Rangell (1959).

8　Most of the theoretical arguments I have borrowed from Melanie Klein are from the various essays collected in Klein (1975; 1980). For an overview of Klein's psychoanalytic theories, see Segal (1964; 1979).

9　Though an emphasis upon reparation appears throughout Klein's work, the key essay is Klein (1937).

10　For an account of the Turin Shroud and some of the claims made on its behalf, see Rogo (1983, 135–40).

11　For an introduction to the literature dealing with the differing views towards the Eucharist held by the more important Protestant groups, see Nischan (1984); Rothkrug (1979, 79–86).

12　I would like to thank Professor Alan Dundes, director of the Folklore Archives at Berkeley, for permitting me access to the material there, most of which has been gathered by his students over the past twenty-five years.

13 See, for example, Zika's (1988) account of "bleeding host shrines" in fourteenth- and fifteenth-century Germany.

14 The explanations of inedia offered by both Bell and Bynum obviously bear a resemblance to the typical explanations offered for *anorexia nervosa* among modern adolescent females. Both authors, however, make the point that there are both similarities and differences between the inedia experienced by Catholic mystics and *anorexia nervosa*.

CHAPTER SIX

1 For more detail on the nature and history of Eucharistic cults and devotions in the Western Church, see Bertaud (1961); King (1965).

2 By contrast, the elevation of the chalice during the consecration of the wine was only included in the liturgy of the Mass at a much later date.

3 For a good account of the importance of the host in *Corpus Christi* processions during the fifteenth century, at least in Germany, see Zika (1988).

4 My account of the history of the Forty Hours is based mainly upon Cargnoni (1986); Corblet (1886, 450–3; Dompnier (1981); Thurston (1904c, 110–48); Weil (1974). An account of the ceremonial details that have surrounded this devotion in the modern era can be found in Fortescue (1943).

5 For a translation of Clement viii's pronouncement on the Forty Hours, see Thurston (1904, 117-20).

6 For a detailed discussion of the reparation theme that runs through all versions of the Forty Hours devotion, see Dompnier (1981, 20–6).

7 My account of the history and development of the various types of monstrances is based upon Andrieu (1950); Corblet (1886, 315–21); Darcel (1861); de Girardot and Didron (1851); Howell (1967); Thurston (1901e; 1913e).

8 These "tower" monstrances are the ones that appear in almost all depictions of a Corpus Christi procession executed before the sixteenth century. See, for example, the Corpus Christi procession depicted in the illustrated manuscript reproduced as the frontispiece for Nelson (1974).

9 See the summary of these regulations in Fortescue (1943, 51).

CHAPTER SEVEN

1 The idea that the Virgin Mary would wait until the Saturday following a person's death has always bothered Catholic commentators, since it suggests that heavenly beings like Mary observe the same temporal categories which are observed on earth. Zimmerman (1904b, 349–51) tried to solve this problem by suggesting that the original text of the Sabbatine Promise said that Mary would descend into Purgatory *subito* ("immediately") not *Sabbato* ("on Satur-

day"). The original promise, he argued, was probably only a promise of an immediate release from Purgatory. In talking of Zimmerman's proposed "Subitine" Indulgence, Thurston (1904b, 75) asked sarcastically why the Virgin Mary would have chosen to speak Italian (which is the language in which *subito* means "immediately") to a French-speaking pope like John XXII.

2 The original tradition might not even have been associated with the Virgin Mary. In trying to discover the "bedrock" tradition from which the scapular legends are derived, Zimmerman (1927, 325–7) argues that these legends do indeed derive from an apparition that reportedly occurred in the thirteenth century. But the apparition in question was to "a certain brother of the Carmelite order" who was *not* Simon Stock and who was having doubts about his vocation. Furthermore, the person who appeared was not the Virgin Mary, but rather a recently deceased Carmelite monk who wanted to reassure the doubter that remaining in the Carmelite Order would be efficacious in achieving salvation. In Zimmerman's reconstruction, it was only later that the Carmelite seer became St Simon Stock and the recently deceased Carmelite became the Virgin Mary.

3 See, for example, the references listed under "Carmelites" in the index to Erasmus's correspondence by Mynors and Thomson (1974).

4 There is no "scapular" entry in Lundeen's (1986) index to Luther's Collected Works. Nevertheless, Luther did use the word in at least three places (see Pelikan 1959, 273; Pelikan 1969, 244; Spitz 1960, 100). In each case, however, the reference is explicitly to the scapular worn by monks.

5 St John of the Cross and St Teresa of Avila together introduced the reforms that led to the establishment of the Discalced Carmelites.

6 An *Agnus Dei* was a small wax disc impressed with the figure of a lamb and blessed by the Pope. The use of these discs dates from the ninth century, and are frequently mentioned in other laws – besides the one mentioned here – enacted by Elizabeth against Catholics in the late sixteenth century. For a fuller discussion of the *Agnus Dei* see Thurston (1913a).

7 The reference seems to be to Thurston (1904b).

8 Since 1910 the Church has permitted the use of a "scapular medal" in place of the Brown Scapular, or in place of the Brown Scapular and several other scapulars simultaneously. Devotees of the Brown Scapular, however, have always discouraged the substitution of the medal for the traditional cloth scapular; see, for instance, Cattelona (1949); Fox (1985, 87); Haffert (1942, 19–20); Lynch (1950, 138–9); Magennis (1923: 50–4).

9 Notice that this passage associates *both* scapular promises, involving Hell and Purgatory, with the apparition to St Simon Stock. Strictly speaking this is incorrect, since in the original traditions only Mary's promise regarding Hell was made to St Simon Stock; her promise involving Purgatory was made to John XXII. Still, this is a simplification of the scapular traditions that appears often in twentieth century devotional literature.

CHAPTER EIGHT

1 Unless otherwise noted, all quotations relating to Alacoque's apparitions are taken from the account of those apparitions in Bainvel (1924, 17–23). My concern in this book is with how the content of Alacoque's apparitions shaped popular devotion to the Sacred Heart, and not with the idiosyncratic processes that led Alacoque to experience these particular apparitions. Still, for readers who are interested in speculating on just what life experiences might have predisposed Alacoque to see and hear what she did, there is a wealth of relevant information in the autobiography she wrote at the command of her spiritual adviser (Alacoque 1961).

2 Though these *sauvegardes* were called "scapulars" in everyday discourse and had been associated with an indulgence since 1872, Church authorities have not considered them to be "true" scapulars, and so traditionally they were not subject to the regulations governing scapulars (Beringer 1925a, 520–1).

3 For the names of some of these people see the discussion later in this chapter.

4 The Sacred Heart has sometimes been displayed exteriorly on the chest of Jesus as a child (see, Grimoüard de Saint Laurent 1880, 154–66; also the plate opposite p. 213), but the dominant iconographic tradition associates the Sacred Heart with the adult Christ.

5 Klein did not deny that *some* of the woman-with-a-penis images found in fantasy material represented the phallic mother (see for instance, Klein 1923, 95; 1925, 115), only that they *more often* reflected the mother who had absorbed the father's penis.

6 This tendency to see the penis as a substitute for the breast was also noted by Freud (1910) in his discussion of Leonardo da Vinci's "vulture dream."

7 The account of the *Kulturkampf* that follows is based primarily upon Anderson (1986); Freudenthal (1967); Lamberti (1986), and Spahn (1913).

CHAPTER NINE

1 For more on the various devotions centred on the Blessed Sacrament, see Beringer, 1925b: 87–109).

2 Three issues in particular seemed to have attracted the attention of scholars interested in Catholic/Protestant differences. The first has to do with the distinctive "ethos" that underlies Protestantism, and the ways in which this distinctive ethos is (or is not) related to social or economic processes. Quite apart from Weber's (1920) classic formulation and the enormous literature that it alone has generated, there is Troeltsch's (1911) argument linking "neo-Calvinism" to "bourgeois-capitalistic" values and more recent work (overviews of which can be found in Brady 1982, 167–8; Scribner 1986) linking Protestantism to distinctively urban values. A second body of literature has focused upon the Catholic doctrine of *immanence*, the belief that the essence of a supernatural

force can merge with the essence of particular physical objects. For Swanson (1967), the Catholic belief in immanence and the Protestant rejection of that belief accounted for most of the other doctrinal differences between the two traditions. Although Swanson's theory has proven controversial (see Colie 1968; Davis 1970; Flint 1968; François 1972), no one has seriously challenged the view that the issue of immanence was at least *one* of the doctrinal issues that most sharply divided Catholicism and Protestantism at the time of the Reformation; see in particular Eire (1986). Finally, there are a number of studies concerned with demonstrating that many of the differences between Catholicism and Protestantism reflect pre-Reformation patterns. Rothkrug's (1979) careful study of the differences in popular piety between north Germany and south Germany in the pre-Reformation period is a good example of this type of research.

3 See, for example, the evaluation of Klein's work expressed in Grosskurth (1986, 373–5).

4 In the context of Klein's overall theory, the type of splintering being discussed here is considered a special case of "splitting," a process that has received a great deal of attention in the psychoanalytic literature. For a comparison between Klein's general view of splitting processes and the views held by others, including Freud, see Grotstein (1981).

5 The material on Italian Catholicism presented in this section is taken from a much longer and more extensive article which I have written on the same subject; see Carroll (forthcoming).

6 See, for instance, Banfield (1958, 129–45); Bianco (1974, 84–106); Brögger (1971); Chapman (1971, 158–207); Gross (1973, 203–12); Maraspini (1968, 221–55); Orsi (1985); Silverman (1975, 149–77); Vecoli (1969, 227–9; 1977, 26–34); Williams (1938, 135–59). For other studies, see the bibliography presented in Tomasi and Stibili (1978).

7 In its simplist terms, the festa was a public celebration, usually in honor of some saint or madonna. Typically, the celebration involved the "official" Church clergy in two ways: first, it was usually held on and around the feast-day which the Church had established for the saint or madonna in question, and second, some portion of the celebration involved a ceremony, like a Mass, held on church property and/or officiated over by a priest. But the central elements in the festa were the processions and other activities which took place outside the church and which were organized by lay associations. For more on the institution of the festa, see the references in Carroll (19xx).

8 On the association between the Evil Eye and envy among Italians, see Brögger (1971, 139–48); DiStasi (1981, 49–53). For discussion of this association among the members of other cultures, see Cosminsky (1976, 165–6); Dionisopoulos-Mass (1976, 44); Foster (1972, 174), Schoeck (1955, 194); Teitelbaum (1976, 64–5).

9 Klein's most important statement on envy is her *Envy and Gratitude* (1957), but discussions of envy appear throughout most of what she wrote between 1946 and her death in 1960; see the essays in Klein (1980).

10 The argument just presented leads to another conclusion, though not one directly relevant to the issue of splintering. If chronic envy does activate the memory of the envy experienced during the paranoid-schizoid position, and given the already mentioned association between envy and the Evil Eye, then we might expect that the memories formed during the paranoid-schizoid position would strongly influence the content of the beliefs surrounding the Evil Eye. In fact, this hypothesis can been used to explain many of the beliefs that do surround the Evil Eye; see Carroll (1984).

11 When Cardinal Roncalli took the name "John XXIII" upon his election as pope in 1958, he was obviously reinforcing the now-standard Catholic interpretation of history, namely, that the "Pisan" John XXIII was not a legitimate pope.

Bibliography

Abraham, Karl. 1921. "Contributions to the Theory of the Anal Character." In *Selected Papers of Karl Abraham*, 338–92. New York: Basic, 1953.

- 1922. "The Spider As Dream Symbol." In D. Bryan and A. Strachey, 1953, trans., *Selected Papers of Karl Abraham*, 326–32. New York: Basic.

Adriányi, Gabriel, *et al.* 1981. *The Church in the Modern Age*. New York: Crossroad.

Alacoque, Margaret Mary. 1961. *Autobiography*. Trans. and intro. by V. Kerns. Westminster, Md.: Newman.

Alfano, G.B., and A. Amitrano. 1951. *Notizie storiche ed osservazioni sulle reliquie di sangue*. Naples: Arti Graiche Adriana.

Alston, G.C. 1913. "Way of the Cross." In *The Catholic Encyclopedia*, vol. 15, 569–71. New York: Encyclopedia Press.

Ambrasi, Domenico. 1970. "Il 'Miracolo di San Gennaro' nell'ultimo cinquantennio." In D. Ambrasi (ed.), *Campania sacra: Studi e documenti*, 187–92. Naples: M. D'Auria.

Anderson, Margaret L. 1986. "The Kulturkampf and the Course of German History." *Central European History* 19 (1): 82–115.

Andrieu, Michel. 1950. "Aux Origines du culte du saint-sacrement: Reliquaires et monstrances eucharistiques." *Analecta Bollandiana* 63: 397–418.

"The Angelus." 1913. *Irish Ecclesiastical Record* 2 (Oct.): 417–18.

Attwater, Donald. 1956. *A Dictionary of Mary*. New York: P.J. Kenedy.

Austin, Rev. H. 1883. *The Stigmata: A History of Various Cases*. London: Thomas Richardson.

Baedeker, Karl. 1900. *Handbook for Travellers: Southern Italy and Sicily*. Leipzig: Karl Baedeker.

Bainvel, Rev. J.W., S.J. 1913a. "Heart of Jesus, Devotion to the." In *The Catholic Encyclopedia*, vol. 2, 163–8. New York: Encyclopedia Press.

- 1913b. "Heart of Mary, Devotion to the." In *The Catholic Encyclopedia*, vol. 7, 168–9. New York: Encyclopedia Press.

- 1924. *Devotion to the Sacred Heart: The Doctrine and Its History*. Trans. from 5th French ed. by E. Leahy. London: Burns, Oates and Washbourne.

Banfield, Edward C. 1958. *The Moral Basis of A Backward Society*. Glencoe, Ill.: Free Press.

Bell, R. 1985. *Holy Anorexia*. Chicago: Univ. of Chicago Press.

Belmonte, Thomas. 1979. *The Broken Fountain*. New York: Columbia Univ. Press.

Bergier, Abbé Nicolas-Sylvestre. 1863. *Dictionnaire de théologie*, vol. 5. Paris: A. Jouby.

Beringer, R.P., S.J. 1925a. *Les Indulgences, leur nature et leur usage*. 4th French ed., vol. 1. Paris: P. Lethielleux.

- 1925b. *Les Indulgences, leur nature et leur usage*, vol. 2. Paris: P. Lethielleux.

Bertaud, Emile. 1961. "Dévotion eucharistique." In *Dictionnaire de Spiritualité*, vol. 4, cols 1621-37. Paris: Beauchesne.

Besutti, G.M. 1972. "Santuari, apparizioni, culto locale, ex voto: Rassegna Bibliografica 1962-1971." *Marianum* 105 (1): 42-141.

Bianco, Carla. 1974. *The Two Rosetos*. Bloomington: Indiana Univ. Press.

Biot, R. 1962. *The Enigma of the Stigmata*. New York: Hawthorn.

Blue Army. 1982. *The Blue Army Manual*. Washington Township, N.J.: The Blue Army of Lady Fatima.

Boe, G. 1949. "Ostensorio." In *Enciclopedia Italiana*, vol. 25, 732-3. Rome: Instituto della Enciclopedia Italiana.

Bouwsma, William J. 1968. "Swanson's Reformation." *Comparative Studies in Society and History* 10 (Sept.): 487-91.

Brady, Thomas A. 1982. "Social History." In S. Ozment (ed.), *Reformation Europe: A Guide to Research*, 161-81. St. Louis: Center for Reformation Research.

Breuer, J., and S. Freud. 1895. "Studies in Hysteria." In *The Standard Edition of the Complete Psychological Works of Sigmund Freud*, vol. 2 (entire). London: Hogarth, 1955.

Brögger, Jan. 1971. *Montevarese: A Study of Peasant Society and Culture in Southern Italy*. Bergen, Norway: Universitetsforlaget.

Brown, B. 1967. "Way of the Cross." In *The New Catholic Encyclopedia*, vol. 14, 832-5. New York: McGraw-Hill.

Brown, Mary Elizabeth. 1987. "The Making of Italian-American Catholics: Jesuit Work on the Lower East Side, New York, 1890's-1950's." *Catholic Historical Review* (Apr.): 195-210.

Brown, Norman O. 1959. *Life Against Death*. Middleton, Conn.: Wesleyan Univ. Press.

Bunker, Henry Alden. 1951. "Psychoanalysis and the Study of Religion." *Psychoanalysis and the Social Sciences* 3: 7-34.

Bynum, C. 1982. *Jesus as Mother: Studies in the Spirituality of the High Middle Ages*. Berkeley: Univ. of California Press.

Bynum, Caroline W. 1987. *Holy Feast and Holy Fast*. Berkeley, Calif.: Univ. of California Press.

Cabrol, Fernand. 1947. *The Roman Missal*. New York: P.J. Kenedy.

Cabussut, André. 1953. "Coeurs (Changement des, Échange des)." In *Dictionnaire de Spiritualité*, vol. 2, cols 1046-51. Paris: Beauchesne.

Callahan, Annice. 1985. *Karl Rahner's Spirituality of the Pierced Heart: A Reinterpretation of Devotion to the Sacred Heart*. Lanham, Md: Univ. Press of America.

Cargnoni, Costanzo. 1986. "Quarante-Heures." In *Dictionnaire de Spiritualité*, vol. 13, cols 2703-23. Paris: Beauchesne.

Carroll, Michael P. 1978. "Freud on Homosexuality and the Super-Ego: Some Cross-Cultural Tests." *Behavior Science Research* 13 (4): 255–71.

- 1984. "On the Psychological Origins of the Evil Eye." *Journal of Psychoanalytic Anthropology* 7 (Spring): 171–87.

- 1986a. *The Cult of the Virgin Mary: Psychological Origins*. Princeton, N.J.: Princeton Univ. Press.

- 1986b. "The Bear Cult That Wasn't." *Journal of Psychoanalytic Anthropology* 9 (1): 19–34.

- 1987a. "Heaven-Sent Wounds: A Kleinian View of the Stigmata in the Catholic Mystical Tradition." *Journal of Psychoanalytic Anthropology* 10 (1): 17–38.

- 1987b. "The Scourging of Psychoanalysis." *Journal of Psychoanalytic Anthropology* 10 (2): 139–45.

- 1987c. "Praying the Rosary: The Anal-Erotic Origins of a Popular Catholic Devotion." *Journal for the Scientific Study of Religion* 26 (4): 486–98.

- 1987d. *"Moses and Monotheism* Revisited: A New Ending to an Old Beginning." *American Imago* 44 (1): 15–35.

Carty, C. 1953. *Padre Pio, the Stigmatist*. St. Paul, Minn.: Radio Replies Press.

Cascone, Gina. 1982. *Pagan Babies and Other Catholic Memories*. New York: St. Martin's.

Le Catéchisme des Provinces Ecclésiatiques de Québec, Montréal et Ottawa. [Le Catéchisme]. 1888. Sherbrooke, Que.: Éditions St-Raphael, 1976.

Cattelona, Jude J. 1949. "How the Scapular or Medal Is Worn." In Carmelite Fathers and Tertiaries, *Take This Scapular!*, 46–52. Chicago: Carmelite Third Order Press.

Ceroke, C.P. 1964. "The Credibility of the Scapular Promise." *Carmelus* 11: 81–123.

Chapman, Charlotte G. 1971. *Milocca: A Sicilian Village*. Cambridge, Mass.: Schenkman.

Cheshire, N. 1975. *The Nature of Psychodynamic Interpretation*. London: John Wiley.

Christian, William A., Jr. 1972. *Person and God in a Spanish Valley*. New York: Seminar.

- 1981a. *Local Religion in Sixteenth-Century Spain*. Princeton: Princeton Univ. Press.

- 1981b. *Apparitions in Late Medieval and Renaissance Spain*. Princeton: Princeton Univ. Press.

- 1984. "Religious Apparitions and the Cold War in Southern Europe." In E. Wolf (ed.), *Religion, Power and Protest in Local Communities*, 239–66. Berlin: Mouton.

Clarke, Edith. 1957. *My Mother Who Fathered Me*. London: Allen and Unwin.

Colie, Rosalie L. 1968. "Review of *Religion and Regime*." *American Historical Review* 73 (Apr.): 1132–4.

Conners, Humphrey. 1949. "The Scapular in Life's Greatest Hour." In Carmelite Fathers and Tertiaries, *Take this Scapular!* 31–6. Chicago: Carmelite Third Order Press.

Corblet, Jules. 1886. *Histoire dogmatique, liturgique, et archéologique du Sacrement de l'Eucharistie*, vol. 2. Paris: Société Générale de Librairie Catholique.

Cosminksy, Sheila. 1976. "The Evil Eye in a Quiche Community." In C. Maloney (ed.), *The Evil Eye*, 163–74. New York: Columbia Univ. Press.

"Covering of Scapulars." 1911. *Irish Ecclesiastical Record* 11 (Jan.): 94–5.

Crehan, Joseph. 1952. *Father Thurston: A Memoir with a Bibliography of His Writings*. London: Sheed and Ward.

Cruz, Joan Carroll. 1984. *Relics*. Huntington, Ind.: Our Sunday Visitor.

Dalgairns, John B. 1857. *The Devotion to the Heart of Jesus, with an Introduction to the History of Jansenism*. London: Richardson.

D'Antonio, Nino. 1979. *Gli ex voto dipinti e il rituale dei fujenti a Madonna dell'Arco*. Cava dei Tirreni, Italy: Di Mauro.

Darcel, Alfred. 1861. "Trésor de Conques." *Annales Archéologiques* 21 (Jan./Feb.): 34–46.

Davis, Natalie Z. 1970. "Deforming the Reformation." *New York Review of Books* 12 (Apr. 10): 35–8.

de Giradot, Auguste, and Adolphe Didron. 1851. "Ostensoirs du moyen age." *Annales Archéologiques* 11: 316–24.

Dehne, Carl. 1975. "Roman Catholic Popular Devotions." *Worship* 49 (8): 446–60.

Delaney, John J. 1980. *Dictionary of Saints*. Garden City, N.J.: Doubleday.

Delumeau, Jean. 1971. *Catholicism between Luther and Voltaire: A New View of the Counter-Reformation*. London: Burns and Oates, 1977.

De Marco, A.A. 1967. "Angelus." In *The New Catholic Encyclopedia*, vol. 1, 521. New York: McGraw-Hill.

Didry, M., and A. Wallemacq. 1931. *Louise Lateau of Bois-d'Haine*. New York: Benziger.

Dineen, D. 1906. "Devotion to the Sacred Heart." *Irish Ecclesiastical Record* 19 (Mar.): 231–46.

Dionisopoulos-Mass, Regina. 1976. "The Evil Eye and Bewitchment in a Peasant Village." In C. Maloney (ed.), *The Evil Eye*, 42–62. New York: Columbia Univ. Press.

DiStasi, Lawrence. 1981. *Mal Occhio*. San Francisco: North Point.

Domhoff, William G. 1970. "Two Luthers: the Traditional and the Heretical in Freudian Psychology." *Psychoanalytic Review* 57: 5–17.

Dompnier, Bernard. 1981. "Un Aspect de la dévotion eucharistique dans la France du xviie siècle: Les Prières de quarante-heures." *Revue d'Histoire de l'Église de France* 67 (Jan.): 5–31.

Drane, Augusta T. 1880. *The History of St. Catherine of Siena and Her Companions*, 2nd ed., vol. 1. London: Burns and Oates.

Dundes, Alan. 1976. "A Psychoanalytic Study of the Bullroarer." *Man* 11: 220–38.

– 1981. "The Hero Pattern and the Life of Jesus." *Psychoanalytic Study of Society* 9: 49–83.

– 1984. *Life is like a Chicken Coop Ladder: A Portrait of German Culture through Folklore*. New York: Columbia Univ. Press.

Duval, André. 1964. "François, Michel." In *Dictionnaire de Spiritualité*, vol. 5, cols 1109–15. Paris: Beauchesne.

Eire, Carlos M.N. 1986. *The War Against the Idols: The Reformation of Europe from Erasmus to Calvin*. Cambridge: Cambridge Univ. Press.

Elwell, Right Rev. Msgr Clarence E. *et al.* 1956. *Our Quest for Happiness*. Vol. 2, *Through Christ Our Lord*. Chicago: Mentzer, Bush.

– 1960. *Our Quest for Happiness*. Vol. 4, *Toward the Eternal Commencement*. Chicago: Mentzer, Bush.

Erikson, Erik H. 1962. *Young Man Luther: A Study in Psychoanalysis and History*. New York: Norton.

Eudes, St John. 1946. *The Sacred Heart of Jesus*, trans. by Dom. Richard Flower. New York: P.J. Kenedy.

Fenichel, Otto. 1945. *The Psychoanalytic Theory of Neurosis*. London: Routledge and Kegan Paul.

Fenlon, Dermot. 1982. "Interpretations of Catholic History." *Journal of Ecclesiastical History* 33 (Apr.): 256–65.

Ferenczi, Sandor. 1914. "The Ontogenesis of the Interest in Money." In his *Sex in Psychoanalysis*, 269–79. New York: Dover, 1956.

Finley, Mitch. 1983. "Recovering the Rosary." *America*, 7 May, 351.

Flint, John T. 1968. "Handbook for Historical Sociologists." *Comparative Studies in Society and History* 10 (Sept.): 492–504.

Fortescue, Adrian. 1943. *The Ceremonies of the Roman Rite Described*. 7th ed. Rev. and augmented by J. O'Connell. London: Burns, Oates and Washbourne.

Foster, George M. 1965. "Peasant Society and the Image of Limited Good." *American Anthropologist* 67: 293–315.

– 1972. "The Anatomy of Envy: A Study in Symbolic Behavior." *Current Anthropology* 13: 165–86.

Fox, Robert J. 1985. *The Marian Catechism*. Washington, N.J.: AMI.

– 1986. *Call of Heaven*. Front Royal, Va.: Christendom College Press.

François, Martha. 1972. "Reformation and Society: An Analysis of Guy Swanson's *Religion and Regime*." *Comparative Studies in Society and History* 14 (June): 287–305.

Freud, Sigmund. 1900. *The Interpretation of Dreams*. In *The Standard Edition of the Complete Psychological Works of Sigmund Freud* (hereafter *S.E.*), vols 4 and 5, 1–751. London: Hogarth, 1953.

– 1901. *The Psychopathology of Everyday Life*. In *S.E.*, vol. 6, 1–310. London: Hogarth, 1960.

– 1905. *Jokes and Their Relation to the Unconscious*. In *S.E.*, vol. 8 (entire). London: Hogarth, 1953.

– 1907. "Obsessive Actions and Religious Practices." In *S.E.*, vol. 9, 115–27. London: Hogarth, 1959.

– 1908a. "Hysterical Phantasies and Their Relation to Bisexuality." In *S.E.*, vol. 9, 155–66. London: Hogarth, 1959.

– 1908b. "Character and Anal-Eroticism." In *S.E.*, vol. 9, 167–75, 1959.

– 1908c. "On the Sexual Theories of Children." In *S.E.*, vol. 9, 205–26. London: Hogarth, 1959.

– 1908d. "Some General Remarks on Hysterical Attacks." In *S.E.*, vol. 9, 227–34. London: Hogarth, 1959.

– 1910. "Leonardo da Vinci and a Memory of his Childhood." In *S.E.*, vol. 11, 57–137. London: Hogarth, 1953.

– 1911. "Psychoanalytic Notes on an Autobiographical Account of Paranoia." In *S.E.*, vol. 12, 1–82. London: Hogarth, 1958.

– 1912–13. "Totem and Taboo." In *S.E.*, vol. 13, 1–161. London: Hogarth, 1953.

– 1913. "The Predisposition to Obsessional Neurosis: A Contribution to the Problem of the Option of Neurosis." In *S.E.*, vol. 12, 311–26. London: Hogarth, 1958.

– 1916–17. "Introductory Lectures on Psychoanalysis." In *S.E.*, vols 15 and 16 (entire). London: Hogarth, 1963.

– 1919. "'A Child Is Being Beaten': A Contribution to the Study of the Origin of Sexual

Perversions." In *S.E.*, vol. 17, 179–204. London: Hogarth, 1955.

- 1924. "The Economic Problem of Masochism." In *S.E.*, vol. 19, 157–72. London: Hogarth, 1961.

- 1926. "Inhibition, Symptoms and Anxiety." In *S.E.*, vol. 20, 75–175. London: Hogarth, 1959.

- 1927. "The Future of an Illusion." In *S.E.*, vol. 21, 1–56. London: Hogarth, 1953.

- 1930. "Civilization and Its Discontents." In *S.E.*, vol. 21, 57–145. London: Hogarth, 1961.

- 1931. "Female Sexuality." In *S.E.*, vol. 21, 221–43. London: Hogarth, 1961.

- 1932. *New Introductory Lectures on Psychoanalysis.* In *S.E.*, vol. 22, 1–182. London: Hogarth, 1964.

- 1939. *Moses and Monotheism.* In *S.E.*, vol. 23, 1–137. London: Hogarth, 1953.

Freudenthal, H.W.L. 1967. "Kulturkampf." In *The New Catholic Encyclopedia*, vol. 8, 267–9. New York: McGraw-Hill.

Froeschlé-Chopard, M.H. 1982. "The Iconography of the Sacred Universe in the Eighteenth Century: Chapels and Churches in the Dioceses of Vence and Grasse." In *Ritual, Religion, and the Sacred: Selections from the Annales.* Vol. 7, edited by Robert Forster and Orest Ranum, 146–81. Baltimore: Johns Hopkins Univ. Press.

"The Gaining of Cumulative Indulgences by the Recital of the Rosary." ["Gaining of Indulgences."] 1909. *Irish Ecclesiastical Record* 25 (July): 88–90.

Gallup, George, Jr, and David Polling. 1980. *The Search for America's Faith.* Nashville: Abingdon.

Gambasin, A. 1967. "Italy: 1789–1965." In *The New Catholic Encyclopedia*, vol. 7, 766–72. New York: McGraw-Hill.

Gay, Volney P. 1975. "Freud's Essay 'Obsessive Actions and Religious Practices.'" *Psychoanalytic Review* 62 (3): 493–507.

Geary, Patrick. 1985. "The Humiliation of Saints." In Stephen Wilson (ed.), *Saints and Their Cults*, 123–40. Cambridge: Cambridge Univ. Press.

Germanus, Father. 1913. *Blessed Gemma Galgani, the Holy Maid of Lucca.* Trans. by Rev. A.M. O'Sullivan, 3rd ed. St Louis, Mo.: B. Herder, 1933.

Gilmore, David D. 1982. "Anthropology of the Mediterranean." In B. Siegel (ed.), *Annual Reviews in Anthropology*, vol. 11, 175–205. Palo Alto: Annual Reviews.

Gilmore, M.M., and David Gilmore. 1979. "Machismo: A Psycho-Dynamic Approach (Spain)." *Journal of Psychological Anthropology* (2): 281–300.

Graber, Robert Bates. 1986. "The Triads of *Passio Domini*: A Footnote to Psychoanalyses of Christianity." *Journal of Psychoanalytic Anthropology* 9 (1): 35–40.

Graef, H. 1951. *The Case of Therese Neumann.* Westminster, Md: Newman Press.

Grant, Ian R. 1929. *The Testimony of Blood.* London: Burns Oates and Washbourne.

Grimoüard de Saint-Laurent, H.J. 1880. *Les Images du Sacré-Coeur, au point de vue de l'histoire et de l'art.* Paris: Bureaux de l'Oeuvre de Voeu National.

Gross, Feliks. 1973. *Il Paese: Values and Change in an Italian Village.* New York: New York Univ. Press.

Grosskurth, Phyllis. 1986. *Melanie Klein: Her World and Her Work.* Toronto: McClelland and Stewart.

Grotstein, James S. 1981. *Splitting and Projective Identification*. New York: Jason Aronson.

Gutheil, T. 1985. "Hysteria." In A. Kuper and J. Kuper (eds), *The Social Science Encyclopedia*, 374. London: Routledge and Kegan Paul.

Haffert, John M. 1942. *Mary In Her Scapular Promise*. Sea Isle City, N.J.: Scapular Press.

Hallman, Barbara McClung. 1985. *Italian Cardinals, Reform, and the Church as Property*. Berkeley: Univ. of California Press.

Hall, J.W. 1946. "The Analysis of a Case of Night-Terror." *The Psychoanalytic Study of the Child* 1 (Annual): 189–227.

Hamon, Auguste. 1953. "Coeur (Sacré). In *Dictionnaire de spiritualité* vol. 3, cols 1032–46. Paris: Beauchesne.

Hay, Denys. 1977. *The Church in Italy in the Fifteenth Century*. Cambridge: Cambridge Univ. Press.

Hennesey, J.J. 1967. "Vatican Council I." *The New Catholic Encyclopedia*, vol. 14, 559–63. New York: McGraw-Hill.

Henry, W. 1924. "Angelus." In *Dictionnaire d'Archéologie Chrétienne et de Liturgie*, vol. 1, edited by F. Cabrol and H. LeClercq, cols 2068–78. Paris: Librairie Letouzey et Ané.

Hilgers, Joseph, S.J. 1913a. "Sabbatine Privilege." In *The Catholic Encyclopedia*, vol. 13, 289–90. New York: Encyclopedia Press.

– 1913b. "Scapular." In *The Catholic Encyclopedia*. Vol. 13, 508–14. New York: Encyclopedia Press.

Hinnesbusch, W.A. 1967. "The Rosary." In *The Catholic Encyclopedia*, vol. 12, 667–70. New York: McGraw-Hill.

Holmes, J. Derek, and Bernard W. Bickers. 1983. *A Short History of the Catholic Church*. London: Burns and Oates.

Howell, C.W. 1967. "Monstrance." In *The New Catholic Encyclopedia*, vol. 9, 1070–1. New York: McGraw-Hill.

Imbert-Gourbeyre, A. 1894a. *La Stigmatisation, l'extase divine, et les miracles de Lourdes*, vol. 1, *Les Faits*. Paris: Clermont-Ferrand.

– 1894b. *La Stigmatisation, l'extase divine, et les miracles de Lourdes*, vol. 2, *Analyse et Discussion*. Paris: Clermont-Ferrand.

Jameson, Anna Brownell. 1903. *Legends of the Madonna*. 2nd ed. London: Unit Library.

Jamison, E.M. *et al.*, 1917. *Italy, Mediaeval and Modern: A History*. Oxford: Clarendon.

Jarry, E. and R. Mori. 1967. "States of the Church: 1600–1870." In *The New Catholic Encyclopedia*, vol. 13, 658–62. New York: McGraw-Hill.

Jedin, Hubert. 1960. *Ecumenical Councils of the Catholic Church*. Freiberg, West Germany: Herder.

– 1965. *Crise et Dénouement du Concile de Trente, 1562–1563*. Paris: Desclée.

– 1980. "Spiritual Life, Popular Devotion and Art." In E. Iserloh, J. Glazik, and H. Jedin (eds), *Reformation and Counter Reformation*, 555–66. New York: Seabury.

– 1981. "Spiritual Life, Popular Devotion and Art." In *The History of the Church*, vol. 5, edited by H. Jedin and J. Dolan, 555–66. New York: Seabury.

Jones, Ernest. 1914. "The Madonna's Conception Through the Ear." In *Essays in Applied Psychoanalysis*, 266–357. London: Hogarth, 1951.

– 1918. "Anal-Erotic Character Traits." In *Papers on Psycho-Analysis*, 413–37. Boston:

Beacon, 1961.

Kaftal, George. 1952. *Iconography of the Saints in Tuscan Painting*. Florence: Sansoni.

– 1965. *Iconography of the Saints in Central and South Italian Schools of Painting*. Florence: Sansoni.

– 1978. *Iconography of the Saints in the Painting of North East Italy*. Florence: Sansoni.

– 1985. *Iconography of the Saints in the Painting of North West Italy*. Florence: Casa Editrice Le Lettere.

Kehoe, Alice B. 1979. "The Sacred Heart: A Case for Stimulus Diffusion." *American Ethnologist* 6 (Nov.): 763–71.

Kehoe, Lawrence. 1871. *The Liquefaction of the Blood of St. Januarius at Naples: An Historical and Critical Examination of the Miracle*. New York: Catholic Publication Society.

Kent, W.H. 1913. "Indulgences." In *The Catholic Encyclopedia*, vol. 7, 783–8. New York: Encyclopedia Press.

King, Archdale A. 1965. *Eucharistic Reservation in the Western Church*. New York: Sheed and Ward.

Klauser, Theodor. 1969. *A Short History of the Western Liturgy*. New York: Oxford Univ. Press.

Klein, Melanie. 1923. "Early Analysis." In *Love, Guilt and Reparation and Other Works, 1921–1945*, 77–105. New York: Delta, 1975.

– 1925. "A Contribution to the Psychogenesis of Tics." In *Love, Guilt and Reparation and Other Works, 1921–1945*, 106–27. New York: Delta, 1975.

– 1927. "Criminal Tendencies in Normal Children." In *Love, Guilt and Reparation and Other Works, 1921–1945*, 170–85. New York: Delta, 1975.

– 1928. "Note on a Dream of Forensic Interest." In *Envy and Gratitude and Other Works, 1946–1963*, 315–17. London: Hogarth, 1975.

– 1931. "A Contribution to the Theory of Intellectual Inhibition." In *Love, Guilt and Reparation and Other Works, 1921–1945*, 236–47. New York: Delta, 1975.

– 1936. "Weaning." In *Love, Guilt and Reparation and Other Works, 1921–1945*, 290–305. New York: Delta, 1975.

Klein, Melanie. 1937. "Love, Guilt and Reparation." In *Love, Guilt and Reparation and Other Works, 1921–1945*, 306–43. New York: Delta, 1975.

– 1945. "The Oedipus Complex in Light of Early Anxieties." In *Love, Guilt and Reparation and Other Works, 1921–1945*, 370–419. New York: Delta, 1975.

– 1946. "Notes on Some Schizoid Mechanisms." In *Envy and Gratitude and Other Works: 1946–1963*, 1–24. London: Hogarth, 1980.

– 1952. "Some Theoretical Conclusions Regarding the Emotional Life of the Infant." In *Envy and Gratitude and Other Works: 1946–1963*, 57–93. London: Hogarth, 1980.

– 1957. "Envy and Gratitude." In *Envy and Gratitude and Other Works: 1946–1963*, 176–235. London: Hogarth, 1980.

– 1959. "Our Adult World and Its Roots in Infancy." In *Envy and Gratitude and Other Works: 1946–1963*, 247–63. London: Hogarth, 1980.

– 1975. *Love, Guilt and Reparation and Other Works, 1921–1945*. Intro. by R.E. Money-Kyrle. New York: Delta.

- 1980. *Envy and Gratitude and Other Works: 1946-1963*, London: Hogarth.

Kline, Paul. 1981. *Fact and Fantasy in Freudian Theory*. 2nd ed. London: Methuen.

Kselman, Thomas A. 1983. *Miracles and Prophecies in Nineteenth-Century France*. New Brunswick, N.J.: Rutgers Univ. Press.

Kselman, Thomas A., and Steven Avella. 1986. "Marian Piety and the Cold War in the United States." *Catholic Historical Review* 72: 403-24.

Lamberti, Marjorie. 1986. "State, Church and the Politics of School Reform During the Kulturkampf." *Central European History* 19 (1): 62-81.

Lançon, Pierre. 1984. "Les Confréries du rosaire en Rouergue aux xvie et xviie siècles." *Annales du Midi* 96 (Apr./June): 121-33.

Larkin, F. 1967. "Sacred Heart, Enthronement of the." In *The New Catholic Encyclopedia*, vol. 12, 820. New York: McGraw-Hill.

Latourette, Kenneth Scott. 1953. *A History of Christianity*. New York: Harper and Row.

Lea, Henry C. 1896. *A History of Auricular Confession and Indulgence in the Latin Church*, vol. 3. Philadelphia: Lea.

Lewis, Oscar. 1959. *Five Families: Mexican Case Studies in the Culture of Poverty*. New York: Basic.

- 1965. *La Vida*. New York: Random House.

Lundeen, Joel W. 1986. *Luther's Works*, vol. 55: index. Philadelphia: Fortress.

Lynch, Most Rev. E.K. 1950. *Your Brown Scapular*. Westminster, Md.: Newman Press.

McClelland, David. 1961. *The Achieving Society*. New York: Free Press.

McGuire, M.R.P. 1967. "Popes, List of." In *The New Catholic Encyclopedia*, vol. 11, 574-6. New York: McGraw-Hill.

McKenna, Rev. Joseph. 1933. "Quarant'Ore or the Forty Hours Prayer." 1933. *Clergy Review*, vol. 6, 186-209.

Magennis, P.E. 1923. *The Scapular Devotion: Origin, Legislation and Indulgences attached to the Scapulars*. Dublin: M.H. Gill and Son.

Maraspini, A.L. 1968. *The Study of an Italian Village*. Paris: Mouton.

Markam, J.J. 1967. "Indulgences, Canon Law of." In *The New Catholic Encyclopedia*, vol. 7, 485-6. New York: McGraw-Hill.

Marmor, J. 1953. "Orality in the Hysterical Personality." *Journal of the American Psychoanalytic Association* 1 (4): 656-71.

May, H.G. and Metzger, B.B. (eds). 1973. *The New Oxford Annotated Bible*. New York: Oxford Univ. Press.

Meara, Mary, Jeffrey Stone, Maureen Kelly, and Richard Davis. 1986. *More Growing Up Catholic*. Garden City, N.Y.: Doubleday.

Merton, Thomas. 1950. *What Are These Wounds?* Milwaukee: Bruce.

Minchinton, Walter. 1974. "Patterns and Structure of Demand: 1500-1750." In Carlo M. Cipola (ed.), *The Fontana History of Europe: The Sixteenth and Seventeenth Centuries*, 79-176. Glasgow: Collins/Fontana.

Mioni, Ugo. 1908. *Il Culto delle reliquie nella chiesa cattolica*. Torino: Tipografia Pontificia.

Moell, C.J. 1967. "Sacred Heart, Devotion to." In *The New Catholic Encyclopedia*, vol. 12, 818-20. New York: McGraw-Hill.

Molloy, G. 1873. *A Visit to Louise Lateau in the Summer of 1872*. London: Burns, Oates.

Mols, Roger. 1974. "Population in Europe: 1500–1700." In Carlo M. Cipola (ed.), *The Fontana History of Europe: The Sixteenth and Seventeenth Centuries*, 15–78. Glasgow: Collins/Fontana.

Mori, R. 1967. "The Roman Question." In *The New Catholic Encyclopedia*, vol. 12, 607–8. New York: McGraw-Hill.

Morris, J.U. 1967. "Sacred Heart, Iconography of." In *The New Catholic Encyclopedia*, vol. 12, 820–2. New York: McGraw-Hill.

Morrisroe, P. 1911. "Sabbatine Indulgence." *Irish Ecclesiastical Record* 29 (Jan.): 98.

Mulhern, P.F. 1967. "Medals, Religious." In *The New Catholic Encyclopedia*, vol. 9, 547–9. New York: Macmillan.

Muller, Wolfgang. 1981. "Liturgy and Popular Piety: New Religious Orders." In *The History of the Church*, vol. 6, edited by H. Jedin and J. Dolan, 547–56. New York: Crossroad.

Murphy, J.F. 1967. "Immaculate Heart of Mary." In *The New Catholic Encyclopedia*, vol. 7, 383–4. New York: McGraw-Hill.

Murray, Collin. 1981. *Families Divided: The Impact of Migrant Labor in Lesotho*. Cambridge: Cambridge Univ. Press.

Mynors, R.A.B., and D.F.S. Thomson (eds). 1974. *The Correspondence of Erasmus*. Toronto: Univ. of Toronto Press.

Nelson, Alan. 1974. *The Medieval English Stage: Corpus Christi Pageants and Plays*. Chicago: Univ. of Chicago Press.

Newman, John Henry. 1836. "On the Mode of Conducting the Controversy with Rome." In *The Via Media of the Anglican Church*, vol. 2, 93–141. London: Longmans, Green, 1908.

– 1841. "A Letter Addressed to the Rev. R.W. Jelf, D.D." In *The Via Media of the Anglican Church*, vol. 2, 365–93. London: Longmans, Green, 1908.

– 1864. "Apologia Pro Vita Sua." Oxford: Clarendon, 1967.

– 1865. "A Letter Addressed to the Rev. E.B. Pusey, D.D., On the Occasion of His Eirenicon." In *Certain Difficulties Felt by Anglicans in Catholic Teaching Considered*, vol. 2, 1–170. London: Longmans, Green, 1910.

Nischan, Bodo. 1984. "The 'Fractio Panis': A Reformed Communion Practice in Late Reformation Germany." *Church History* 53 (Mar.): 17–29.

Oligny, Rev. Paul (trans.). 1980. *Papal Teachings: The Holy Rosary*. Boston: The Daughters of St. Paul.

O'Loan, D. 1894. "The 'Angelus,'" *Irish Ecclesiastical Record* 15 (Mar.): 255–7.

O'Malley, John W. 1982. "Social History." In Ozment, Steven (ed.), *Reformation Europe: A Guide to Research*, 161–81. St. Louis: Center for Reformation Research.

O'Neil, Mary R. 1986. "From 'Popular' to 'Local' Religion: Issues in Early Modern European History." *Religious Studies Review* 12 (July/Oct.): 222–6.

Orsi, Robert A. 1985. *The Madonna of 115th Street*. New Haven: Yale Univ. Press.

Ousterhout, Robert. 1981. "The Church of Santo Stefano: A "Jerusalem" in Bologna." *Gesta* 20 (2): 311–21.

Ozment, Steven. 1982. *Reformation Europe: A Guide to Research*. St. Louis: Center for Reformation Research.

Pacquin, Jo. 1949. "Simon Stock, Saint of the Scapular." In Carmelite Fathers and Tertiaries, *Take This Scapular!* 3–15. Chicago: Carmelite Third Order Press.

Parsons, Anne. 1969. *Belief, Magic and Anomie: Essays in Psychological Anthropology*. New York: Free Press.

Pater, Thomas. 1946. *Miraculous Abstinence: A Study of One of the Extraordinary Mystical Phenomena*. Washington, D.C.: Catholic University of America Press.

Pelikan, Jaroslav (ed.). 1959. *Luther's Works*, vol. 23. St. Louis: Concordia.

– (ed.). 1969. *Luther's Works*, vol. 16. St Louis: Concordia.

Peters, F.E. 1985. "The Procession That Never Was: The Painful Way in Jerusalem." *Drama Review* 29 (Fall): 31–41.

Petito, Luigi. 1983. *San Gennaro: Storia, Folclore, Culto*. Naples: LER.

Phelan, Gerald B. 1946. "Introduction." In St John Eudes, *The Sacred Heart of Jesus*, xiii–xxx. New York: P.J. Kenedy.

Phillips, C.S. 1936. *The Church in France: 1848–1907*. London: Society for Promoting Christian Knowledge.

Pope, Barbara C. 1988. "A Heroine Without Heroics: The Little Flower of Jesus and Her Times." *Church History* 57 (Mar.): 46–60.

Rahner, Hugo. 1957. "The Beginnings of the Devotion in Patristic Times." In J. Stierli (ed.), *Heart of the Saviour*, 37–57. Freiburg, West Germany: Herder and Herder.

Rahner, Karl. 1957 "Some Theses on the Theology of the Devotion." In J. Stierli (ed.), *Heart of the Saviour*, 36–57. Freiburg: Herder and Herder.

Rangell, L. 1959. "The Nature of Conversion." *Journal of the American Psychoanalytic Association* 7 (4): 632–62.

Réau, Louis. 1958. *Iconographie de l'art chrétien*, vol. 3. Paris: Presses Universitaires de France.

"Recitation of Angelus." 1909. *Irish Ecclesiastical Record* 25 (Jan.): 90–1.

Rogo, D. Scott. 1983. *Miracles*. Chicago: Contemporary.

Róheim, Géza. 1945. "Aphrodite, or the Woman with a Penis." *Psychoanalytic Quarterly* 14 (July): 350–90.

Rosenman, Stanley. 1986. "The Fundament of German Character Structure." *The Journal of Psychohistory* 14 (1): 65–78.

Rothkrug, Lionel. 1979. "Popular Religion and Holy Shrines: Their Influence on the Origins of the German Reformation and Their Role in German Cultural Development." In James Obelkevich (ed.), *Religion and the People, 800–1700*, 20–86. Chapel Hill: Univ. of North Carolina Press.

– 1987. "Holy Shrines, Religious Dissonance, and Satan in the Origins of the German Reformation." *Historical Reflections/Reflexions Historiques* 14 (2): 143–286.

Rushe, James P. 1911. "The 'Scapular Promise' From the Historical Standpoint." *Irish Ecclesiastical Record* 29 (Mar.): 266–88.

Salomone-Marino, Salvatore. 1897. *Customs and Habits of the Sicilian Peasants*. London: Associated Univ. Press, 1981.

Salvatori, F. 1874. *The Lives of S. Veronica Giuliani, Capuchin Nun, and of the Blessed Battista Varani, of the Order of S. Clare*. London: R. Washbourne.

Sarro, Mario. 1966. "La Cattedrale di Avellino e le sue tradizioni millenarie." In *La Cattedrale di Avellino: Nella storia, nel culto, nell'arte*. Cava dei Tirreni: Emilio Mauro.

Saunders, George R. 1981. "Men and Women in Southern Europe: A Review of Some Aspects of Cultural Complexity." *Journal of Psychoanalytic Anthropology* 4 (4): 435–66.

Schiller, Gertrud. 1966. *Iconography of Christian Art*, vol. 1. London: Lund Humphries, 1971.

Schmöger, Rev. K. 1885a. *Life of Anne Catherine Emmerich*, vol. 1. New York: F. Pustet.

– 1885b. *Life of Anne Catherine Emmerich*, vol. 2. New York: F. Pustet.

Schneck, Jerome M. 1958. "A Hypnoanalytic Note on the Heart As a Phallic Symbol." *Journal of Nervous and Mental Disease* 126 (Apr.): 401–2.

Schneider, Daniel E. 1954. "The Image of the Heart and the Synergic Principle in Psychoanalysis (Psychosynergy): I." *Psychoanalytic Review* 41 (July): 197–215.

– 1955. "The Image of the Heart and the Synergic Principle in Psychoanalysis (Psychosynergy): II and III." *Psychoanalytic Review* 42 (Oct.): 343–60.

Schoeck, Helmut. 1955. "The Evil Eye: Forms and Dynamics of a Universal Superstition." In A. Dundes (ed.), *The Evil Eye: A Folklore Casebook*, 192–200. New York: Garland, 1981.

Schumacher, M.A. 1945. *I Teach Catechism*, vol. III: *Grades 6–8*. New York: Benziger.

Schwemmer, Wilhelm. 1958. *Adam Kraft*. Nuremberg: Hans Carl.

Scribner, R.W. 1981. *For the Sake of Simple Folk: Popular Propaganda for the German Reformation*. New York: Cambridge Univ. Press.

– 1986. *The German Reformation*. London: Macmillan.

Segal, Hanna. 1964. *An Introduction to the Work of Melanie Klein*. London: Hogarth.

– 1973. *An Introduction to the Work of Melanie Klein*. London: Hogarth.

– 1979. *Klein*. London: Fontana/Collins.

Shaw, J.G. 1954. *The Story of the Rosary*. Milwaukee: Bruce.

Silverman, Sydel. 1975. *Three Bells of Civilization: The Life of an Italian Hill Town*. New York: Columbia Univ. Press.

Siwek, P. 1953. *The Riddle of Konnersreuth: A Psychological and Religious Study*. Milwaukee: Bruce.

– 1967. "Stigmatization." In *The New Catholic Encyclopedia*, vol. 13, 711–13. New York: McGraw-Hill.

Smet, J. 1967. "Carmelites." In *The New Catholic Encyclopedia*, vol. 3, 118–21. New York: McGraw-Hill.

Smith, Raymond. 1956. *The Negro Family in British Guiana*. London: Routledge and Kegan Paul.

Spahn, Martin. 1913. "Kulturkampf." In *The Catholic Encyclopedia*, vol. 8, 703–10. New York: Encyclopedia Press.

Spitz, Lewis (ed.). 1960. *Luther's Works*, vol. 34. Philadelphia: Muhlenburg.

Stephens, William N. 1962. *The Oedipus Complex: Cross-Cultural Evidence*. New York: Free Press of Glencoe.

Stierli, Josef. 1957a. "Devotion to the Sacred Heart from the End of the Patristic Period Down to St. Margaret Mary." In J. Stierli (ed.), *Heart of the Saviour*, 59-107. Freiburg, West Germany: Herder.

- 1957b. "The Development of the Church's Devotion to the Sacred Heart in Modern Times." In J. Stierli (ed.), *Heart of the Saviour*, 109-30. Freiburg, West Germany: Herder.

Swanson, Guy. 1967. *Religion and Regime*. Ann Arbor: Univ. of Michigan Press.

- 1986. "Immanence and Transcendence: Connections With Personality and Personal Life." *Sociological Analysis* 47 (Fall): 189-215.

Tackett, Timothy. 1986. *Religion, Revolution and Regional Culture in Eighteenth-Century France*. Princeton: Princeton Univ. Press.

Taffert, Theodore (ed). 1967. *Luther's Works*, vol. 54. Philadelphia: Fortress.

Tarachow, Sidney. 1955. "St. Paul and Early Christianity: A Psychoanalytic and Historical Study." *Psychoanalysis and the Social Sciences*, vol. 4, 223-81.

Taves, Ann. 1986. *The Household of Faith: Roman Catholic Devotions in Mid-Nineteenth Century America*. Notre Dame: Univ. of Notre Dame Press.

Teitelbaum, Joel. 1976. "The Leer and the Loom: Social Controls on Handloom Weavers." In C. Maloney (ed.), *The Evil Eye*, 63-75. New York: Columbia Univ. Press.

Tentori, Tulio. 1982. "An Italian Religious Feast: The Fujenti Rites of the Madonna dell'Arco, Naples." In James Preston (ed.), *Mother Worship*, 94-122. Chapel Hill: Univ. of North Carolina Press.

Teresa, Saint. 1911. *The Life of St. Teresa of Jesus of the Order of Carmel, Written by Herself*. 4th ed. London: T. Baker.

Thompson, Stith. 1955. *Motif-Index of Folk Literature*. 6 vols. Bloomington: Indiana Univ. Press.

Thomson, John A.F. 1980. *Popes and Princes, 1417-1517: Politics and Polity in the Late Medieval Church*. London: George Allen and Unwin.

Thurston, Herbert S.J. 1900a. "Our Popular Devotions. I. The Stations of the Cross." *The Month* 96 (July): 1-12.

- 1900b. "Our Popular Devotions. I. Stations of the Cross." *The Month* 96 (Aug.): 153-66.

- 1900c. "Our Popular Devotions. I. The Stations of the Cross." *The Month* 96 (Sept.): 282-93.

- 1900d. "Our Popular Devotions. II. The Rosary." *The Month* 96 (Oct.): 403-18.

- 1900e. "Our Popular Devotions. II. The Rosary." *The Month* 96 (Nov.): 513-27.

- 1900f. "Our Popular Devotions. II. The Rosary." *The Month* 96 (Dec.): 620-37.

- 1901a. "Our Popular Devotions. II. The Rosary." *The Month* 97 (Jan.): 67-79.

- 1901b. "Our Popular Devotions. II. The Rosary." *The Month* 97 (Feb.): 172-88.

- 1901c. "Our Popular Devotions. II. The Rosary." *The Month* 97 (Mar.): 286-304.

- 1901d. "Our Popular Devotions. II. The Rosary." *The Month* 97 (Apr.): 383-404.

- 1901e. "Our Popular Devotions. IV. Benediction of the Blessed Sacrament. 2. Exposition." *The Month* 98 (July): 58-69.

- 1901f. "Our Popular Devotions. V. The Angelus. 1. The Hail Mary." *The Month* 97 (Nov.): 483-99.

- 1901g. "Our Popular Devotions. v. The Angelus. 2. The Curfew Bell." *The Month* 97 (Dec.): 607-16.
- 1902a. "Our Popular Devotions. v. The Angelus. 3. Compline or Curfew Bell - Which?" *The Month* 98 (Jan.): 60-73.
- 1902b. "Our Popular Devotions. v. The Angelus. 4. The Midday Angelus." *The Month* 99 (May): 518-32.
- 1902c. "Our Popular Devotions. vi. The So-Called Bridgettine Rosary." *The Month* 100 (July): 189-203.
- 1903. "The Nine Fridays." *The Month* 101 (June): 635-49.
- 1904a. "The Antiquity of the Angelus." *The Month* 103 (Jan.): 57-66.
- 1904b. "The Origin of the Scapular: A Criticism." *Irish Ecclesiastical Record* 16 (July): 59-75.
- 1904c. *Lent and Holy Week*. London: Longmans, Green.
- 1906. *The Stations of the Cross*. London: Burns and Oates.
- 1908a. "The Name of the Rosary. i." *The Month* iii (May): 518-29.
- 1908b. "The Name of the Rosary. ii." *The Month* iii (June): 610-23.
- 1909a. "The Miracle of St. Januarius (i)." *The Tablet*, May 22, 803-5.
- 1909b. "The Miracle of St. Januarius (ii)." *The Tablet* May 29, 842-4.
- 1911a. "The Scapular Tradition and Its Defenders." *Irish Ecclesiastical Record* 29 (May): 492-504.
- 1911b. "A Recent Confirmation of the Scapular Tradition." *Irish Ecclesiastical Record* 29 (June): 604-10.
- 1913a. "Agnus Dei." In *The Catholic Encyclopedia*. Vol. 1, 220-1. New York: Encyclopedia Press.
- 1913b. "Angelus." In *The Catholic Encyclopedia*. Vol. 1, 486- 7. New York: Encyclopedia Press.
- 1913c. "Januarius, Saint." In *The Catholic Encyclopedia*. Vol. 8, 295-7. New York: Encyclopedia Press.
- 1913d. "Medals, Devotional." In *The Catholic Encyclopedia*. Vol. 10, 111-15. New York: Encyclopedia Press.
- 1913e. "Ostensorium." In *The Catholic Encyclopedia*. Vol. 11, 344-6. New York: Encyclopedia Press.
- 1913f. "Popular Devotions." In *The Catholic Encyclopedia*. Vol. 12, 275-6. New York: Encyclopedia Press.
- 1913g. "The Rosary." In *The Catholic Encyclopedia*. Vol. 13, 184-7. New York: Encyclopedia Press.
- 1921. "The Blood of St. Januarius." *The Month* 138 (Nov.): 453-7.
- 1926. "The Alleged Liquefaction of the Blood of St. Januarius." *Catholic Medical Guardian* 4 (Apr.): 54-60.
- 1927a. "The Blood Miracles of Naples i." *The Month* 149 (Jan.): 44-55.
- 1927b. "The Blood Miracles of Naples ii." *The Month* 149 (Feb.): 123-35.
- 1927c. "The Blood Miracles of Naples iii." *The Month* 149 (Mar.): 236-47.
- 1927d. "Scapulars i." *The Month* 149 (June): 481-8.

- 1927e. "Scapulars II." *The Month* 150 (July): 44–58.
- 1930. "The 'Miracle' of St. Januarius." *The Month* 155 (Feb.): 119–29.
- 1952. *The Physical Phenomena of Mysticism*. Edited by J. Crehan. London: Burns Oates.
- 1955. *Surprising Mystics*. Edited by J. Crehan. Chicago: Henry Regnery.

Tomasi, Silvano M., and Edward C. Stibili. 1978. *Italian-Americans and Religion: An Annotated Bibliography*. New York: New York Center for Migration Studies.

Trevelyan, Janet P. 1956. *A Short History of the Italian People*. Rev. ed. London: George Allen and Unwin.

Trexler, Richard C. 1980. *Public Life in Renaissance Florence*. New York: Academic.

Vecoli, Rudolph J. 1969. "Prelates and Peasants: Italian Immigrants and the Catholic Church." *Journal of Social History* 2 (Spring): 217–68.

- 1977. "Cult and Occult in Italian-American Culture: The Persistence of a Religious Heritage." In R.M. Miller and T.D. Marzik (eds.), *Immigrants and Religion in Urban America*, 27–47. Philadelphia: Temple Univ. Press.

Verheylezoon, Louis, S.J. 1955. *Devotion to the Sacred Heart*. Rockford, Ill: TAN, 1978.

Vernon, H.M. 1909. *Italy from 1494 to 1790*. Cambridge: Cambridge Univ. Press.

Vinciotti, A. 1962. *I Sanctuari d'Italia*. Città di Castello: Associazione Sanctuari d'Italia.

von Lama, F.R. 1935. *Therese of Konnersreuth*. Milwaukee: Bruce.

Wagner, Richard V. 1979. "Achievement Orientation and the Image of Limited Good in the French Alps. In M. Clark, R.V. Kemper, and C. Nelson (eds.), *From Tzintzuntzan to the "Image of Limited Good": Essays in Honor of George M. Foster*, 119–30. Berkeley: Kroeber Anthropological Society.

Weber, Max. 1920. *The Protestant Ethic and the Spirit of Capitalism*. New York: Charles Scribner, 1958.

Weil, Mark. S. 1974. "The Devotion of the Forty Hours and Roman Baroque Illusions." *Journal of the Warburg and Courtauld Institutes* 37: 218–48.

Willam, Franz Michel. 1953. *The Rosary: Its History and Meaning*. New York: Benziger.

Williams, Phyllis H. 1938. *South Italian Folkways in Europe and America*. New York: Russell and Russell, 1969.

Williamson, B. 1932. *Gemma of Lucca*. London: Alexander-Ouseley.

Wilson, Stephen. 1980. "Cults of the Saints in the Churches of Central Paris." *Comparative Studies in Society and History* 22 (Oct.): 548–75.

Wroth, William. 1982. *Christian Images in Hispanic New Mexico*. Colorado: Colorado Springs Fine Arts Center, Taylor Museum.

Xiberta, Bartholomew, 1949. "Annotations on the Status of the Scapular Question." In Carmelite Fathers and Tertiaries, *Take This Scapular!* 213–43. Chicago: Carmelite Third Order Press.

Yorburg, Betty. 1983. *Families and Societies*. New York: Columbia Univ. Press.

Zika, Charles. 1988. "Hosts, Processions and Pilgrimages: Controlling the Sacred in Fifteenth-Century Germany." *Past and Present* 118 (Feb.): 25–64.

Zimmerman, Benedict. 1904a. "The Origin of the Scapular (From Original Sources)." *Irish Ecclesiastical Record* 15 (Feb.): 142–53.

- 1904b. "The Origin of the Scapular – II (From Original Sources). *Irish Ecclesiastical*

Record 15 (Mar.): 206–34.

- 1904c. "The Origin of the Scapular – III (From Original Sources)." *Irish Ecclesiastical Record* 15 (Apr.): 331–51.

- 1913. "Carmelite Order, the." In *The Catholic Encyclopedia*, vol. 3, 354–70. New York: Encyclopedia Press.

- 1927. "The Carmelite Scapular." *The Month* 150 (Oct.): 321– 30.

Index